The Washington Post

THE
MUELLER REPORT
ILLUSTRATED

The Obstruction Investigation

Illustrations by
JAN FEINDT

Text and Analysis by
ROSALIND S. HELDERMAN

MATEA GOLD, Political Investigations Editor
KATHERINE B. LEE, Art Director

SUZETTE MOYER, Senior Design Editor
BRONWEN LATIMER, Senior Photo Editor
BRIAN GROSS, Deputy Design Director
GREG MANIFOLD, Design Director
JABIN BOTSFORD, Photographer
FRANCES MOODY, Copy Editor
KOLIN POPE, Video Graphics Editor

SCRIBNER

New York   London   Toronto   Sydney   New Delhi

Scribner
An Imprint of Simon & Schuster, Inc.
1230 Avenue of the Americas
New York, NY 10020

First Scribner trade paperback edition December 2019

SCRIBNER and design are registered trademarks of The Gale Group, Inc., used under license by Simon & Schuster, Inc., the publisher of this work.

For information about special discounts for bulk purchases, please contact Simon & Schuster Special Sales at 1-866-506-1949 or business@simonandschuster.com.

The Simon & Schuster Speakers Bureau can bring authors to your live event. For more information or to book an event, contact the Simon & Schuster Speakers Bureau at 1-866-248-3049 or visit our website at www.simonspeakers.com.

Interior design by Katherine B. Lee, Suzette Moyer,
Brian Gross and Greg Manifold

Manufactured in the United States of America

10 9 8 7 6 5 4 3 2 1

ISBN 978-1-9821-4927-7 (pbk)
ISBN 978-1-9821-4928-4 (ebook)

Contents

Introduction

Special counsel Robert S. Mueller III spent nearly two years investigating Russia's interference in the 2016 presidential campaign and whether President Trump obstructed the inquiry. His 448-page report, which was released in redacted form to the public in April 2019, laid out a Russian government plot to help elect Trump by weaponizing fake and divisive information on social media and disseminating emails hacked from the Democratic National Committee and Democratic officials.

Mueller made two major conclusions in his report: He found that the Russian effort had been "sweeping and systematic," and he determined the evidence did not establish that Trump or his campaign had conspired with the Kremlin.

However, the special counsel left one significant question unanswered: whether the president broke the law by trying to block the probe.

Mueller decided that because Justice Department policy states that a president cannot be indicted, it would not be fair to take a position on whether Trump committed a crime. But his report laid out a dramatic narrative of an angry and anxious president trying to control a criminal investigation — even after he knew he was under scrutiny.

The special counsel also made a point of saying that his report did not exonerate the president. That inconclusive legal finding was unsatisfying for Trump's supporters and his critics, sparking a debate about his actions that is still raging. But Mueller's factual findings provided the nation with an extraordinary historical record: a fly-on-the-wall account of life in the White House, told through the eyes of the men and women who served the president and who, under penalty of perjury, shared their memories with investigators.

This book is drawn directly from episodes detailed in the Mueller report in which prosecutors found evidence of possible obstruction of justice, as well as congressional testimony and Washington Post reporting. Dialogue in text bubbles is taken from Mueller's report, which cited text messages, contemporaneous notes and investigative interviews with first-hand witnesses who described conversations among key players. Words within quotation marks reflect exact dialogue included in the report, or comments made at public events or in media interviews.

Illustrations of public events are based on news photographs taken at the time. The president's tweets have been reproduced verbatim, although the number of "likes" and "retweets" may have changed over time.

THE
MUELLER REPORT
ILLUSTRATED

The Obstruction Investigation

1

"This Russia thing is far from over"

The investigation that shadowed the first two years of President Trump's administration began quietly during the 2016 campaign. U.S. intelligence agencies suspected Russia was behind efforts to sway American voters, such as WikiLeaks' release of hacked Democratic emails. The FBI began examining ties between Trump associates and the Russian government.

Donald Trump won the election on Nov. 8, 2016. By that time, U.S. intelligence officials had publicly blamed Russia for the release of the hacked emails, describing it as an effort "to interfere with the US election process."

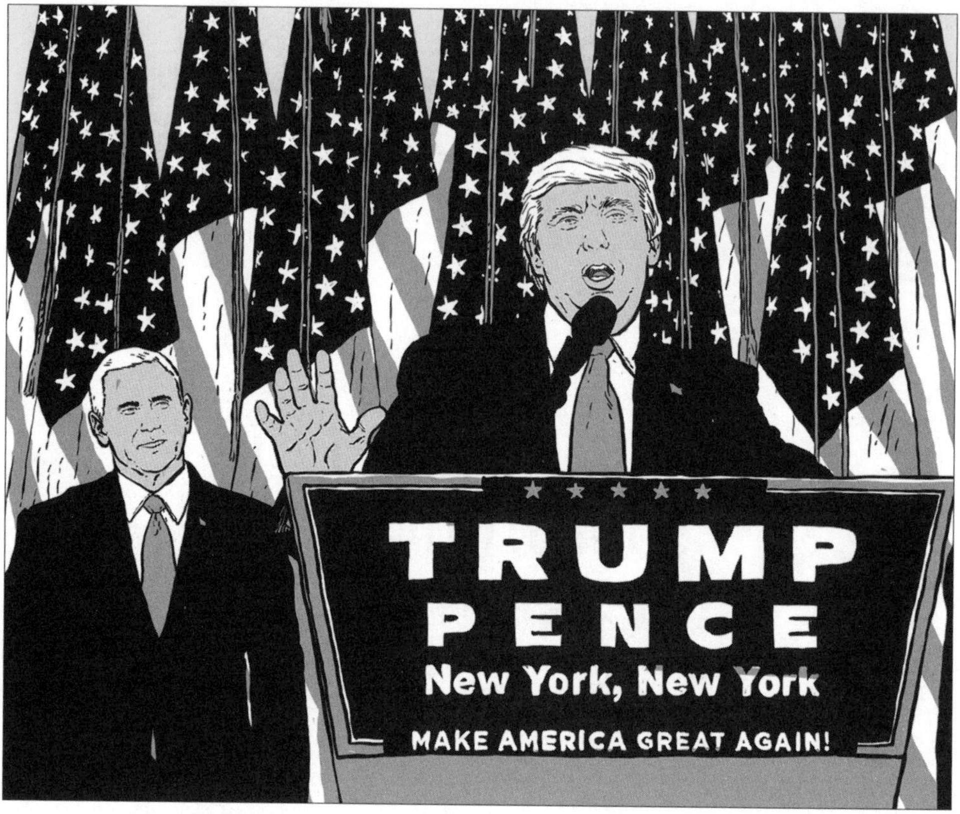
TRUMP
PENCE
New York, New York
MAKE AMERICA GREAT AGAIN!

Trump scoffed at that conclusion, calling it "ridiculous." He said the intelligence agencies did not know who was really responsible. "It could be somebody sitting in a bed some place," he said.

The way Trump and his top advisers responded to the Russia attack set in motion a crisis that would consume his White House — and it led to the investigation of the president himself for obstruction of justice.

The first test came in late December 2016. Barack Obama was still president. With just weeks to go until Trump's inauguration, the Obama administration announced it was imposing sanctions on Russia in response to its interference in the campaign.

"Based on uniform intelligence assessments, the Russians were responsible for hacking the DNC."

THE WHITE HOUSE

Trump's advisers were concerned the fallout would hurt the United States' relationship with Russia. The president-elect saw the move as an attempt to embarrass him by suggesting his election was not legitimate.

Michael Flynn, the incoming White House national security adviser, on vacation in the Dominican Republic, told colleagues he planned to speak with Russia's man in Washington, Ambassador Sergey Kislyak.

He texted an aide.

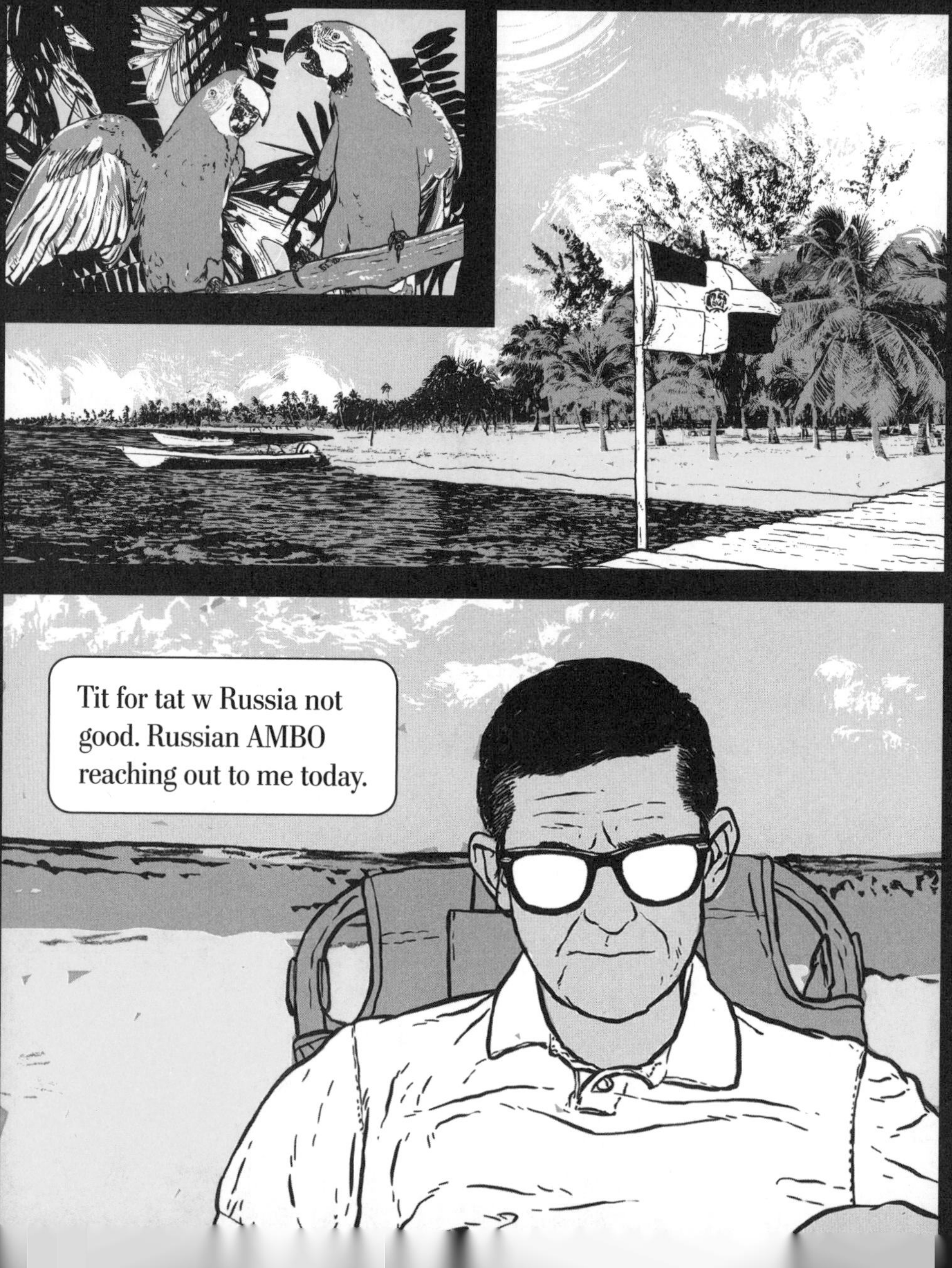
Tit for tat w Russia not good. Russian AMBO reaching out to me today.

Flynn also spoke by phone to his deputy, K.T. McFarland, who was with the president-elect and other advisers at Mar-a-Lago, Trump's private Florida estate.

McFarland told Flynn that the president-elect's team didn't want things with Russia to heat up.

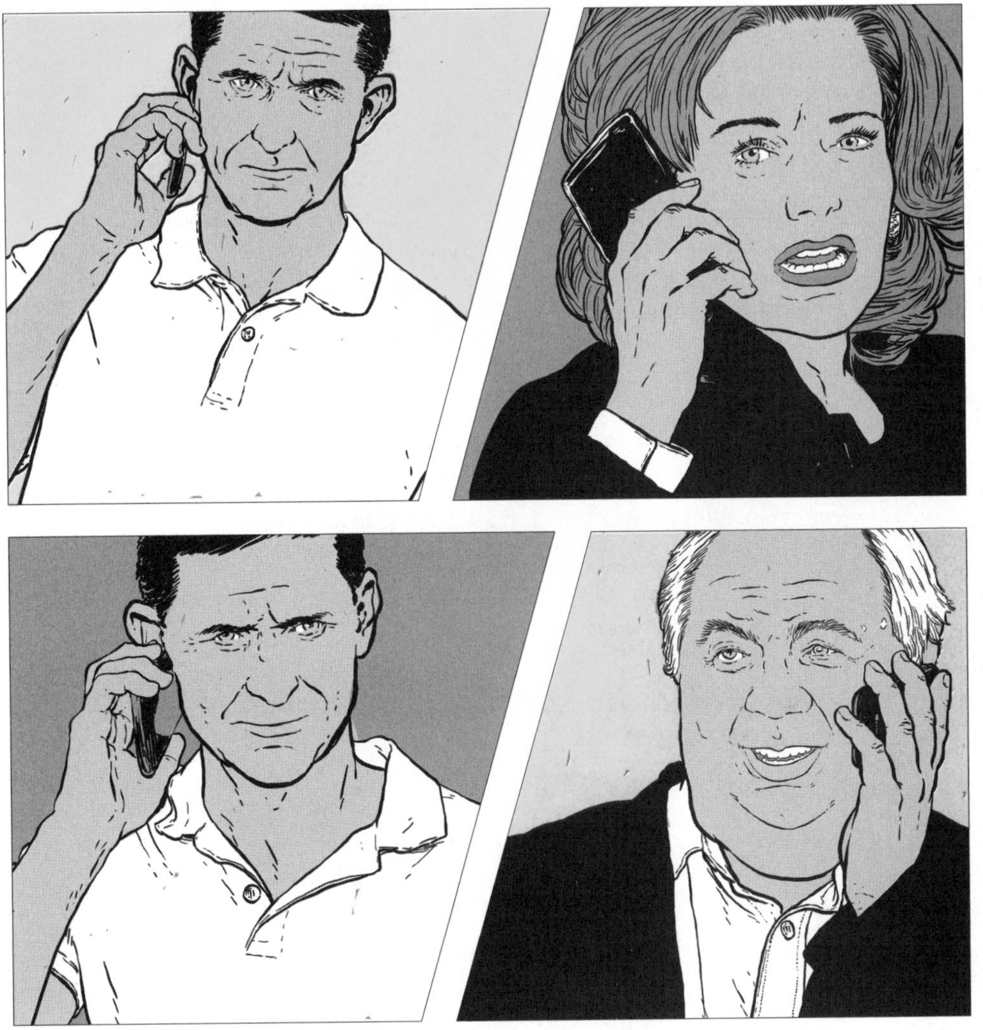

Flynn immediately called Kislyak.

They discussed the sanctions — and Flynn asked Russia not to escalate the situation. It was a highly unorthodox request. Flynn was not yet representing the U.S. government.

The next day, Russian President Vladimir Putin issued a statement saying Russia would not retaliate.

Statement by the President of Russia

December 30, 2016, 15:15

As it proceeds from international practice, Russia has reasons to respond in kind. Although we have the right to retaliate, we will not resort to irresponsible 'kitchen' diplomacy but will plan our further steps to restore Russian-US relations based on the policies of the Trump Administration.

Back in Washington, national security officials in the Obama administration were surprised by Russia's mild reaction. But Trump tweeted an appreciative response.

Donald J. Trump ✔
@realDonaldTrump

Great move on delay (by V. Putin) - I always knew he was very smart!

2:41 PM · Dec 30, 2016

33.3K Retweets   **97.1K** Likes

The following week, the president-elect was briefed by intelligence agencies on Russia's efforts in the previous months to bolster his candidacy. After the meeting, Trump said in a statement that the hacks had "absolutely no effect on the outcome of the election."

On Jan. 12, 2017, Washington Post columnist David Ignatius reported that Flynn and Kislyak had spoken on the day the sanctions were announced. Ignatius wrote that it was unclear what they had discussed, but he questioned whether Flynn had said something to undercut the Obama administration.

> According to a senior U.S. government official, Flynn phoned Russian Ambassador Sergey Kislyak several times on Dec. 29, the day the Obama administration announced the expulsion of 35 Russian officials as well as other measures in retaliation for the hacking. What did Flynn say, and did it undercut the U.S. sanctions? The Logan Act (though never enforced) bars U.S. citizens from correspondence intending to influence a foreign government about "disputes" with the United States. Was its spirit violated? The Trump campaign didn't immediately respond to a request for comment.

The revelation caused a stir. Trump was already facing questions about Russia's interference in the election, and now it appeared his incoming national security adviser might have secretly undermined Obama's attempts to hold the Russians accountable.

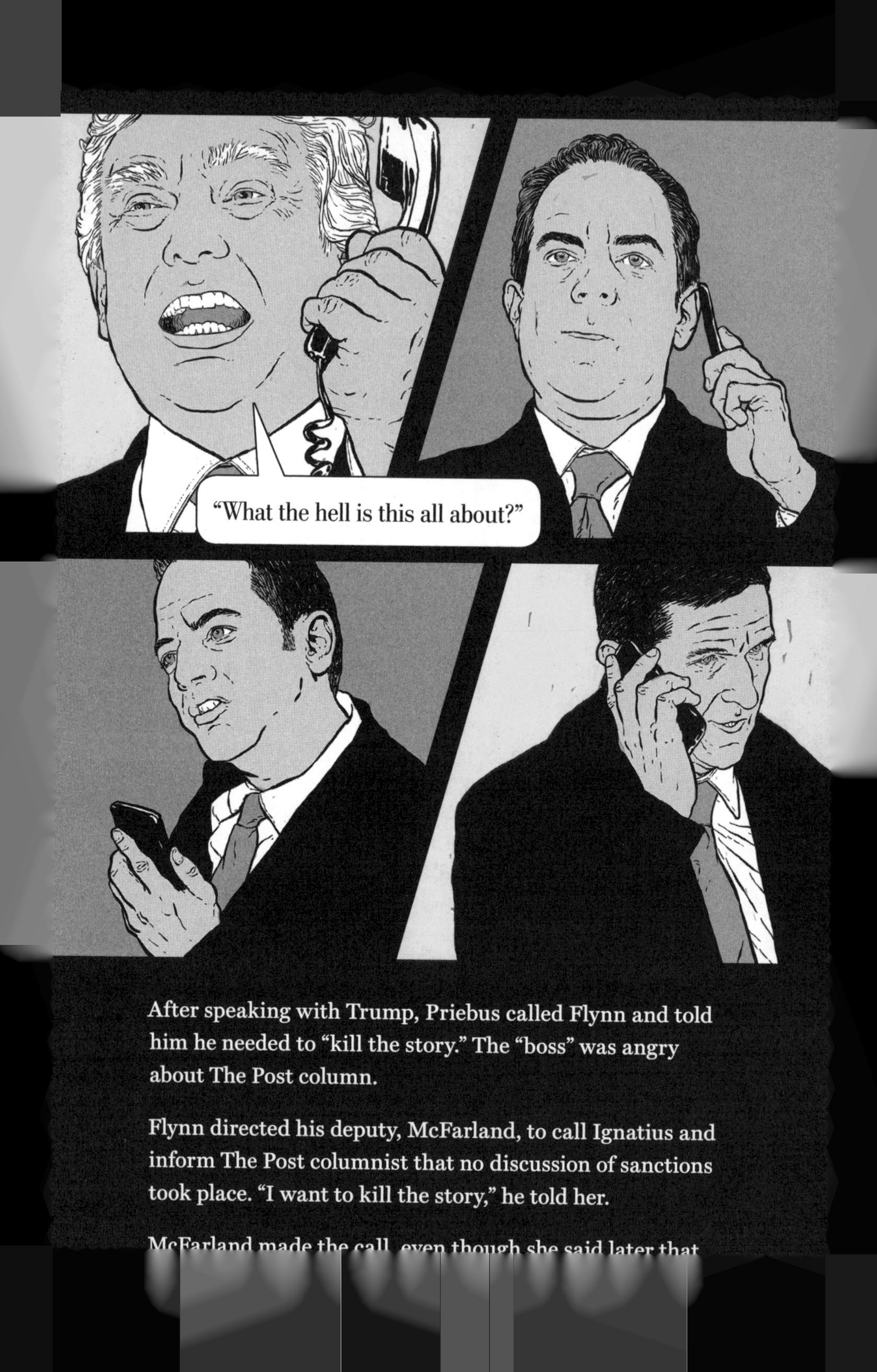
"What the hell is this all about?"

After speaking with Trump, Priebus called Flynn and told him he needed to "kill the story." The "boss" was angry about The Post column.

Flynn directed his deputy, McFarland, to call Ignatius and inform The Post columnist that no discussion of sanctions took place. "I want to kill the story," he told her.

McFarland made the call, even though she said later that

Flynn then told other Trump advisers, including Vice President-elect Mike Pence, that he had not discussed sanctions with Kislyak.

In a round of media interviews, Pence, Priebus and incoming press secretary Sean Spicer denied that Flynn and Kislyak had discussed sanctions.

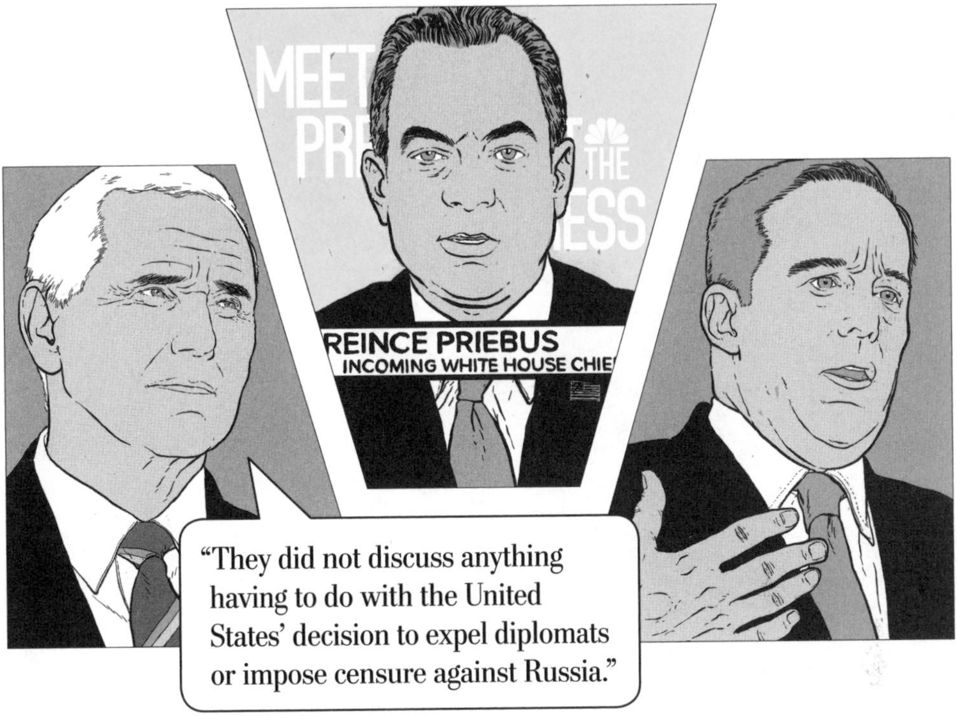
MEET
PR
THE
ESS
REINCE PRIEBUS
INCOMING WHITE HOUSE CHIE
"They did not discuss anything having to do with the United States' decision to expel diplomats or impose censure against Russia."

Senior Justice Department officials were alarmed by their statements, especially the one by Pence. The United States routinely monitors communications of Russian officials. The Justice Department officials knew what Flynn said about his conversations with Kislyak was not true. They feared Flynn's lies gave Russia leverage over him.

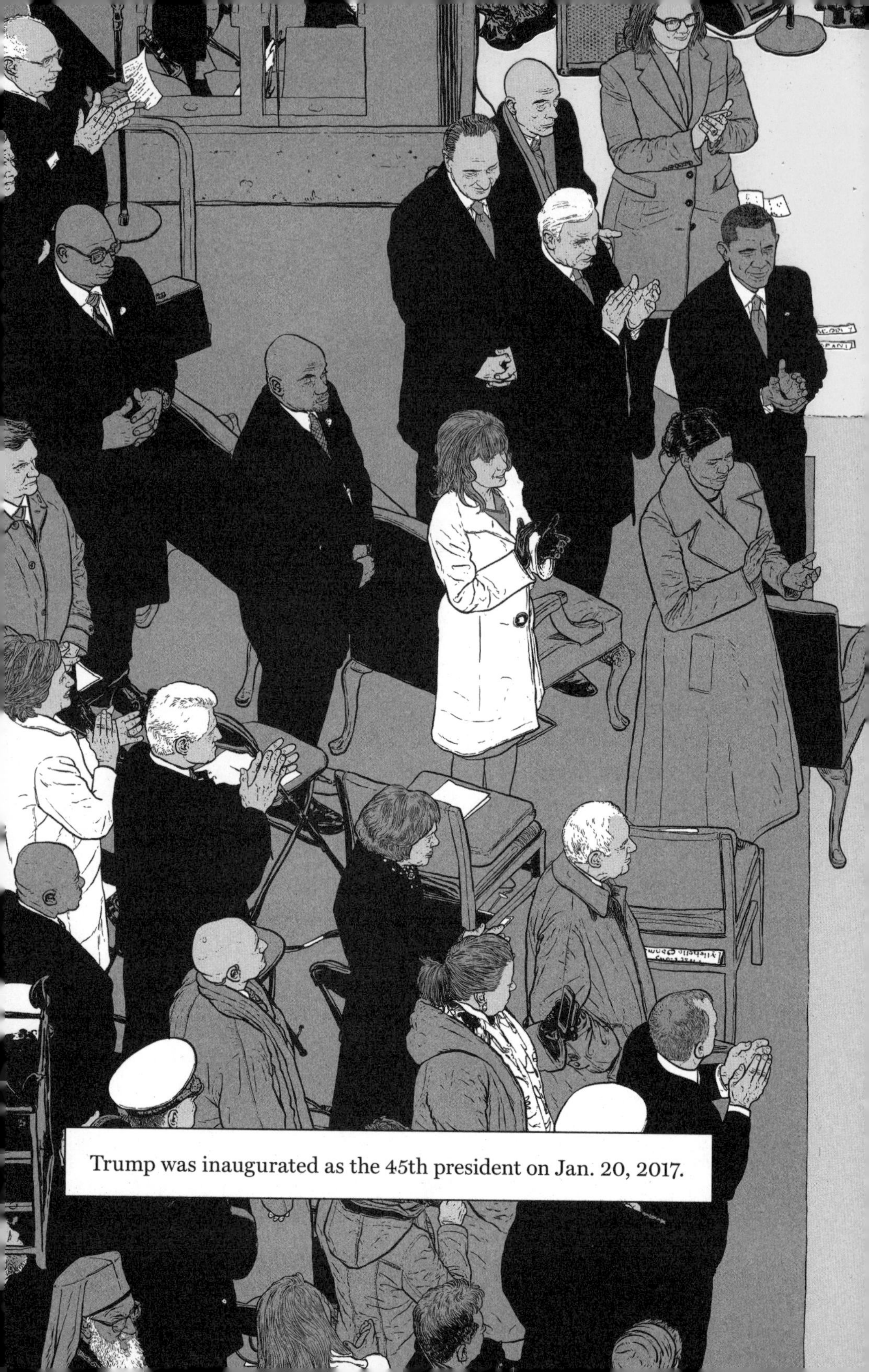

Trump was inaugurated as the 45th president on Jan. 20, 2017.

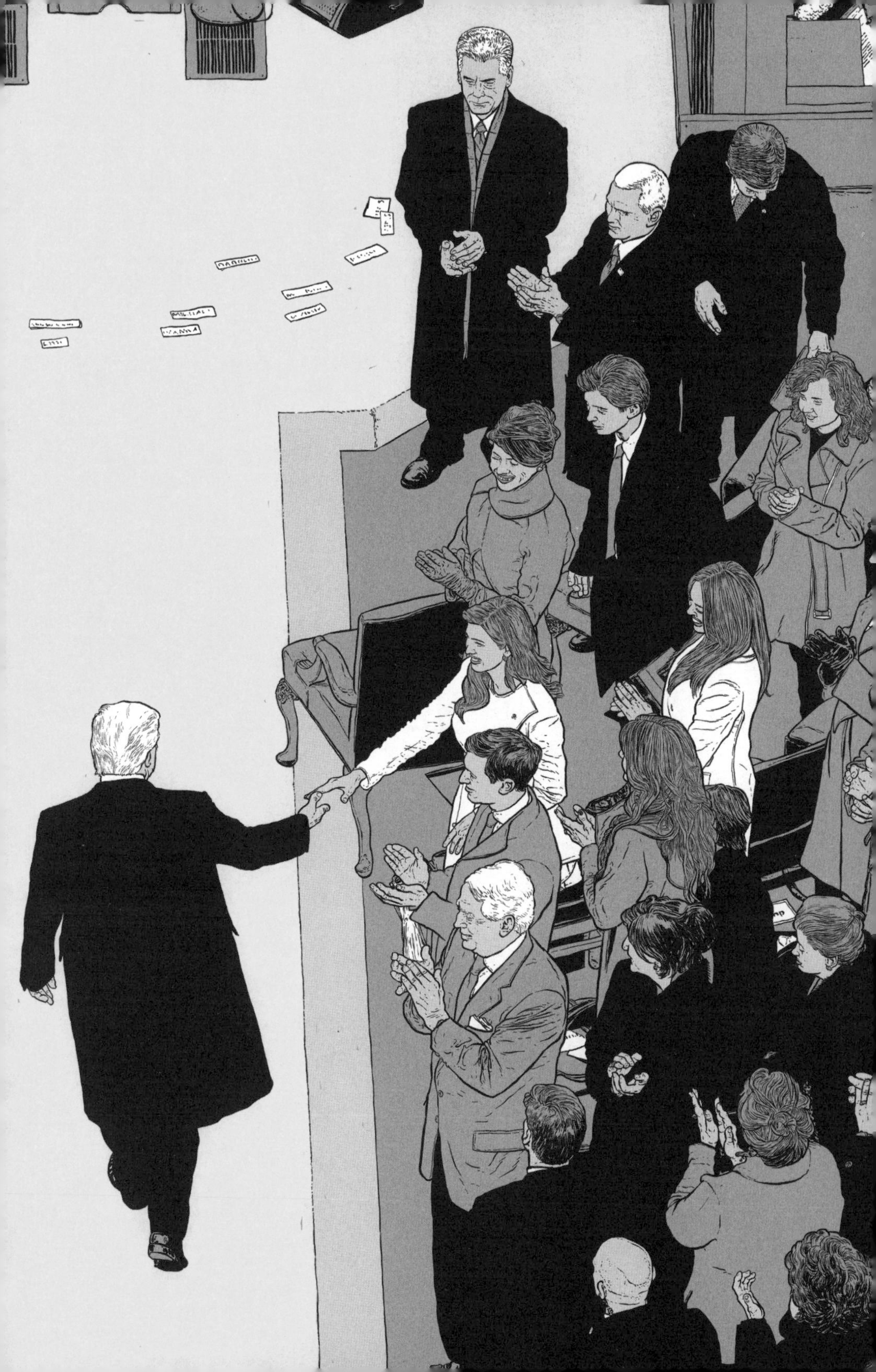

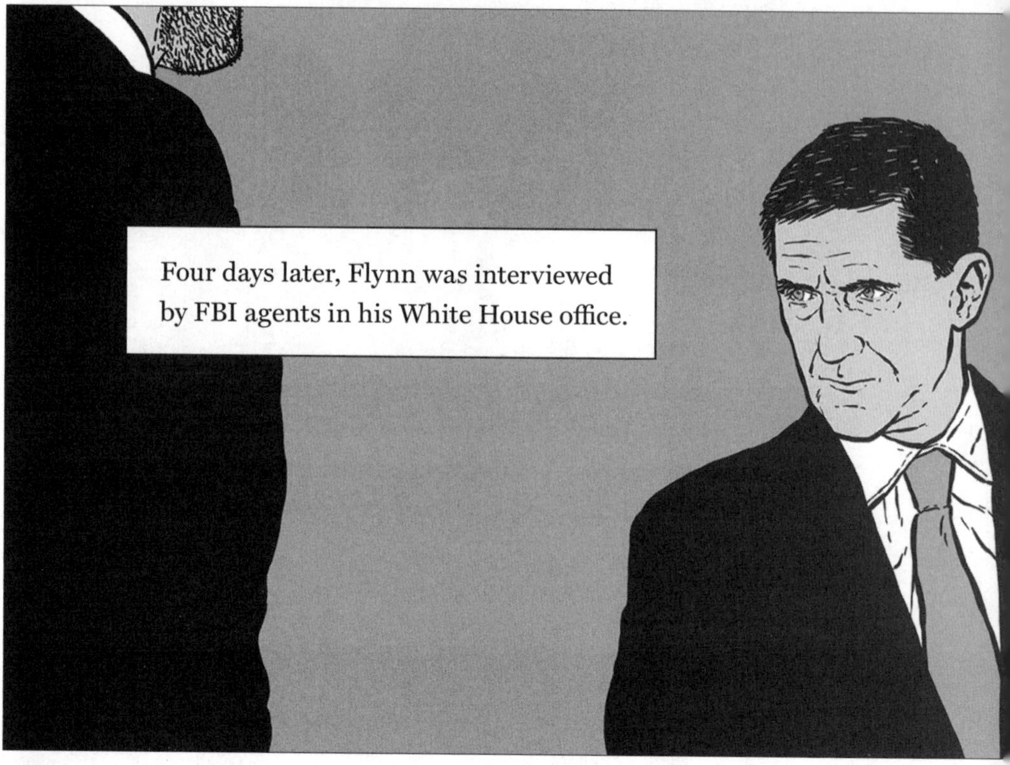
Four days later, Flynn was interviewed by FBI agents in his White House office.

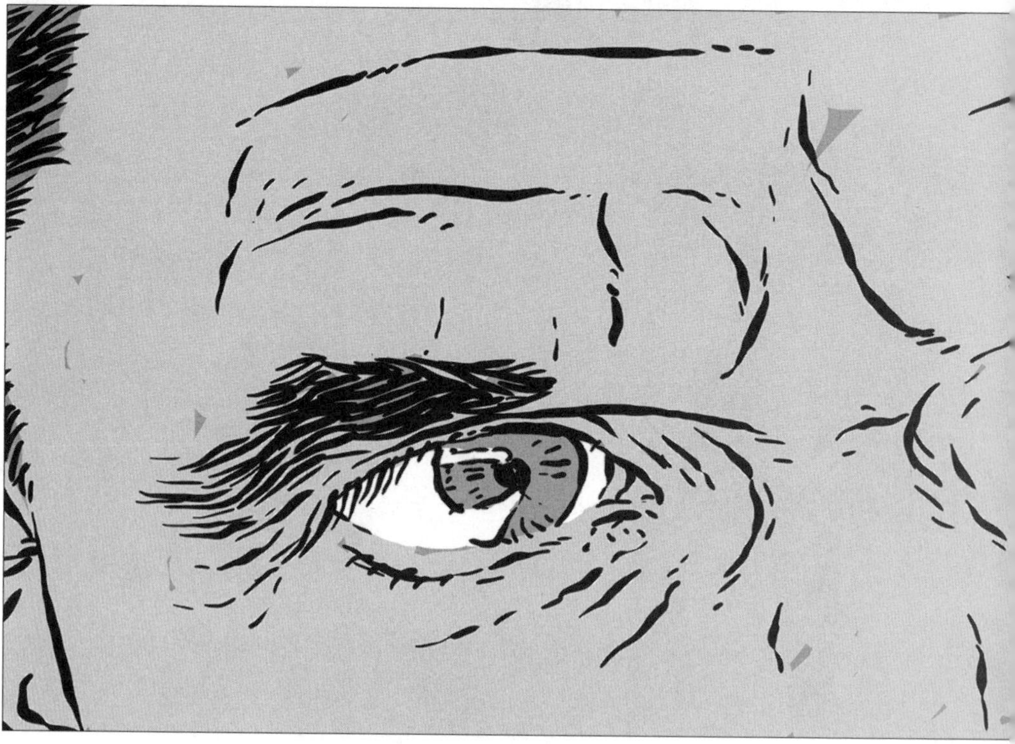

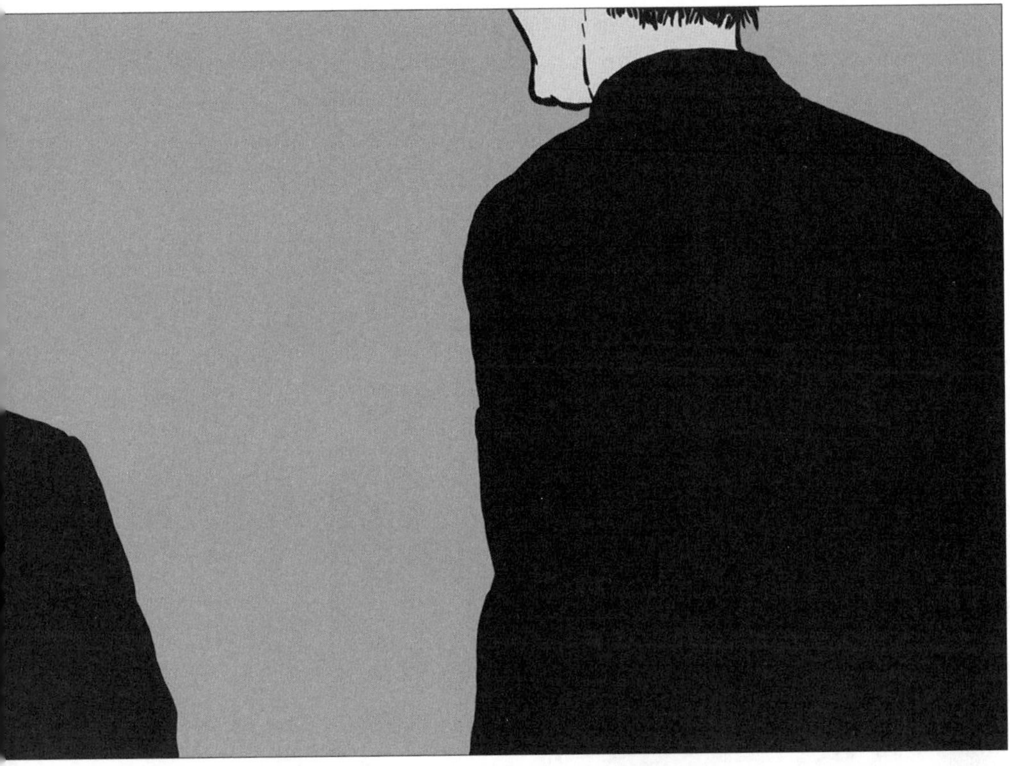

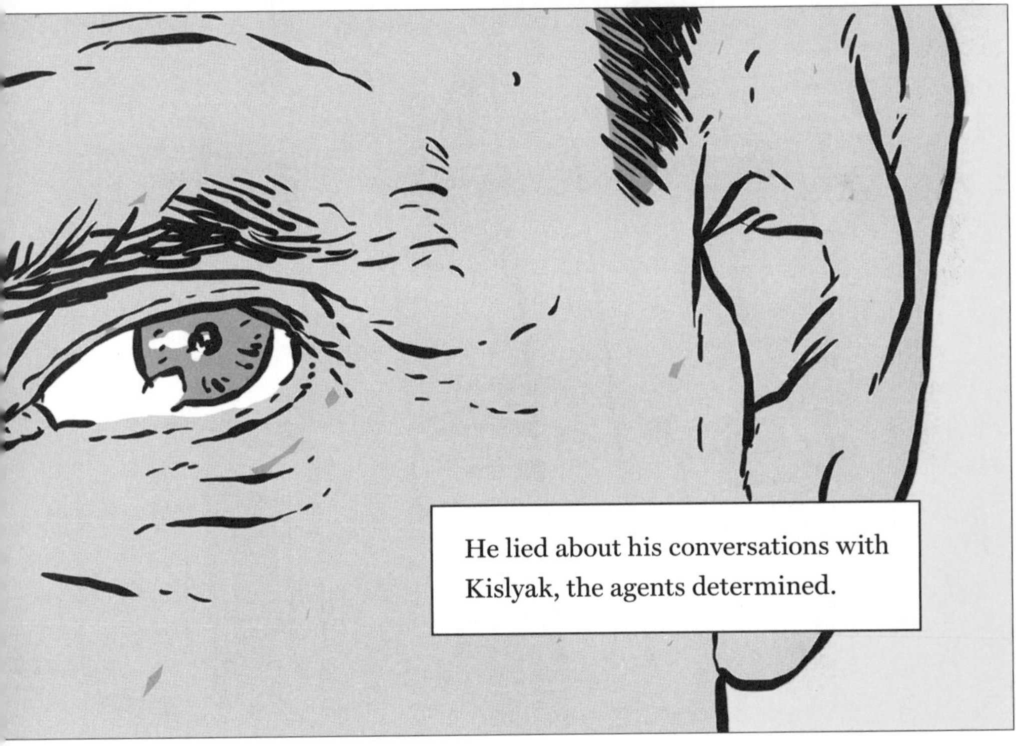
He lied about his conversations with Kislyak, the agents determined.

On Jan. 26, senior Justice Department officials Sally Yates and Mary McCord met with White House Counsel Donald McGahn at the White House. They warned him that Pence's public statements defending Flynn were not true and could make Flynn a target of blackmail by the Russians. Yates also revealed that Flynn had been interviewed by the FBI.

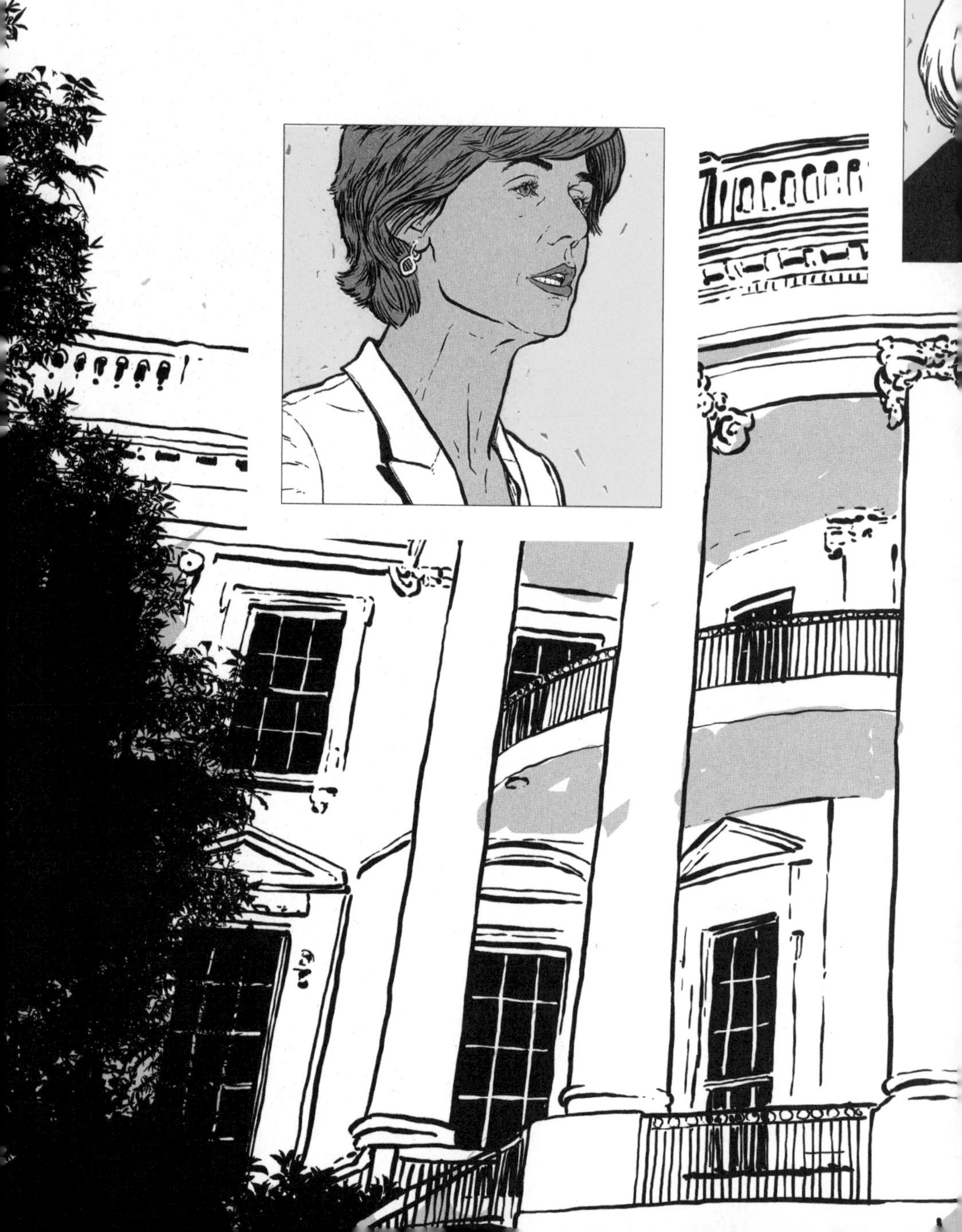

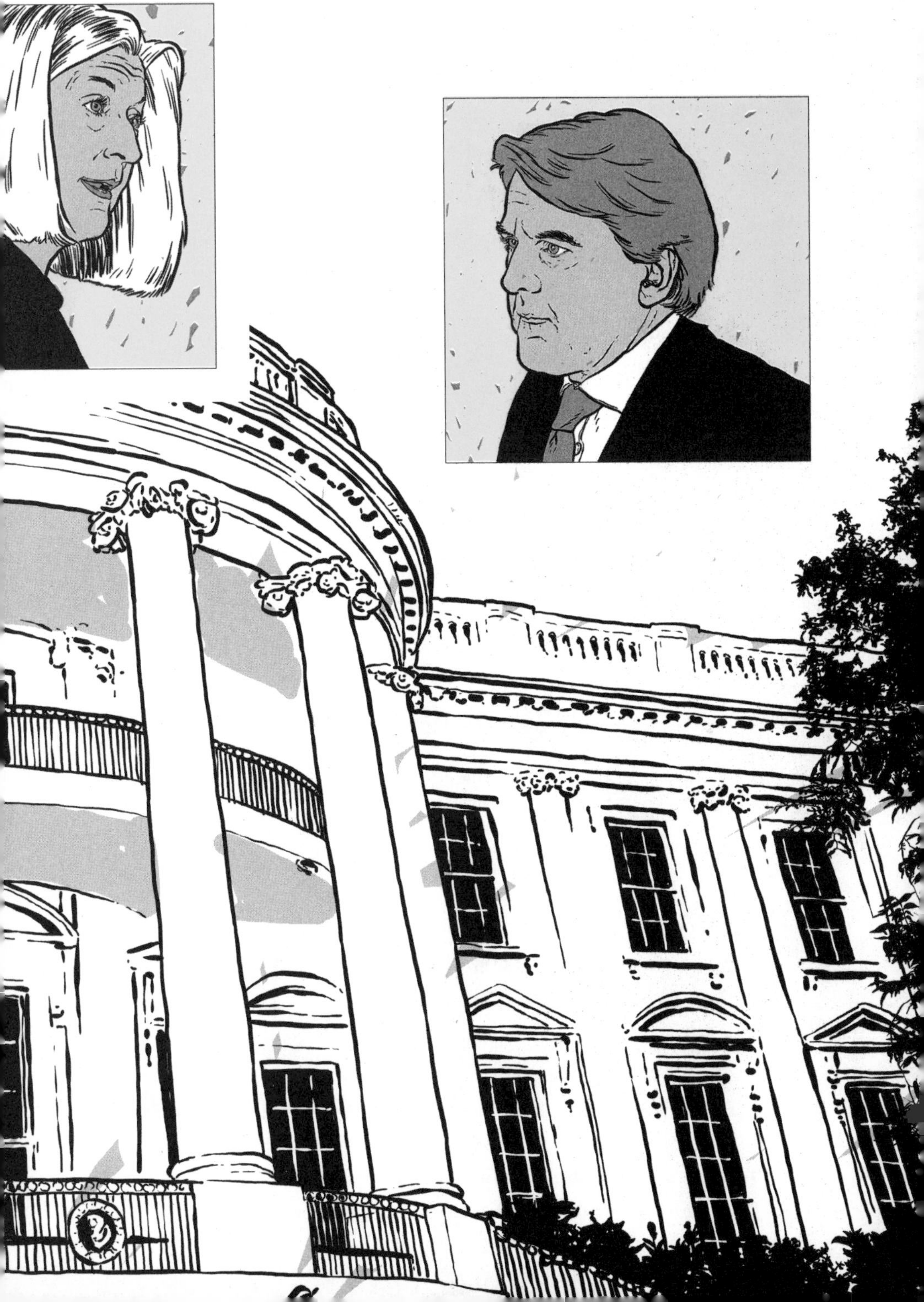

This was serious: The White House now knew that the FBI was examining Flynn's interactions with the Russian ambassador. McGahn immediately told Trump about the Justice Department warnings and that Flynn had been interviewed.

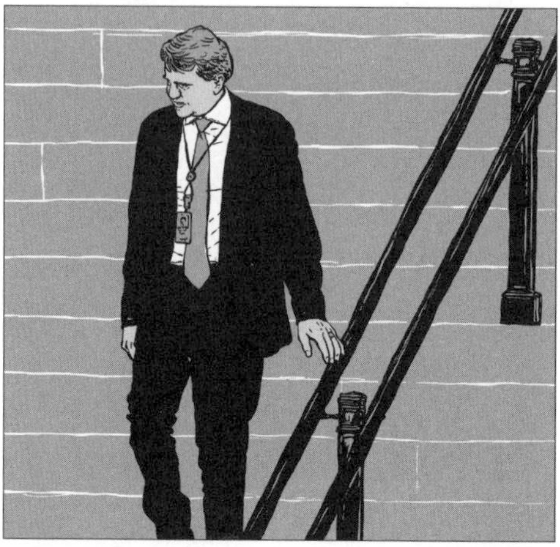

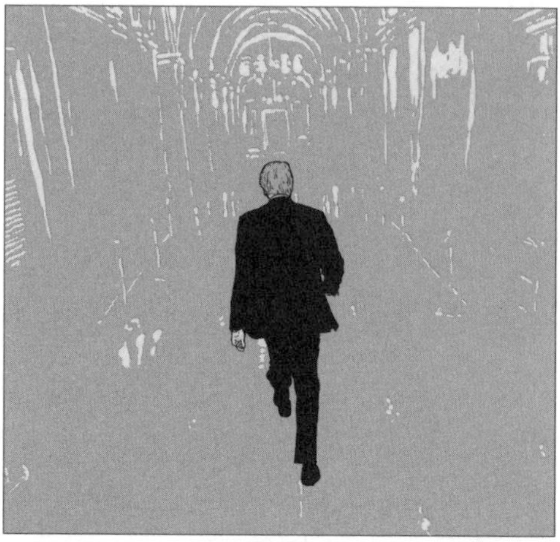

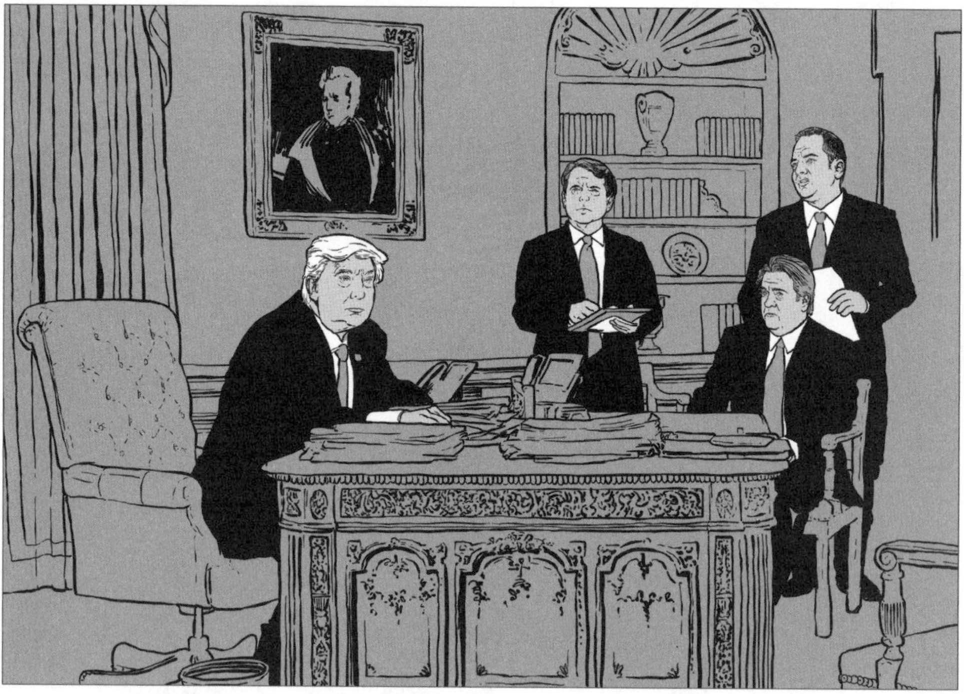

Trump told McGahn, Priebus and senior adviser Stephen K. Bannon to look into the situation — and to keep it quiet.

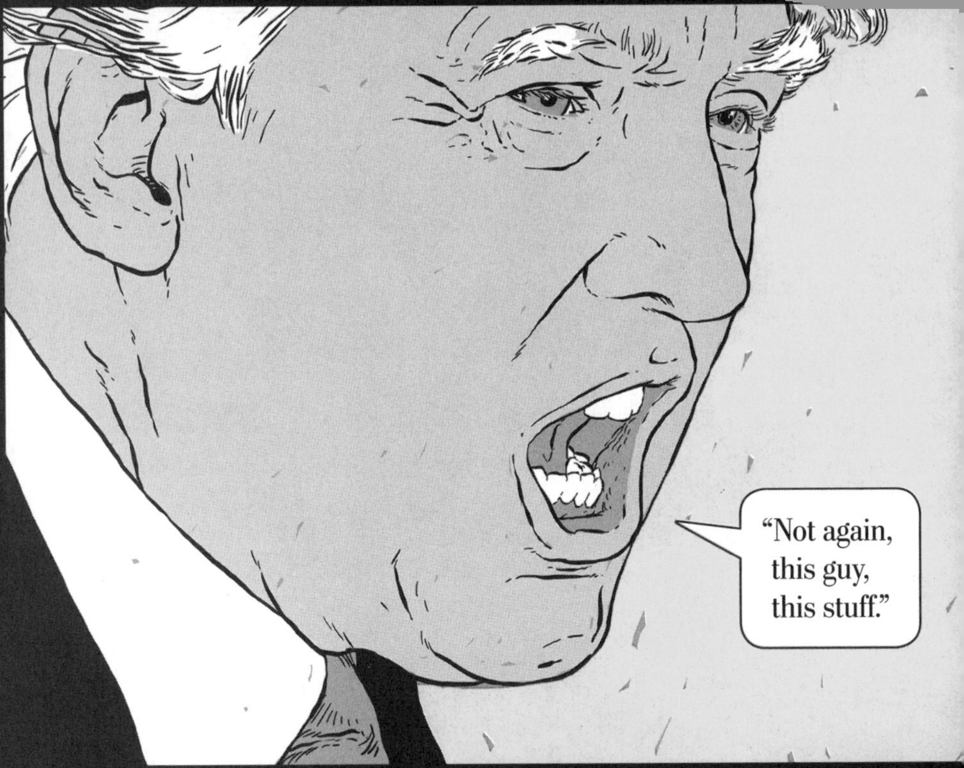
"Not again, this guy, this stuff."

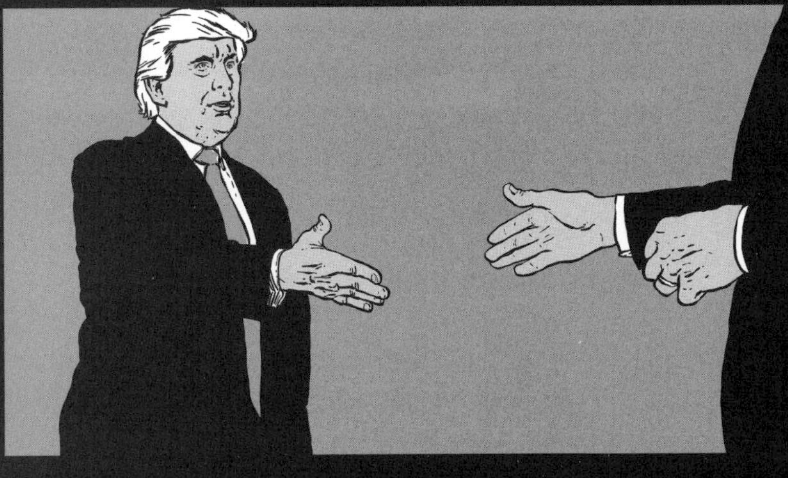

The next day, Jan. 27, Trump invited FBI Director James B. Comey to dinner at the White House. Trump made it clear to aides that he wanted to be alone with Comey, rejecting a suggestion by Bannon that he or Priebus also attend

When Comey arrived, he was taken aback to discover no one else was joining them.

Over dinner, Trump attempted to extract a promise.

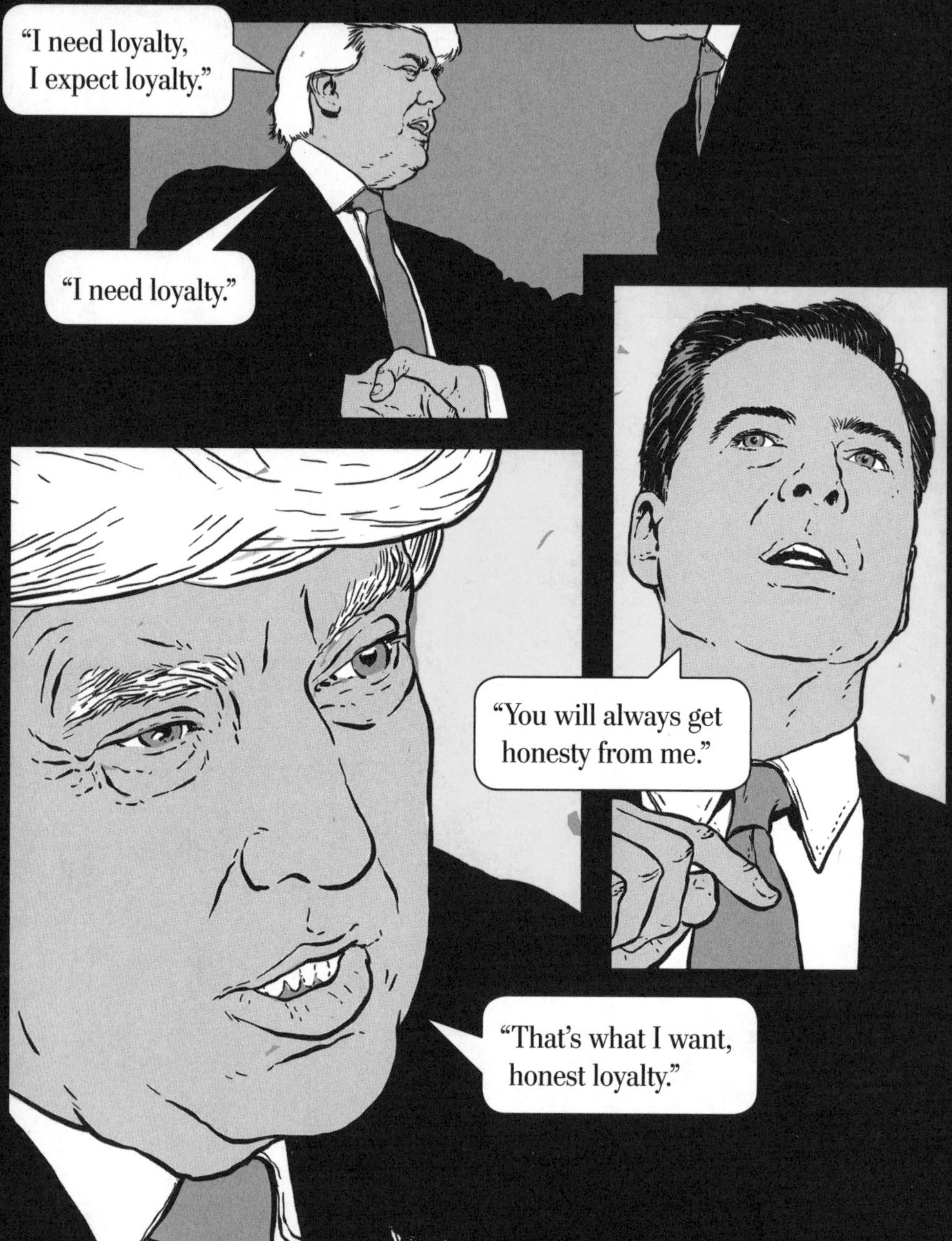
"I need loyalty, I expect loyalty."
"I need loyalty."
"You will always get honesty from me."
"That's what I want, honest loyalty."

Comey was uncomfortable and felt Trump was trying to secure a promise that he would protect the president's interests over anything else.

Days later, Trump and Flynn had a one-on-one conversation in the Oval Office. The president was upset about the stories and asked his national security adviser what he told the Russian ambassador.

Flynn acknowledged to Trump that he might have discussed sanctions with Kislyak.

On Feb. 9, The Washington Post broke the news that Flynn had in fact discussed sanctions with Kislyak before Trump took office, despite the denials from the vice president and top Trump aides.

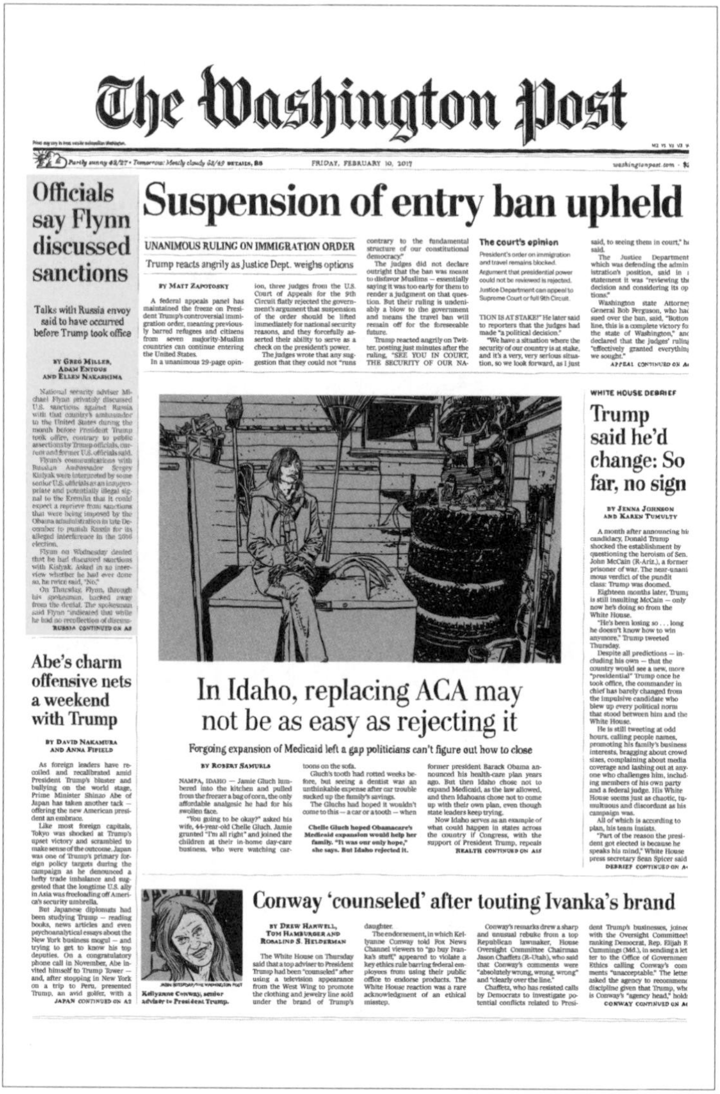

The Washington Post

Partly sunny 42/27 • Tomorrow: Mostly cloudy 62/49 DETAILS, B8 — FRIDAY, FEBRUARY 10, 2017 — washingtonpost.com

Officials say Flynn discussed sanctions

Talks with Russia envoy said to have occurred before Trump took office

BY GREG MILLER, ADAM ENTOUS AND ELLEN NAKASHIMA

National security adviser Michael Flynn privately discussed U.S. sanctions against Russia with that country's ambassador to the United States during the month before President Trump took office, contrary to public assertions by Trump officials, current and former U.S. officials said.

Flynn's communications with Russian Ambassador Sergey Kislyak were interpreted by some senior U.S. officials as an inappropriate and potentially illegal signal to the Kremlin that it could expect a reprieve from sanctions that were being imposed by the Obama administration in late December to punish Russia for its alleged interference in the 2016 election.

Flynn on Wednesday denied that he had discussed sanctions with Kislyak. Asked in an interview whether he had ever done so, he twice said, "No."

On Thursday, Flynn, through his spokesman, backed away from the denial. The spokesman said Flynn "indicated that while he had no recollection of discuss-

RUSSIA CONTINUED ON A8

Suspension of entry ban upheld

UNANIMOUS RULING ON IMMIGRATION ORDER

Trump reacts angrily as Justice Dept. weighs options

BY MATT ZAPOTOSKY

A federal appeals panel has maintained the freeze on President Trump's controversial immigration order, meaning previously barred refugees and citizens from seven majority-Muslim countries can continue entering the United States.

In a unanimous 29-page opinion, three judges from the U.S. Court of Appeals for the 9th Circuit flatly rejected the government's argument that suspension of the order should be lifted immediately for national security reasons, and they forcefully asserted their ability to serve as a check on the president's power.

The judges wrote that any suggestion that they could not "runs contrary to the fundamental structure of our constitutional democracy."

The judges did not declare outright that the ban was meant to disfavor Muslims — essentially saying it was too early for them to render a judgment on that question. But their ruling is undeniably a blow to the government and means the travel ban will remain off for the foreseeable future.

Trump reacted angrily on Twitter, posting just minutes after the ruling, "SEE YOU IN COURT, THE SECURITY OF OUR NATION IS AT STAKE!" He later said to reporters that the judges had made "a political decision."

"We have a situation where the security of our country is at stake, and it's a very, very serious situation, so we look forward, as I just said, to seeing them in court," he said.

The Justice Department, which was defending the administration's position, said in a statement it was "reviewing the decision and considering its options."

Washington state Attorney General Bob Ferguson, who had sued over the ban, said, "Bottom line, this is a complete victory for the state of Washington," and declared that the judges' ruling "effectively granted everything we sought."

APPEAL CONTINUED ON A4

The court's opinion

President's order on immigration and travel remains blocked.

Argument that presidential power could not be reviewed is rejected.

Justice Department can appeal to Supreme Court or full 9th Circuit.

In Idaho, replacing ACA may not be as easy as rejecting it

Forgoing expansion of Medicaid left a gap politicians can't figure out how to close

BY ROBERT SAMUELS

NAMPA, IDAHO — Jamie Gluch lumbered into the kitchen and pulled from the freezer a bag of corn, the only affordable analgesic he had for his swollen face.

"You going to be okay?" asked his wife, 44-year-old Chelle Gluch. Jamie grunted "I'm all right" and joined the children at their in-home day-care business, who were watching cartoons on the sofa.

Gluch's tooth had rotted weeks before, but seeing a dentist was an unthinkable expense after car trouble sucked up the family's savings.

The Gluchs had hoped it wouldn't come to this — a car or a tooth — when former president Barack Obama announced his health-care plan years ago. But then Idaho chose not to expand Medicaid, as the law allowed, and then Idahoans chose not to come up with their own plan, even though state leaders keep trying.

Now Idaho serves as an example of what could happen in states across the country if Congress, with the support of President Trump, repeals

HEALTH CONTINUED ON A15

Chelle Gluch hoped Obamacare's Medicaid expansion would help her family. "It was our only hope," she says. But Idaho rejected it.

WHITE HOUSE DEBRIEF

Trump said he'd change: So far, no sign

BY JENNA JOHNSON AND KAREN TUMULTY

A month after announcing his candidacy, Donald Trump shocked the establishment by questioning the heroism of Sen. John McCain (R-Ariz.), a former prisoner of war. The near-unanimous verdict of the pundit class: Trump was doomed.

Eighteen months later, Trump is still insulting McCain — only now he's doing so from the White House.

"He's been losing so . . . long he doesn't know how to win anymore," Trump tweeted Thursday.

Despite all predictions — including his own — that the country would see a new, more "presidential" Trump once he took office, the commander in chief has barely changed from the impulsive candidate who blew up every political norm that stood between him and the White House.

He is still tweeting at odd hours, calling people names, promoting his family's business interests, bragging about crowd sizes, complaining about media coverage and lashing out at anyone who challenges him, including members of his own party and a federal judge. His White House seems just as chaotic, tumultuous and discordant as his campaign was.

All of which is according to plan, his team insists.

"Part of the reason the president got elected is because he speaks his mind," White House press secretary Sean Spicer said

DEBRIEF CONTINUED ON A4

Abe's charm offensive nets a weekend with Trump

BY DAVID NAKAMURA AND ANNA FIFIELD

As foreign leaders have recoiled and recalibrated amid President Trump's bluster and bullying on the world stage, Prime Minister Shinzo Abe of Japan has taken another tack — offering the new American president an embrace.

Like most foreign capitals, Tokyo was shocked at Trump's upset victory and scrambled to make sense of the outcome. Japan was one of Trump's primary foreign policy targets during the campaign as he denounced a hefty trade imbalance and suggested that the longtime U.S. ally in Asia was freeloading off America's security umbrella.

But Japanese diplomats had been studying Trump — reading books, news articles and even psychoanalytical essays about the New York business mogul — and trying to get to know his top deputies. On a congratulatory phone call in November, Abe invited himself to Trump Tower — and, after stopping in New York on a trip to Peru, presented Trump, an avid golfer, with a

JAPAN CONTINUED ON A2

Conway 'counseled' after touting Ivanka's brand

Kellyanne Conway, senior adviser to President Trump.

BY DREW HARWELL, TOM HAMBURGER AND ROSALIND S. HELDERMAN

The White House on Thursday said that a top adviser to President Trump had been "counseled" after using a television appearance from the West Wing to promote the clothing and jewelry line sold under the brand of Trump's daughter.

The endorsement, in which Kellyanne Conway told Fox News Channel viewers to "go buy Ivanka's stuff," appeared to violate a key ethics rule barring federal employees from using their public office to endorse products. The White House reaction was a rare acknowledgment of an ethical misstep.

Conway's remarks drew a sharp and unusual rebuke from a top Republican lawmaker, House Oversight Committee Chairman Jason Chaffetz (R-Utah), who said that Conway's comments were "absolutely wrong, wrong, wrong" and "clearly over the line."

Chaffetz, who has resisted calls by Democrats to investigate potential conflicts related to President Trump's businesses, joined with the Oversight Committee's ranking Democrat, Rep. Elijah E. Cummings (Md.), in sending a letter to the Office of Government Ethics calling Conway's comments "unacceptable." The letter asked the agency to recommend discipline given that Trump, who is Conway's "agency head," holds

CONWAY CONTINUED ON A6

McGahn and Priebus decided Flynn could not have forgotten about the details of his conversation with Kislyak and must have lied about them. They told Trump that he should fire the national security adviser.

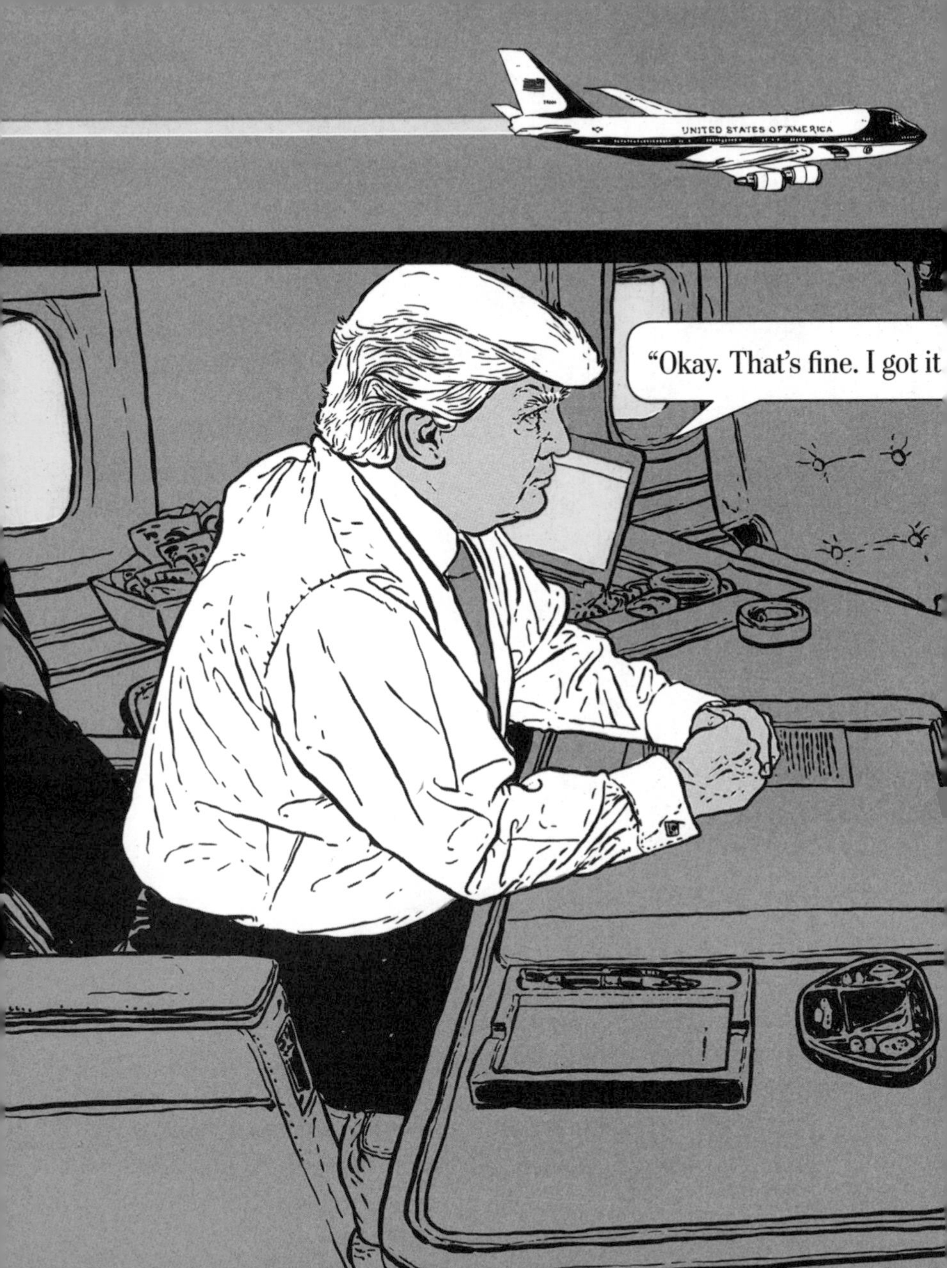
UNITED STATES OF AMERICA
“Okay. That’s fine. I got it

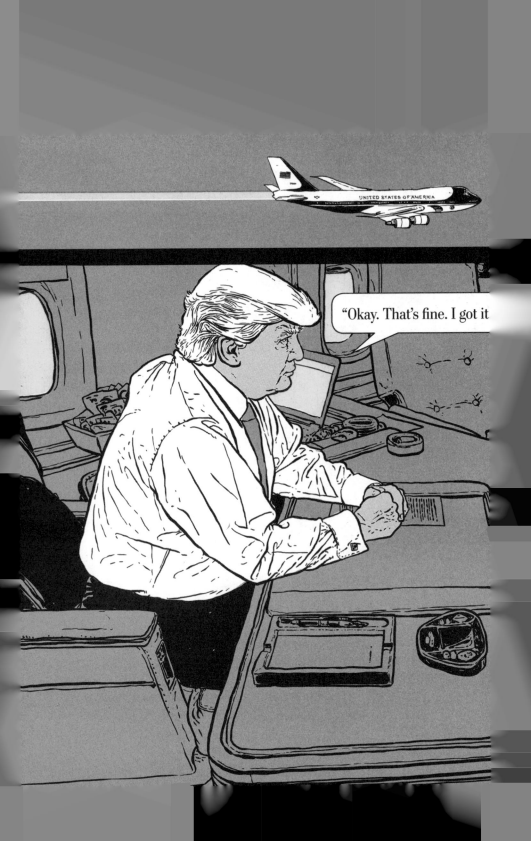

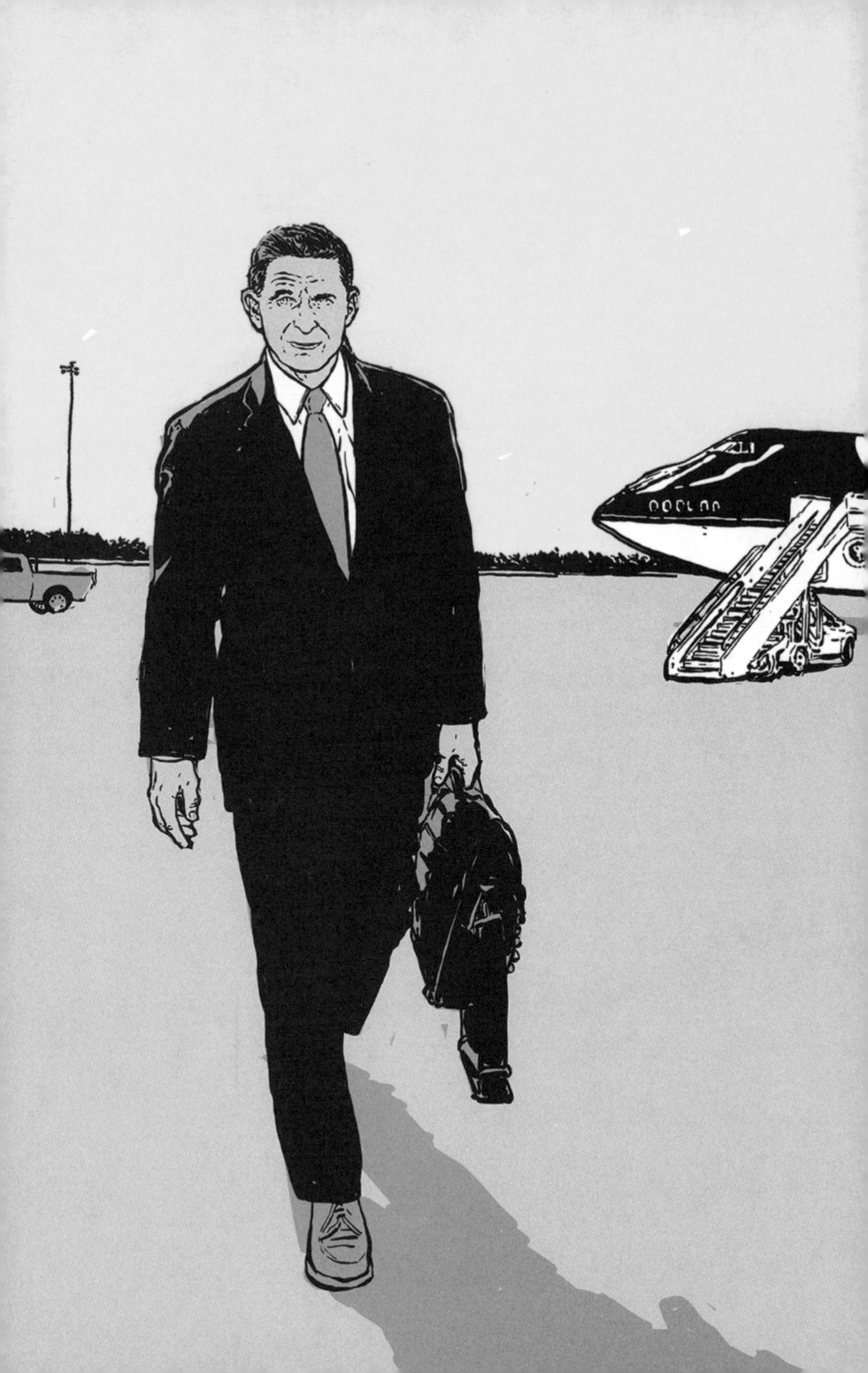

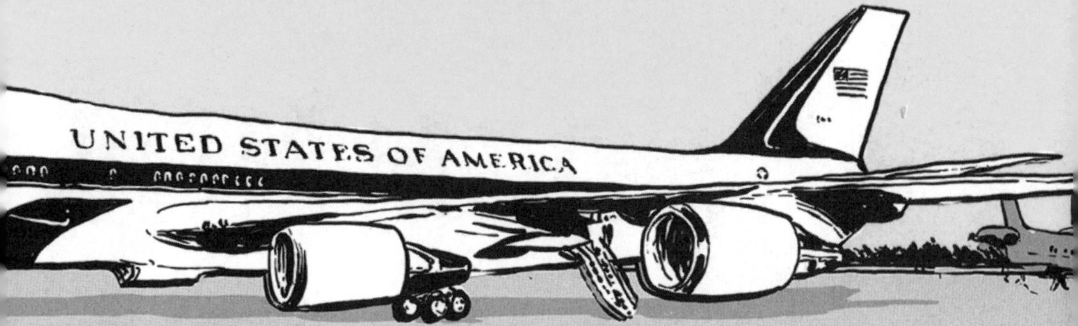
UNITED STATES OF AMERICA

But others in the White House doubted Flynn's story.

The next day, Priebus told Flynn he had to resign.

Flynn said he wanted to say goodbye to the president. Priebus brought Flynn into the Oval Office.

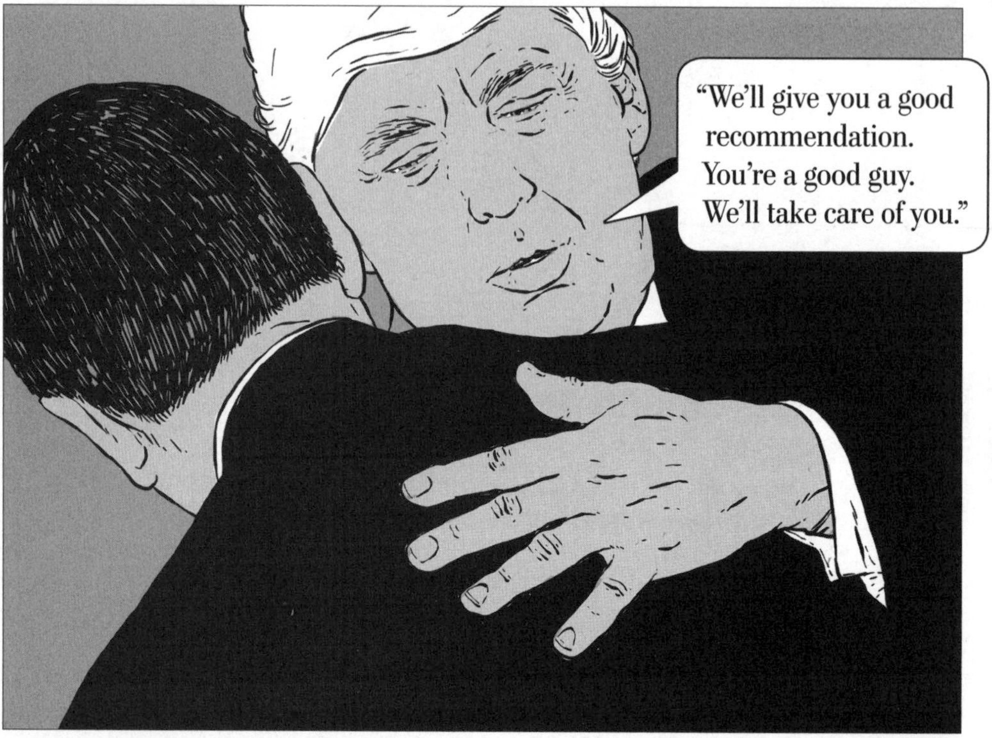
"We'll give you a good recommendation. You're a good guy. We'll take care of you."

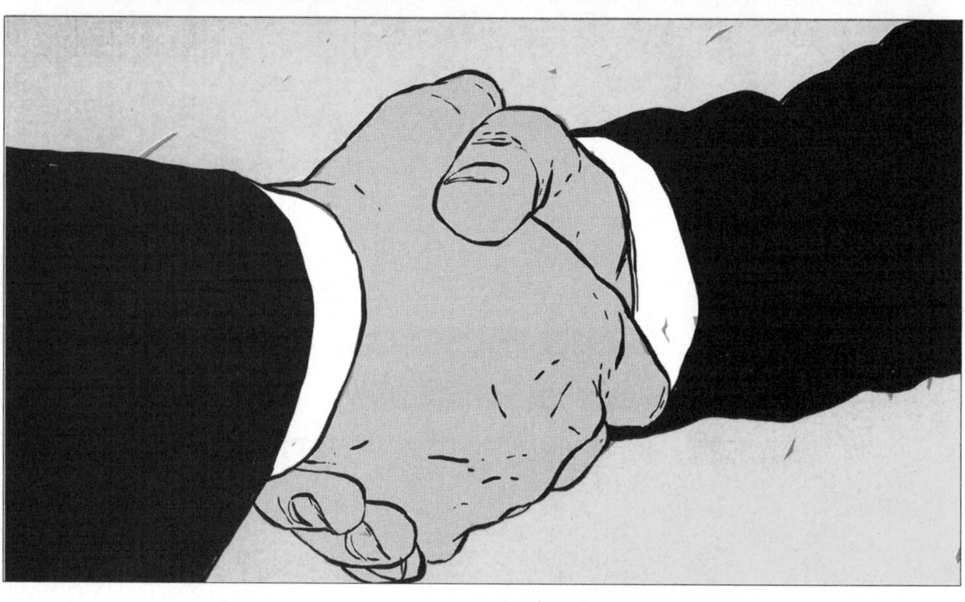

The following day, Feb. 14, New Jersey Gov. Chris Christie came to the White House to visit Trump.

The two men had known each other for years, and Christie was an informal adviser.

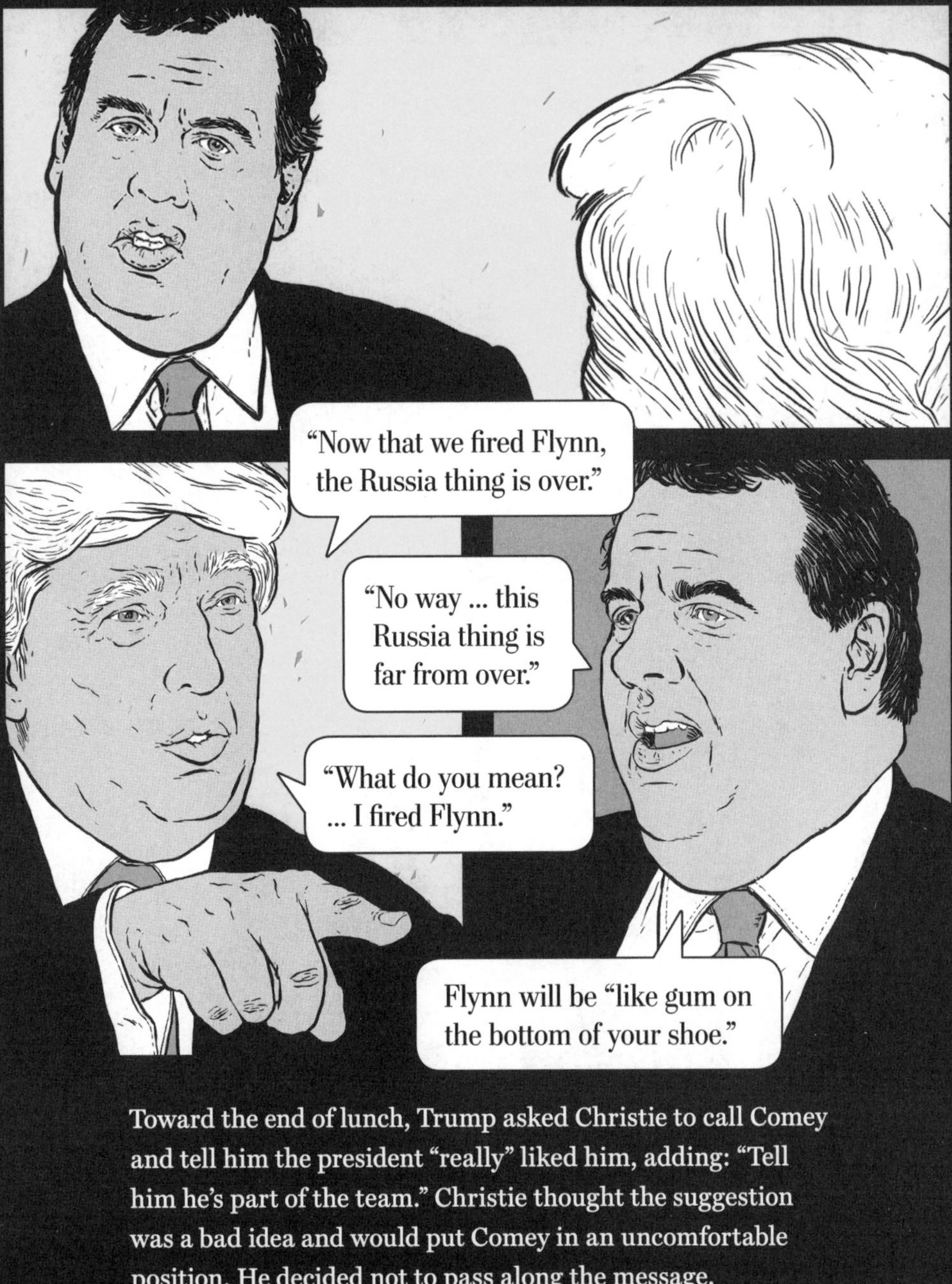
"Now that we fired Flynn, the Russia thing is over."
"No way ... this Russia thing is far from over."
"What do you mean? ... I fired Flynn."
Flynn will be "like gum on the bottom of your shoe."

Toward the end of lunch, Trump asked Christie to call Comey and tell him the president "really" liked him, adding: "Tell him he's part of the team." Christie thought the suggestion was a bad idea and would put Comey in an uncomfortable position. He decided not to pass along the message.

At 4 p.m. that day, the president met with Attorney General Jeff Sessions, Comey, his son-in-law Jared Kushner and other officials for a homeland security briefing in the Oval Office.

At the end, Trump asked to speak to Comey alone. Sessions and Kushner tried to stay, but the president excused them.

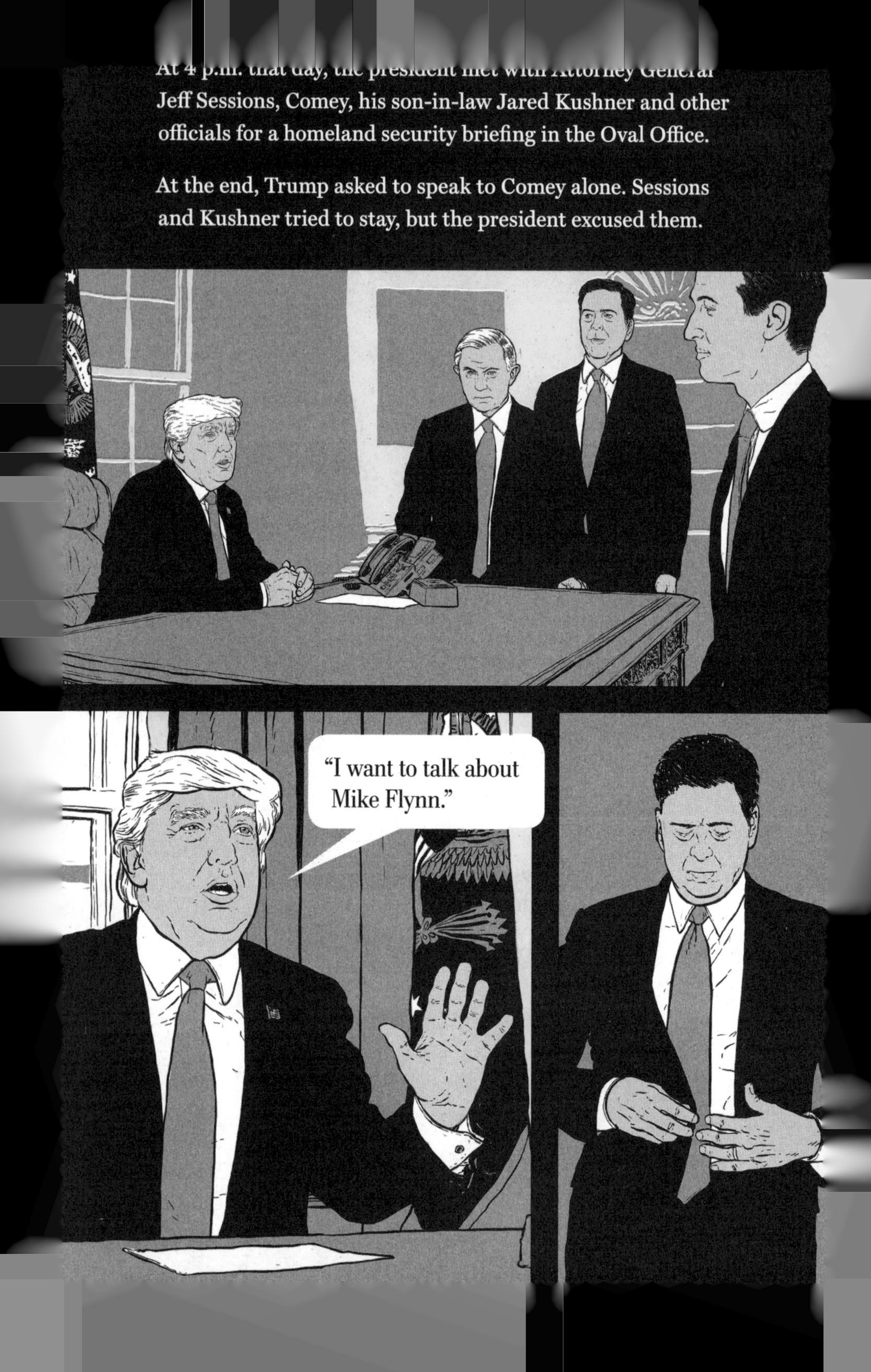
"I want to talk about Mike Flynn."

At one point, Priebus opened the door, but the president did not want to be interrupted. He sent his chief of staff away.

"I hope you can see your way clear to letting this go, to letting Flynn go. He is a good guy. I hope you can let this go."

Flynn "is a good guy."

Comey felt that was as much as he could say. He did not commit to "letting Flynn go" — which he saw as an inappropriate directive to end the investigation.

After his Oval Office meeting with the president, Comey began drafting a memo documenting their conversation.

He also asked Sessions, who as attorney general supervised the FBI, not to leave him alone with Trump again.

About a week later, Bannon and Priebus told McFarland that the president wanted her to resign as deputy national security adviser, but they suggested that she could be appointed ambassador to Singapore.

At Trump's direction, Priebus asked McFarland to put in writing that Trump did not direct Flynn to talk to Kislyak. She refused, saying she did not know whether that was true. She consulted a White House lawyer for advice, who also urged her not to write the letter. He was concerned it could be seen as a quid pro quo for the ambassador position.

McFarland resigned her White House post as requested, but did not write the letter. Trump still nominated her for the ambassadorship, but she ultimately withdrew her name from consideration amid questions about her interactions with Flynn.

On March 31, the news broke that Flynn was offering to cooperate with congressional investigators. In exchange, he wanted immunity.

National Security

Flynn offers to cooperate with congressional probe in exchange for immunity

What Trump and Flynn have said on immunity

Here's what former national security adviser Michael Flynn and President Donald Trump said about immunity in 2016. (Sarah Parnass/The Washington Post)

By **Adam Entous** and **Ellen Nakashima**
March 31, 2017

Former national security adviser Michael Flynn has offered to cooperate with congressional investigators in exchange for immunity from prosecution, a suggestion that has been met with initial skepticism, according to people familiar with the matter.

"General Flynn certainly has a story to tell, and he very much wants to tell it, should the circumstances

Publicly, Trump raged against his enemies.

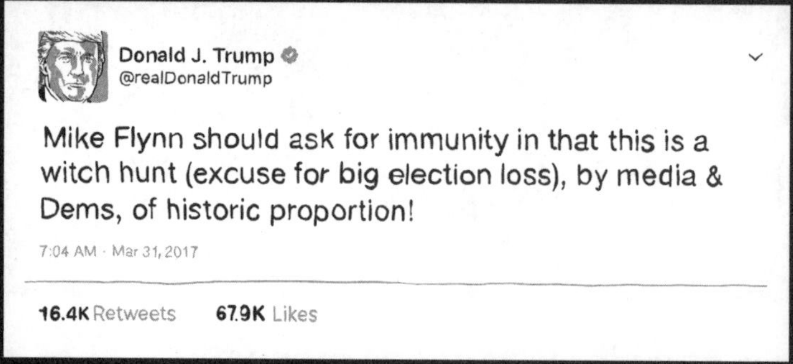

Donald J. Trump
@realDonaldTrump

Mike Flynn should ask for immunity in that this is a witch hunt (excuse for big election loss), by media & Dems, of historic proportion!

7:04 AM · Mar 31, 2017

16.4K Retweets 67.9K Likes

But the FBI and congressional investigations were ramping up, and, privately, Trump appeared concerned about what his ousted national security adviser would say.

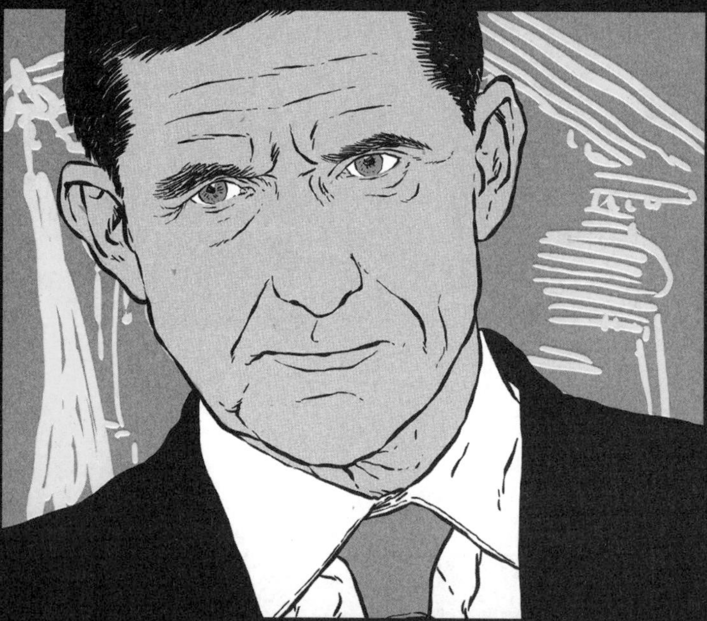

Around that time, Trump asked McFarland to pass a message to Flynn. The president felt bad for Flynn, Trump told McFarland. He should stay strong.

2

The president fires the FBI director

In the spring of 2017, President Trump was brooding. He had been in office fewer than four months, but he felt the weight of the Russia investigation hanging over his young administration.

As FBI Director James B. Comey prepared to testify to Congress in May, Trump saw an opening: The president told his advisers that he wanted Comey to state publicly that Trump was not a subject of the investigation, as the FBI director had previously told him in private. If Comey did not make such a statement, Trump said, it would be the last straw for the director.

Comey did not do as the president hoped. In his May 3 testimony, he confirmed that the FBI was investigating Russia and the 2016 election.

But under questioning from Sen. Richard Blumenthal (D-Conn.), he refused to rule out that the president was under scrutiny as part of the case.

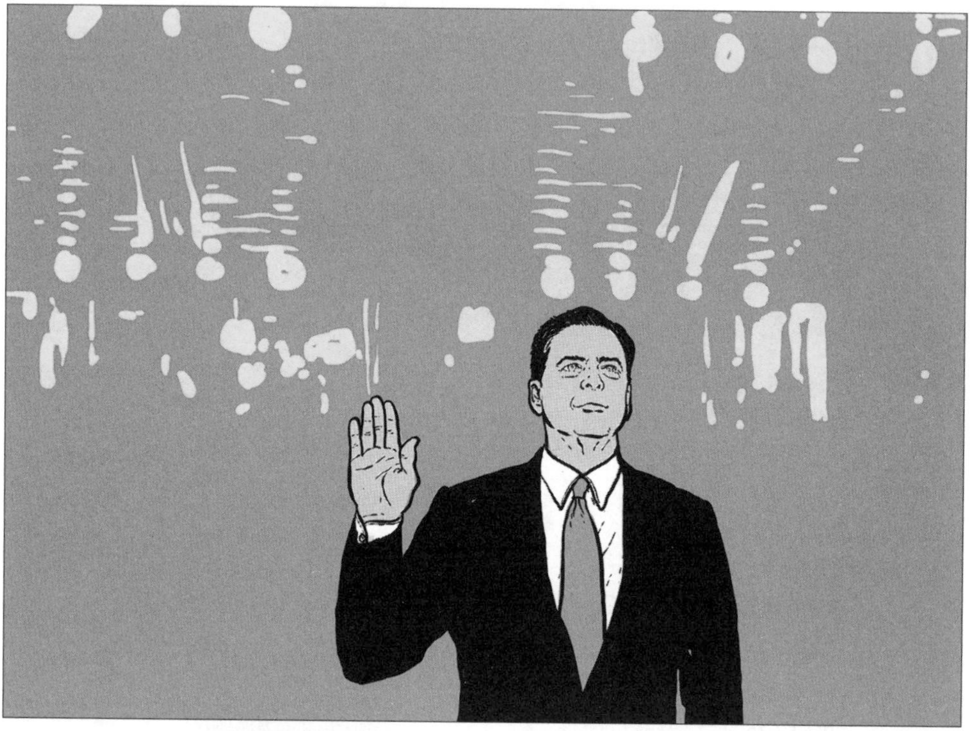

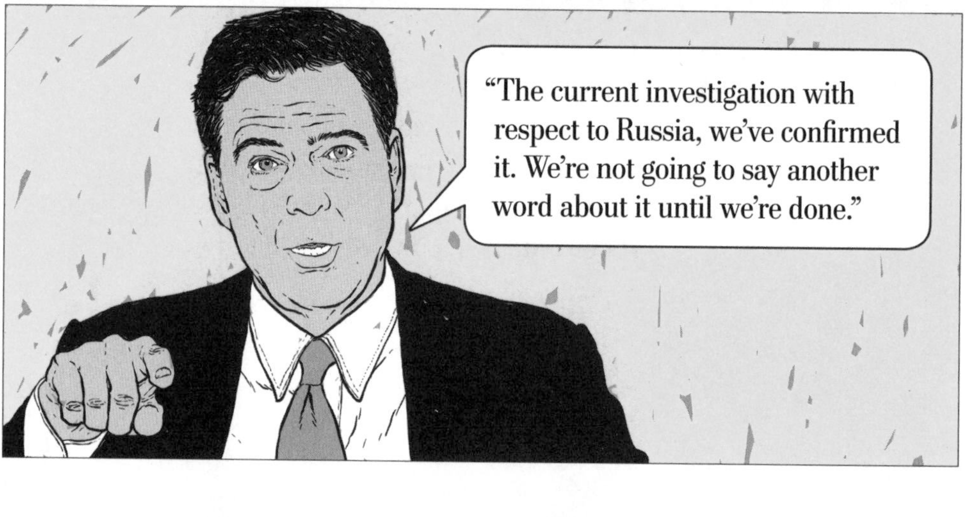
"The current investigation with respect to Russia, we've confirmed it. We're not going to say another word about it until we're done."

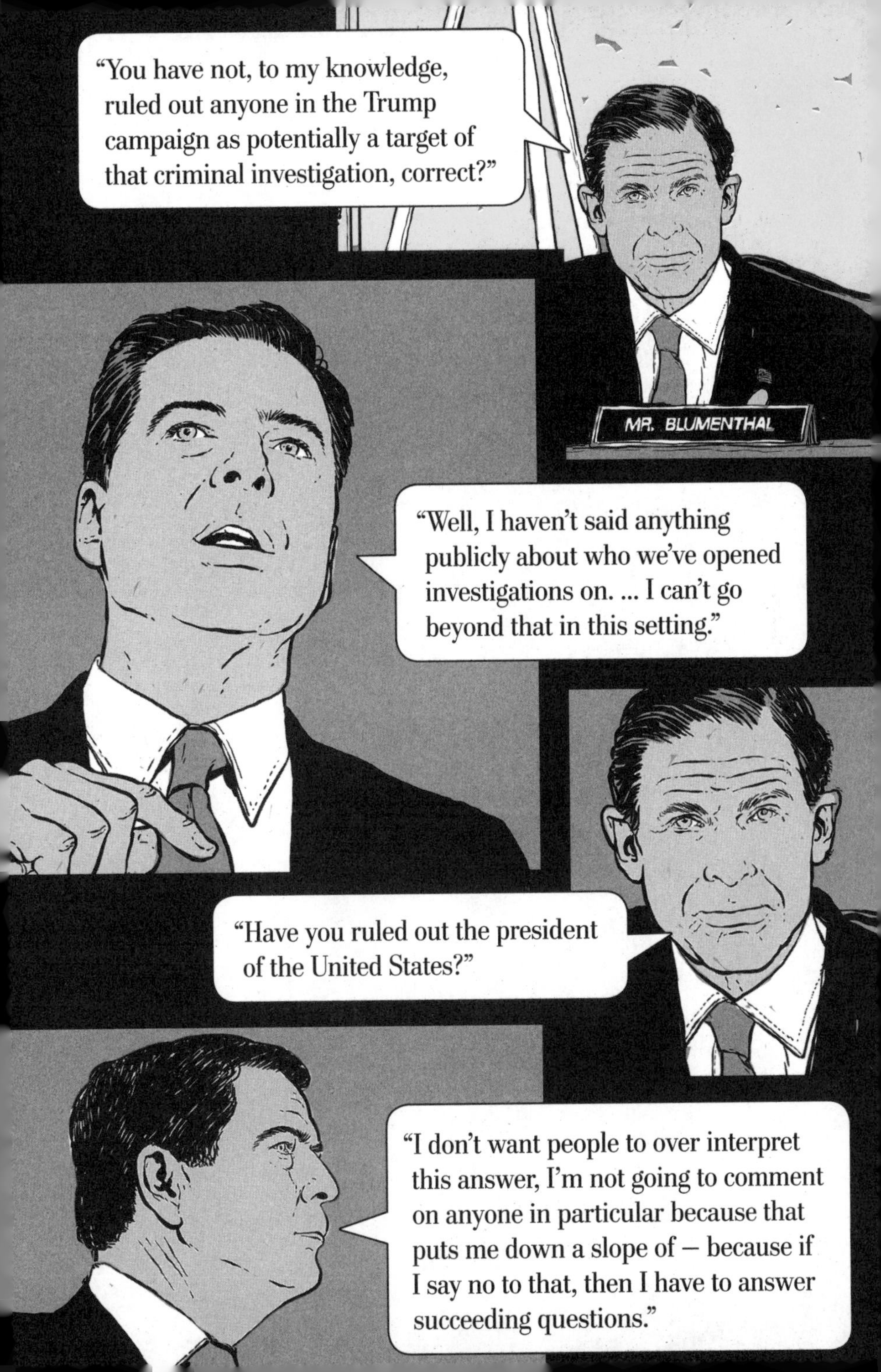
"You have not, to my knowledge, ruled out anyone in the Trump campaign as potentially a target of that criminal investigation, correct?"
MR. BLUMENTHAL
"Well, I haven't said anything publicly about who we've opened investigations on. ... I can't go beyond that in this setting."
"Have you ruled out the president of the United States?"
"I don't want people to over interpret this answer, I'm not going to comment on anyone in particular because that puts me down a slope of – because if I say no to that, then I have to answer succeeding questions."

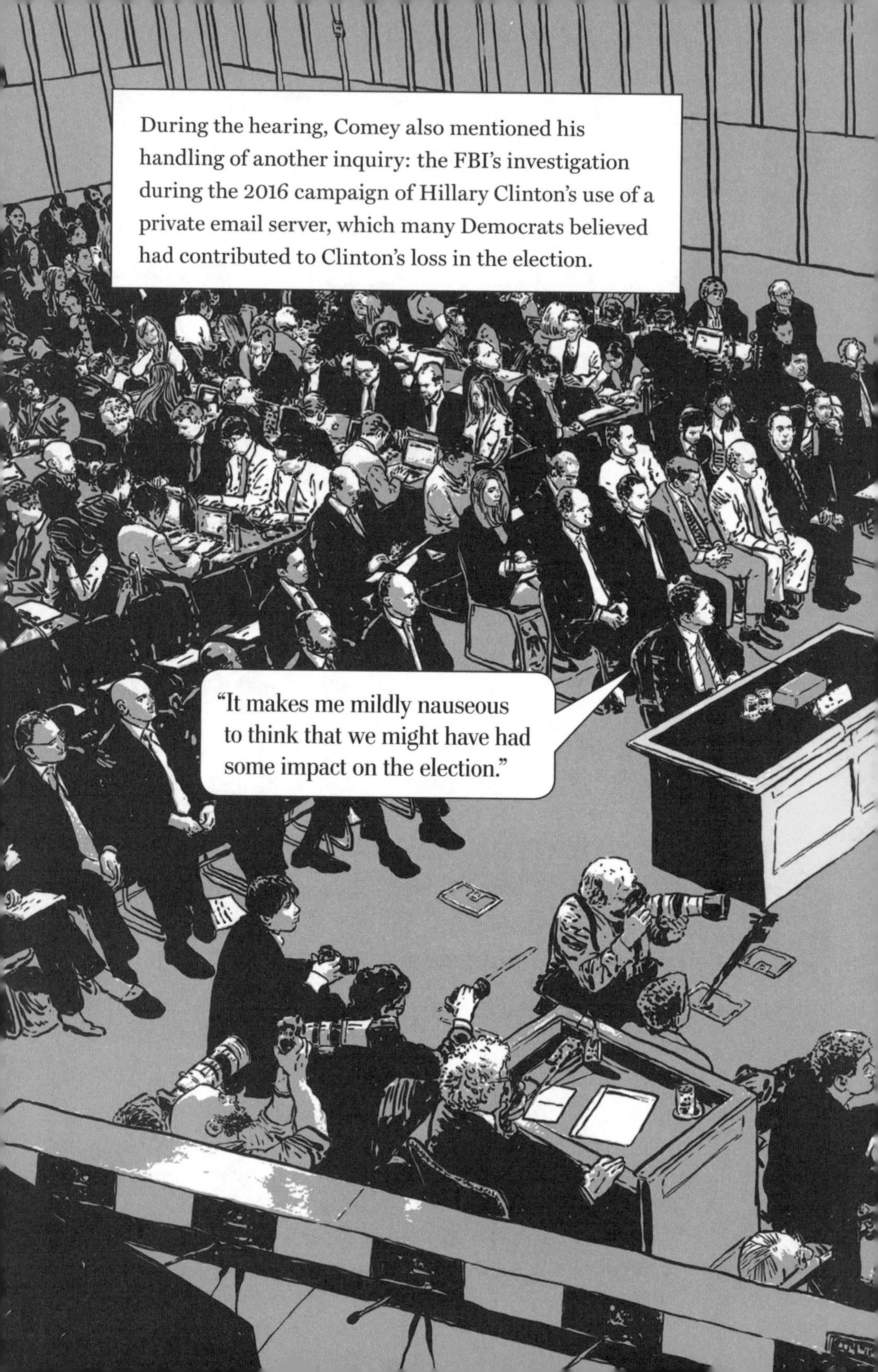
During the hearing, Comey also mentioned his handling of another inquiry: the FBI's investigation during the 2016 campaign of Hillary Clinton's use of a private email server, which many Democrats believed had contributed to Clinton's loss in the election.
"It makes me mildly nauseous to think that we might have had some impact on the election."

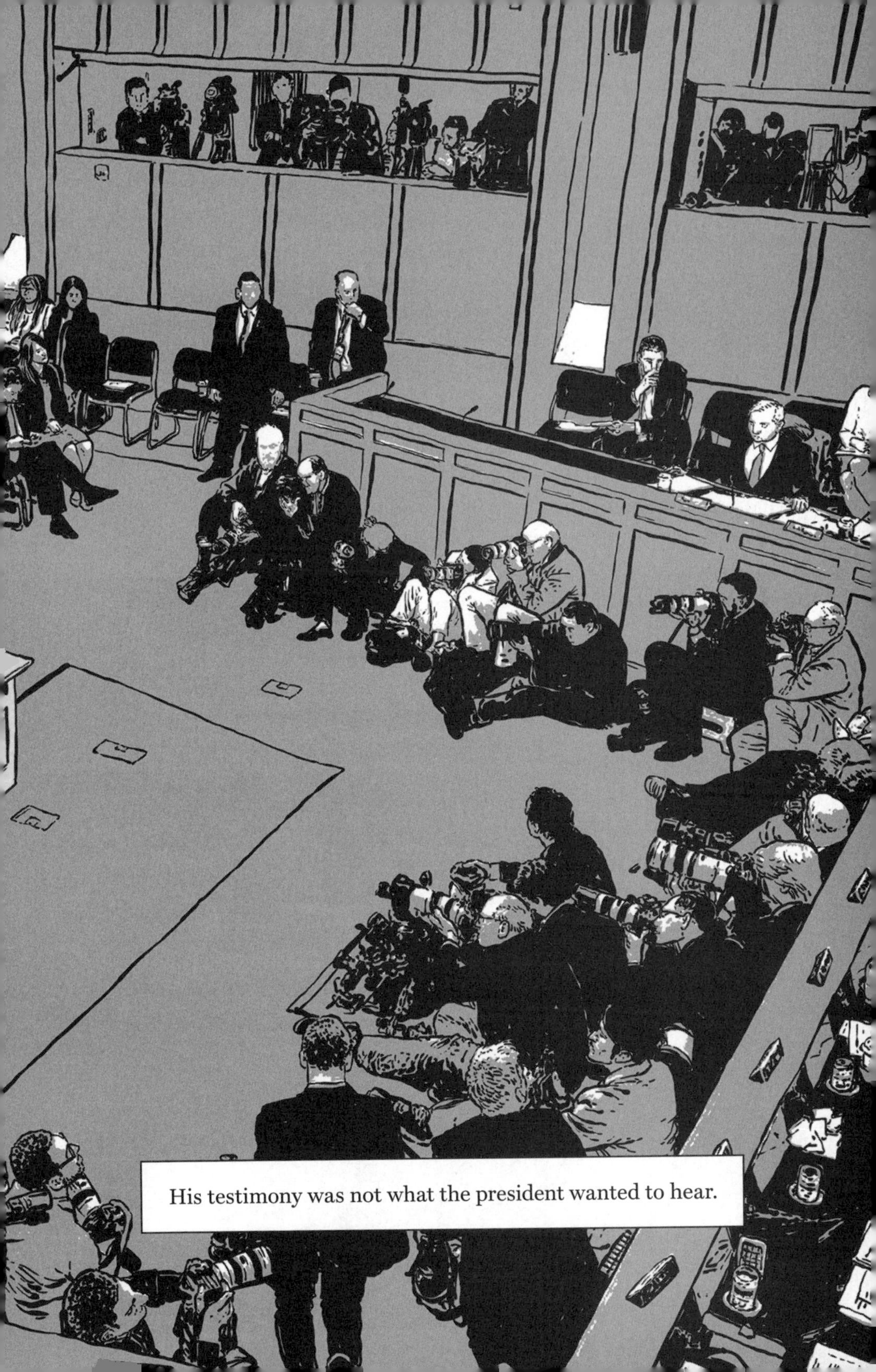
His testimony was not what the president wanted to hear.

Later that day, Trump met with White House Counsel Donald McGahn, Attorney General Jeff Sessions and Sessions's chief of staff, Jody Hunt. McGahn told Trump that Comey had declined to answer questions about whether Trump was under investigation. The president grew angry and blamed his attorney general, who had removed himself from overseeing the probe because he and other Justice Department officials believed his role in Trump's campaign could be a conflict of interest.

"This is terrible, Jeff. It's all because you recused. AG is supposed to be [the] most important appointment. Kennedy appointed his brother. Obama appointed Holder. I appointed you and you recused yourself."

"You left me on an island. I can't do anything."

Trump told Sessions that the recusal was unfair and was undercutting his authority with foreign leaders. Sessions told the president that he had no choice. If Trump wanted a fresh start at the FBI, Sessions said, he should consider

The president made up his mind: The FBI director had to go. That Friday night, Trump dined at his golf course in Bedminster, N.J., with son-in-law Jared Kushner, adviser Stephen Miller and other aides and family members. The president told them he wanted to remove Comey and had ideas about how to announce the decision in a letter. Trump began dictating as Miller took notes.

I, and I believe the American public — including Ds and Rs — have lost faith in you as Director of the FBI.

Based on those notes and further input from Trump, Miller prepared a letter that weekend firing Comey. To avoid leaks, the president was adamant that no one at the White House be told of the plan. He made it clear he wanted the letter to begin by stressing he was not under investigation.

On Monday morning, Trump met with White House Chief of Staff Reince Priebus, Miller and McGahn in the Oval Office and told them he had decided to fire Comey.

The president then read aloud from the letter he had dictated to Miller.

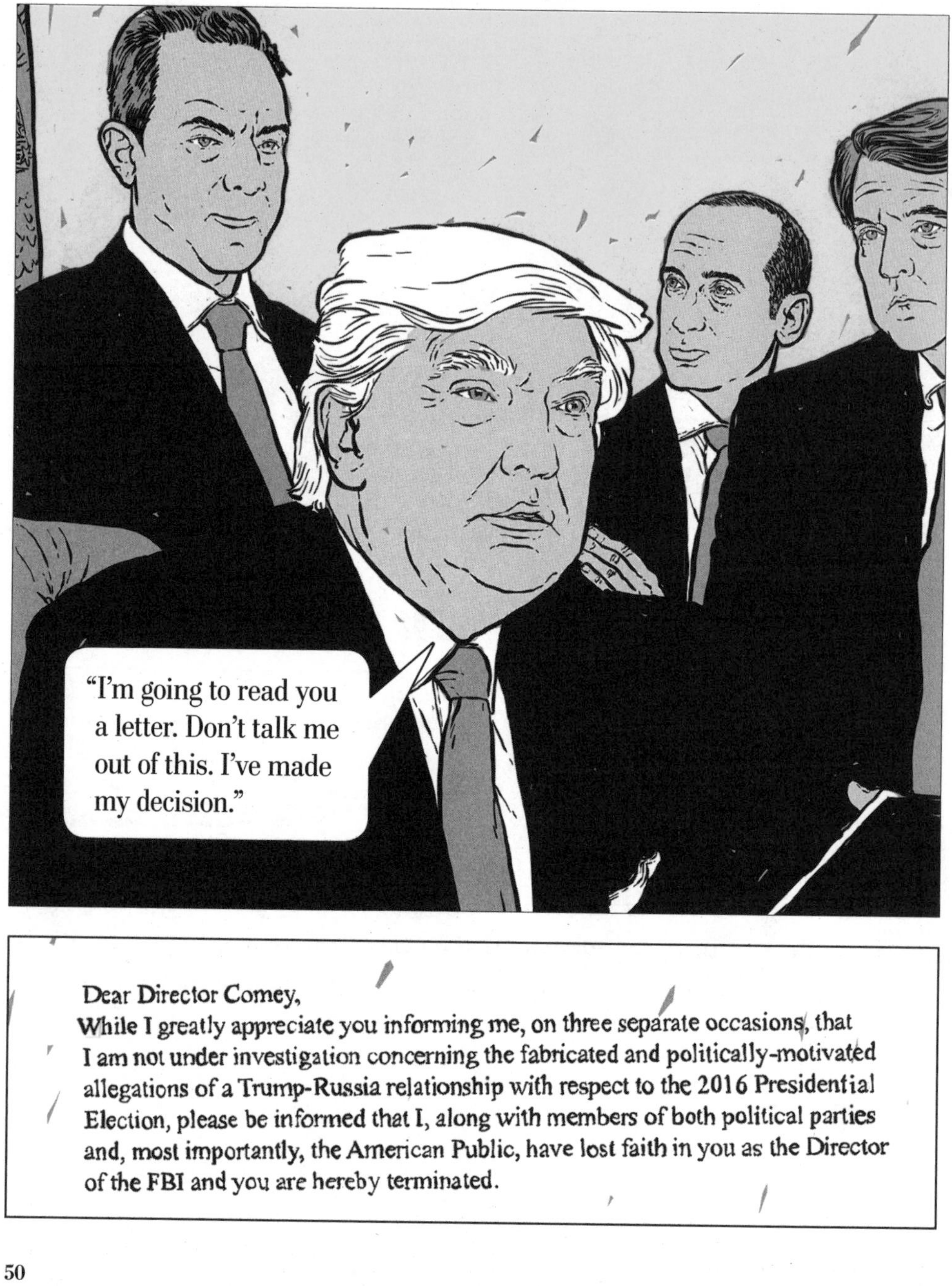
"I'm going to read you a letter. Don't talk me out of this. I've made my decision."

Dear Director Comey,
While I greatly appreciate you informing me, on three separate occasions, that I am not under investigation concerning the fabricated and politically-motivated allegations of a Trump-Russia relationship with respect to the 2016 Presidential Election, please be informed that I, along with members of both political parties and, most importantly, the American Public, have lost faith in you as the Director of the FBI and you are hereby terminated.

Some of Trump's aides were concerned. The president had the power to fire the FBI director, but it had happened only once before in history. If it appeared Trump was dismissing Comey because of the Russia investigation, it could look like he was trying to meddle with the probe.

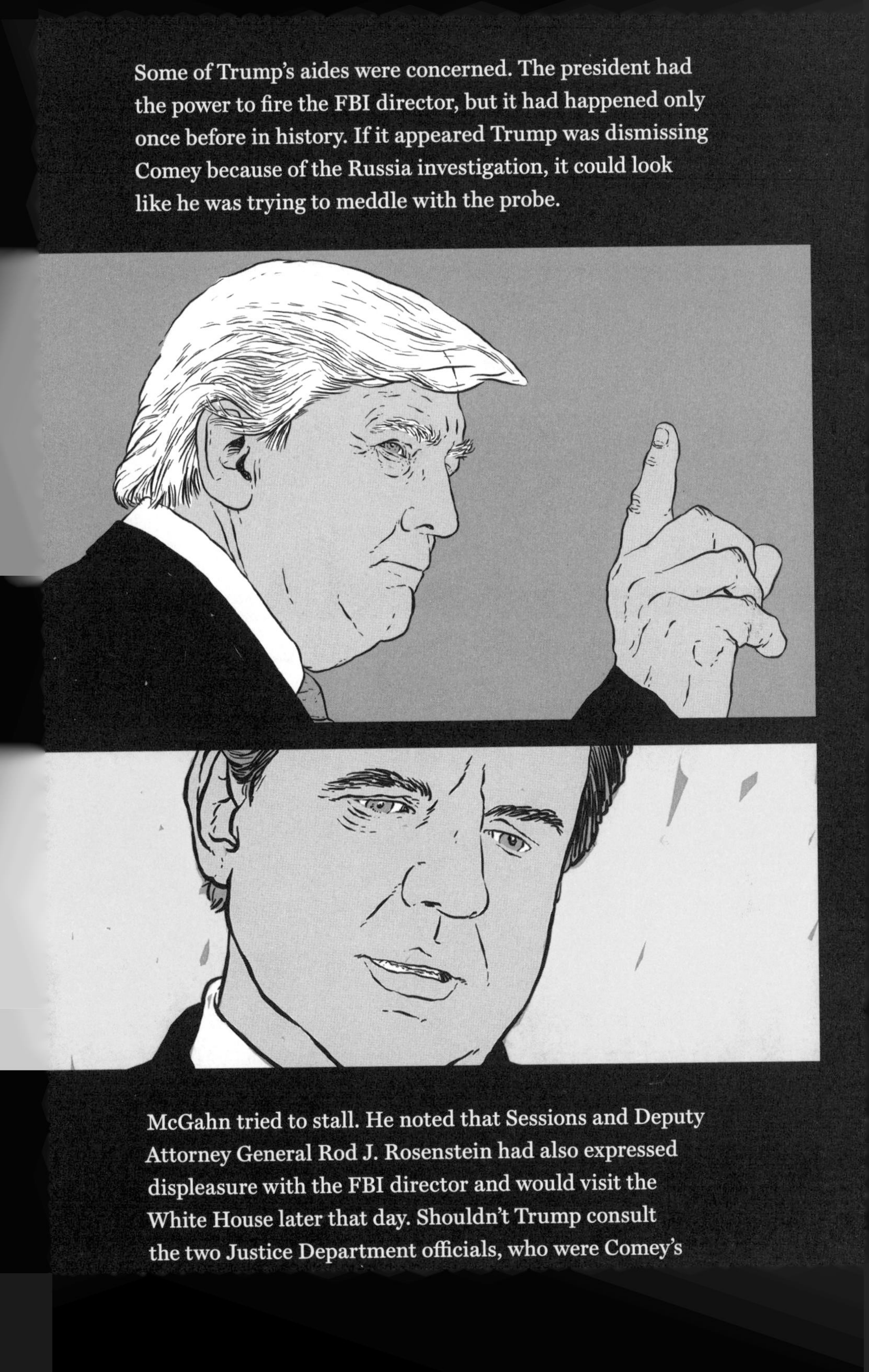

McGahn tried to stall. He noted that Sessions and Deputy Attorney General Rod J. Rosenstein had also expressed displeasure with the FBI director and would visit the White House later that day. Shouldn't Trump consult the two Justice Department officials, who were Comey's

At 5 p.m., Trump and several White House officials met with Sessions and Rosenstein. The president said he had watched Comey's testimony. Something was "not right" with the FBI director. Trump told them Comey should be removed and asked Sessions and Rosenstein what they thought.

Sessions noted that he had previously recommended that Comey be replaced. Rosenstein said he had concerns with how Comey handled the Clinton email investigation.

"Put the Russia stuff in the memo."

Trump distributed copies of the letter he had drafted. McGahn suggested Comey be allowed to resign, but Trump was adamant: He needed to be fired.

Trump asked Rosenstein to draft a memo recommending Comey's removal; he wanted it first thing in the morning. Rosenstein said he did not think the Russia investigation should be mentioned because it was not the basis of his recommendation. Trump said he would appreciate him

After the meeting, Rosenstein knew Comey would be fired —
but not for the reasons he thought the FBI director should go.

U. S. Department of Justice

Office of the Deputy Attorney General

The Deputy Attorney General   Washington, D.C. 20530

May 9, 2017

MEMORANDUM FOR THE ATTORNEY GENERAL

FROM: ROD J. ROSENSTEIN
                   DEPUTY ATTORNEY GENERAL

SUBJECT: RESTORING PUBLIC CONFIDENCE IN THE FBI

The Federal Bureau of Investigation has long been regarded as our nation's premier federal
investigative agency. Over the past year, however, the FBI's reputation and credibility have suffered
substantial damage, and it has affected the entire Department of Justice. That is deeply troubling to
many Department employees and veterans, legislators and citizens.

The current FBI Director is an articulate and persuasive speaker about leadership and the
immutable principles of the Department of Justice. He deserves our appreciation for his public
service. As you and I have discussed, however, I cannot defend the Director's handling of the
conclusion of the investigation of Secretary Clinton's emails, and I do not understand his refusal to
accept the nearly universal judgment that he was mistaken. Almost everyone agrees that the Director
made serious mistakes; it is one of the few issues that unites people of diverse perspectives.

The next morning, May 9, Hunt delivered to the White
House a letter from Sessions recommending Comey's
removal and a memo from Rosenstein titled "Restoring
Public Confidence in the FBI." The memo argued that Comey
had made "serious mistakes" in the handling of the Clinton
matter and was unlikely to change his ways.

Trump liked the Justice Department letters, which did not mention Russia. He decided to present Comey's firing as the result of a recommendation by the department.

The president's actions made his aides nervous. In her daily notes, McGahn's chief of staff, Annie Donaldson, described a fear that the handling of Comey's firing could lead to the end of Trump's presidency. She wrote that staff had determined that no rationales beyond what had been provided by the Justice Department should be cited to justify Comey's firing.

"The beginning of the end?"
Trump's original letter should not see the "light of day."

Trump asked Miller to draft a new cover letter, but insisted it still have language noting that Comey told the president he was not under investigation in the Russia probe. McGahn and Priebus objected, but Trump insisted.

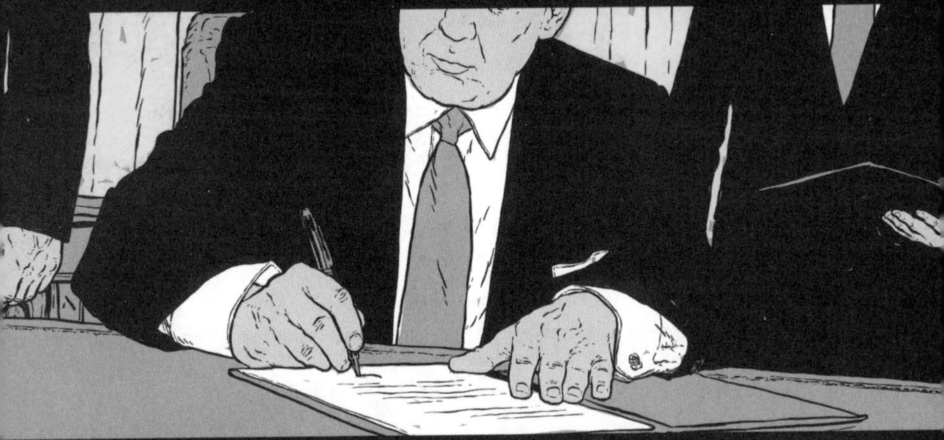

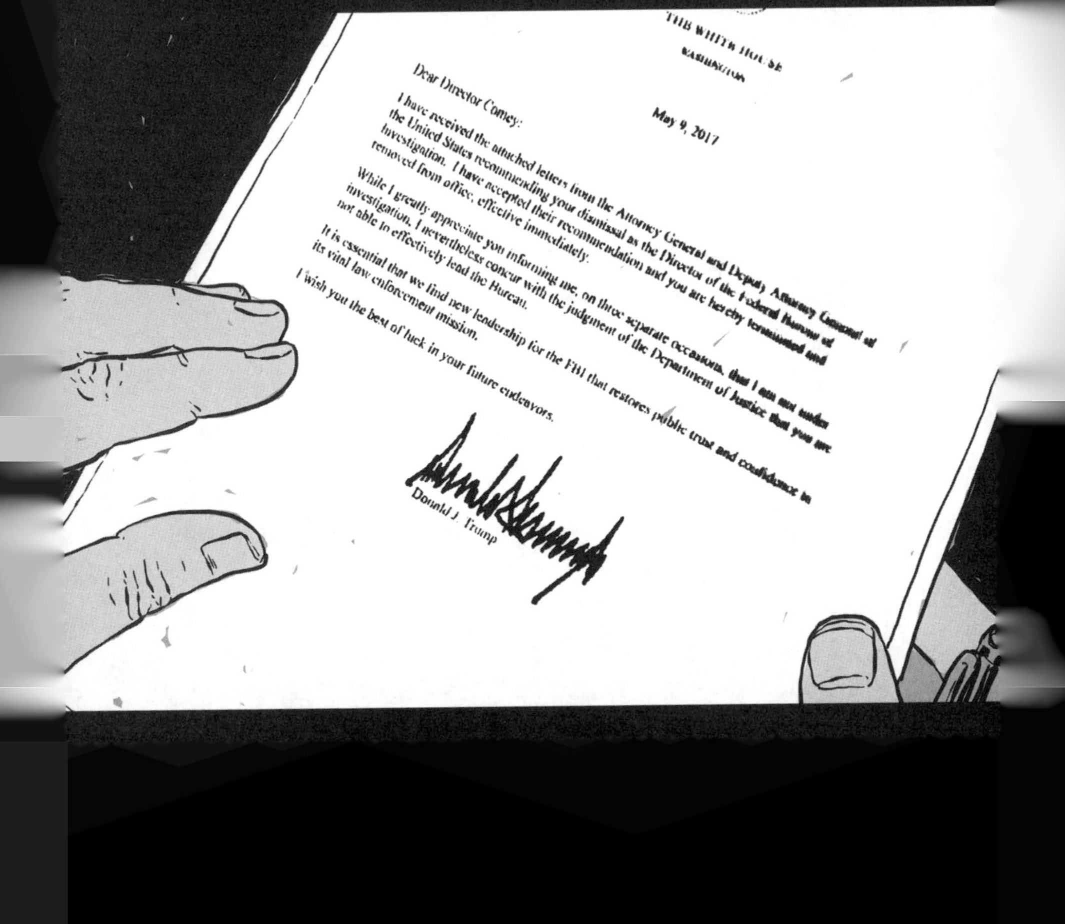
THE WHITE HOUSE
WASHINGTON
May 9, 2017
Dear Director Comey:
I have received the attached letters from the Attorney General and Deputy Attorney General of the United States recommending your dismissal as the Director of the Federal Bureau of Investigation. I have accepted their recommendation and you are hereby terminated and removed from office, effective immediately.
While I greatly appreciate you informing me, on three separate occasions, that I am not under investigation, I nevertheless concur with the judgment of the Department of Justice that you are not able to effectively lead the Bureau.
It is essential that we find new leadership for the FBI that restores public trust and confidence in its vital law enforcement mission.
I wish you the best of luck in your future endeavors.
Donald J. Trump

The White House released a statement saying Trump fired Comey at the Justice Department's recommendation.

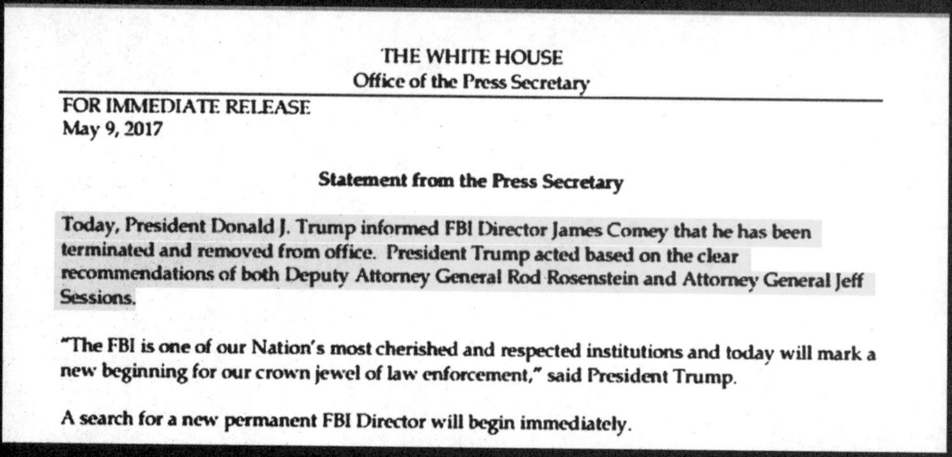

THE WHITE HOUSE
Office of the Press Secretary

FOR IMMEDIATE RELEASE
May 9, 2017

Statement from the Press Secretary

Today, President Donald J. Trump informed FBI Director James Comey that he has been terminated and removed from office. President Trump acted based on the clear recommendations of both Deputy Attorney General Rod Rosenstein and Attorney General Jeff Sessions.

"The FBI is one of our Nation's most cherished and respected institutions and today will mark a new beginning for our crown jewel of law enforcement," said President Trump.

A search for a new permanent FBI Director will begin immediately.

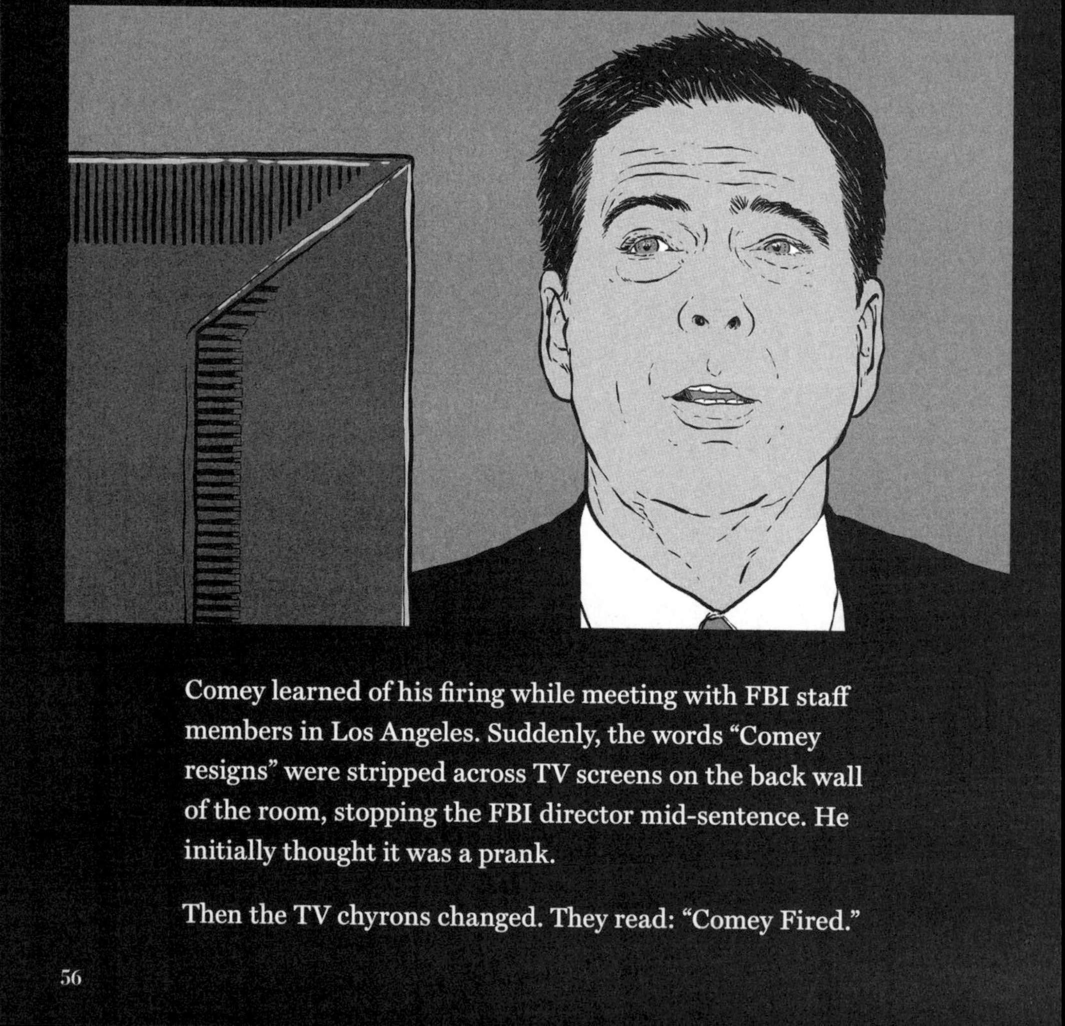

Comey learned of his firing while meeting with FBI staff members in Los Angeles. Suddenly, the words "Comey resigns" were stripped across TV screens on the back wall of the room, stopping the FBI director mid-sentence. He initially thought it was a prank.

Then the TV chyrons changed. They read: "Comey Fired."

Trailed by news helicopters, the now-deposed Comey made his way to the airport and flew home on the FBI's private jet.

After nearly four years leading the FBI, Comey returned to his home in Northern Virginia, now a private citizen.

The story exploded. Trump's critics accused him of trying to hinder the Russia probe, and even his allies seemed worried.

Watching the wall-to-wall coverage in the hours after he fired Comey, the president grew unhappy. Trump called New Jersey Gov. Chris Christie and told Christie that he was getting "killed" in the press. What should he do?

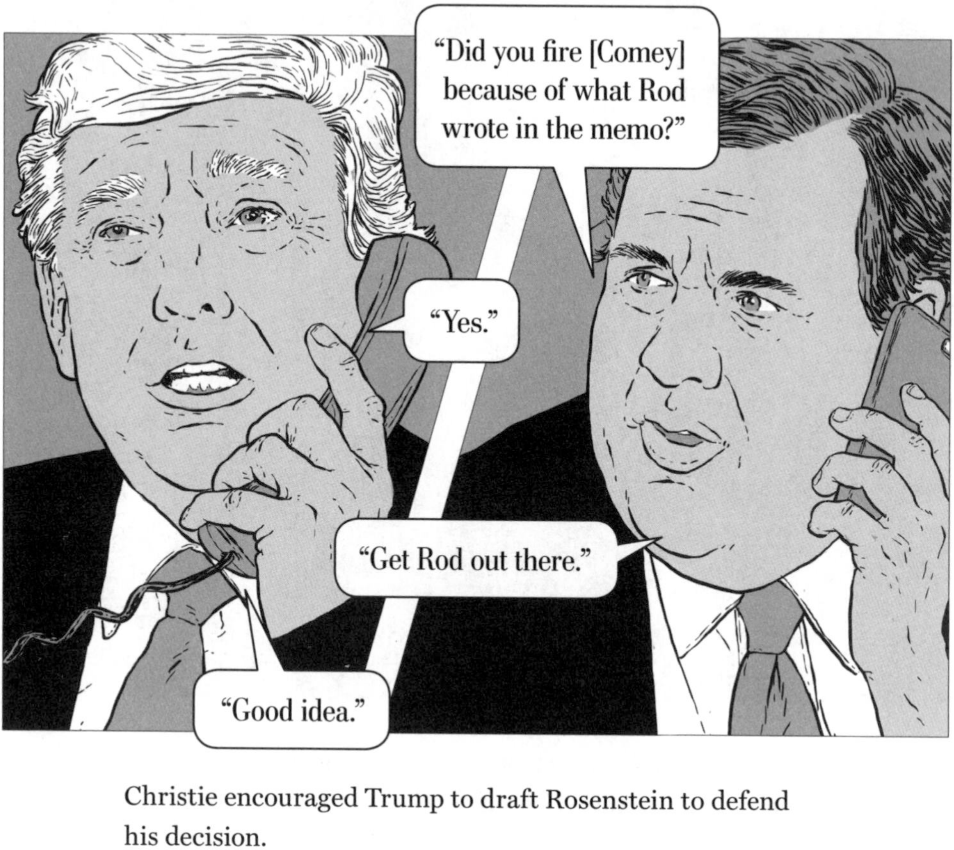
"Did you fire [Comey] because of what Rod wrote in the memo?"
"Yes."
"Get Rod out there."
"Good idea."

Christie encouraged Trump to draft Rosenstein to defend his decision.

That same night, the White House press office called the Justice Department: It wanted to put out a statement saying it was Rosenstein's idea to fire Comey. Rosenstein told his colleagues that he didn't want to be involved in putting out a "false story."

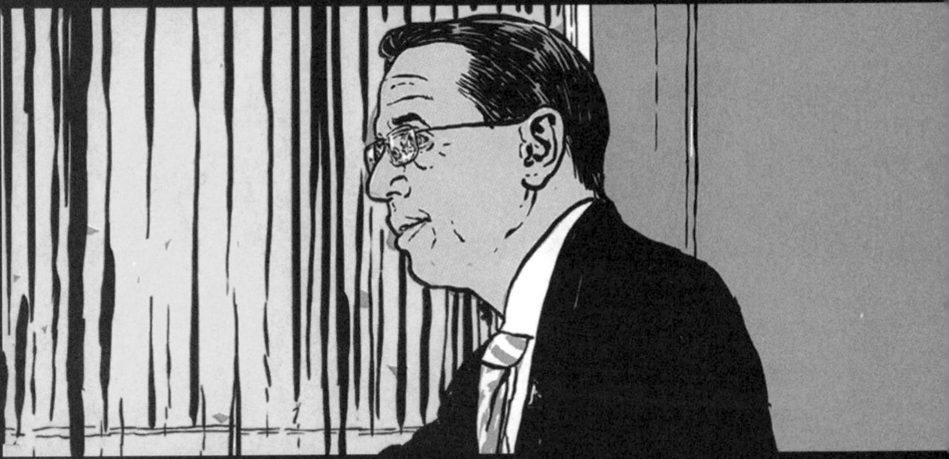

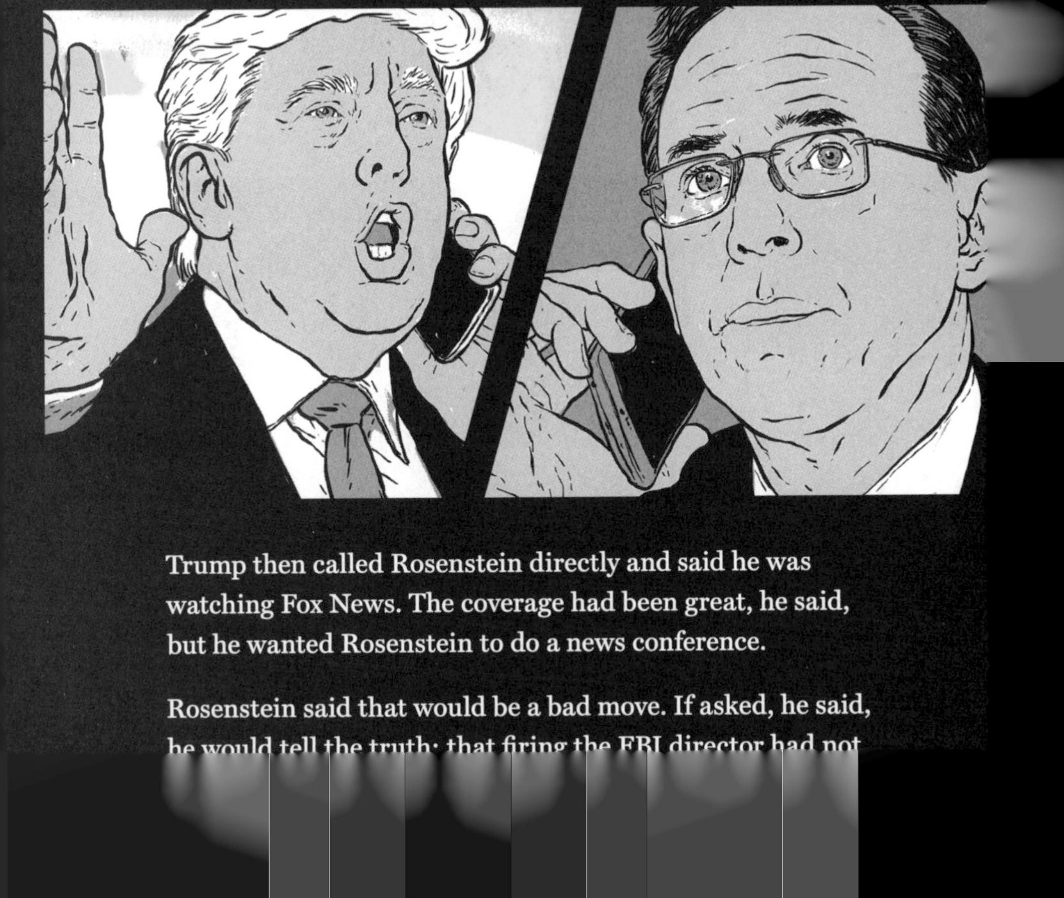

Trump then called Rosenstein directly and said he was watching Fox News. The coverage had been great, he said, but he wanted Rosenstein to do a news conference.

Rosenstein said that would be a bad move. If asked, he said, he would tell the truth: that firing the FBI director had not

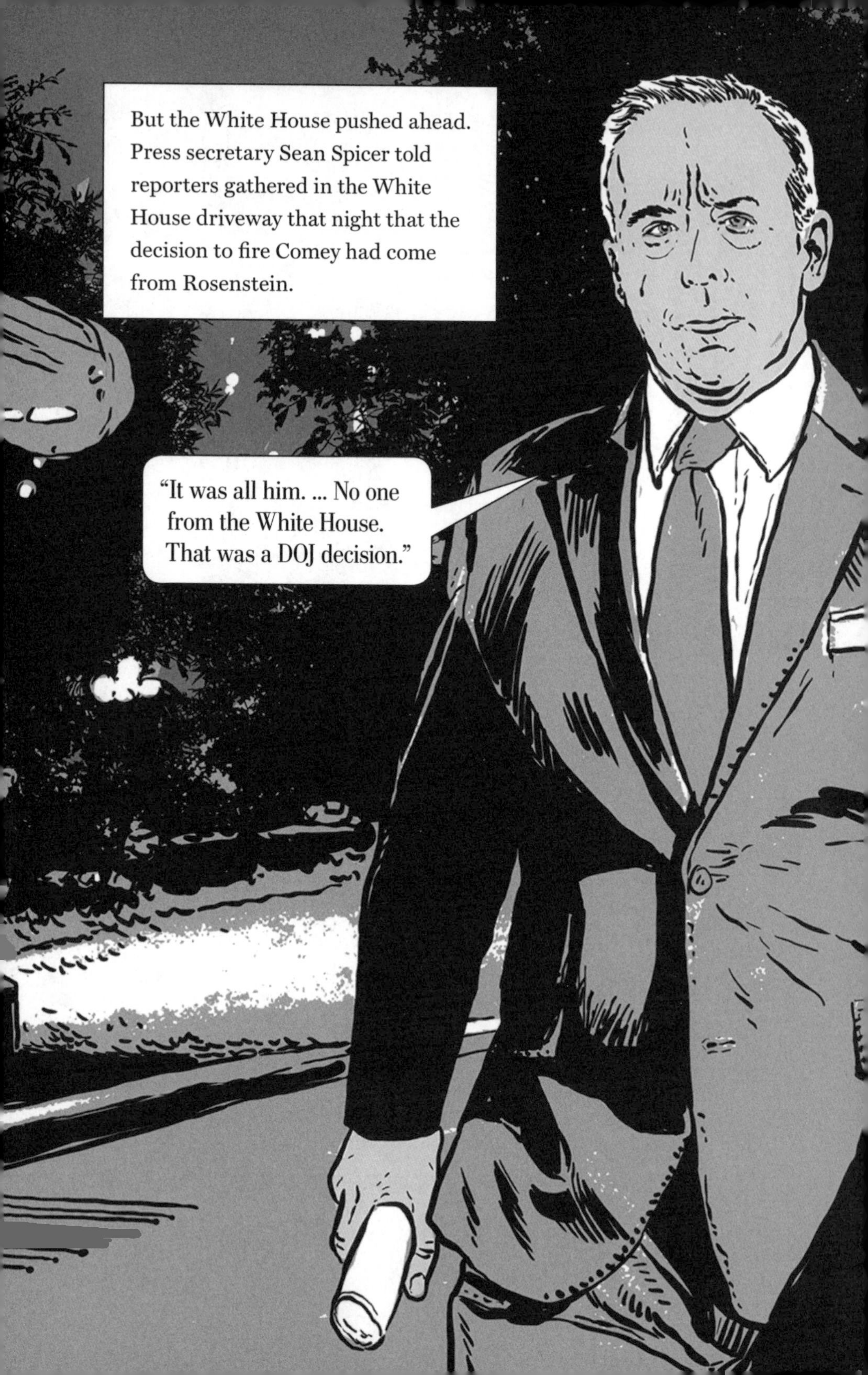
But the White House pushed ahead. Press secretary Sean Spicer told reporters gathered in the White House driveway that night that the decision to fire Comey had come from Rosenstein.
"It was all him. ... No one from the White House. That was a DOJ decision."

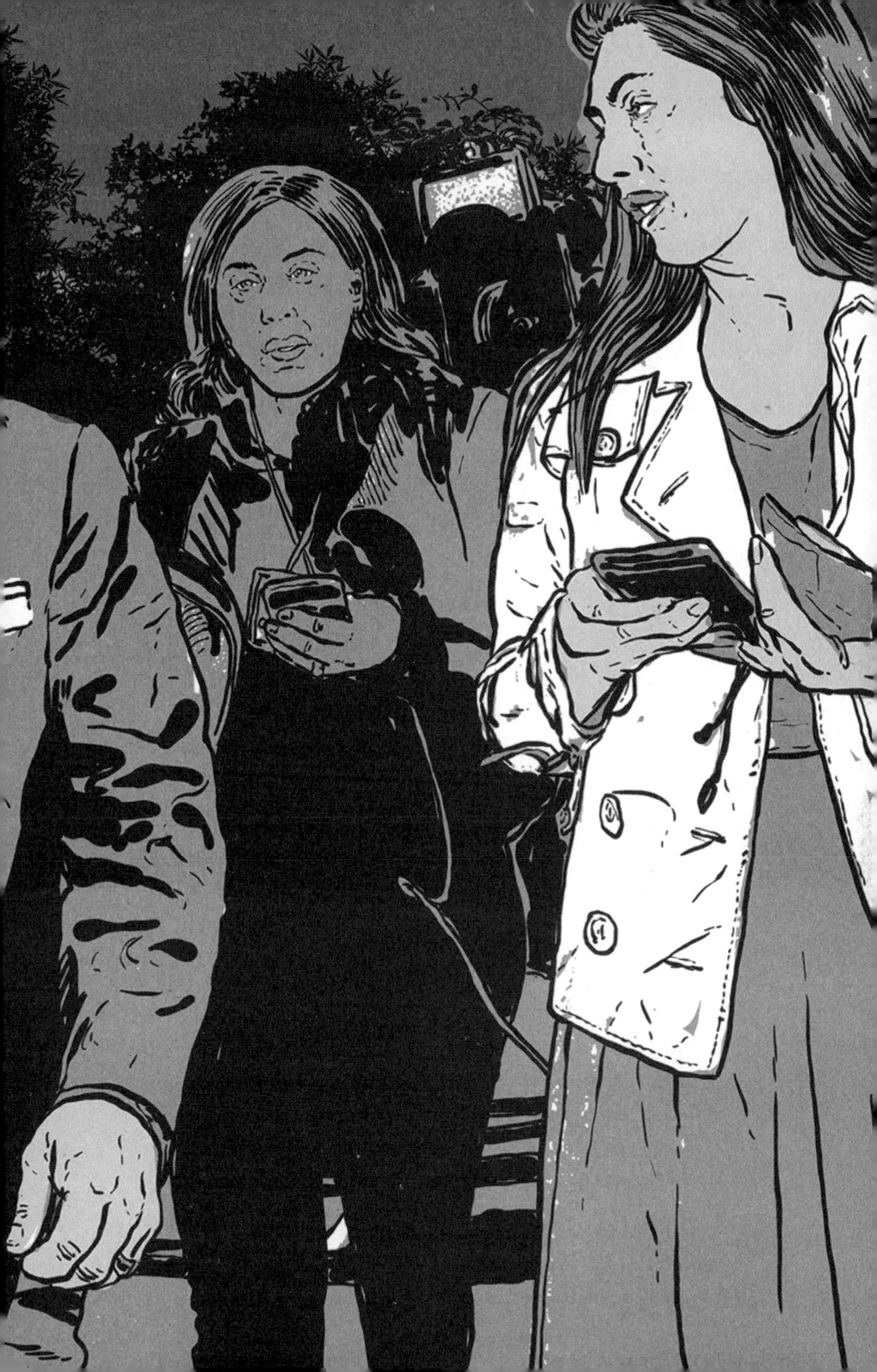

Privately, Trump told a different story the next day, May 10, when he met with Russian Foreign Minister Sergey Lavrov and Russian Ambassador Sergey Kislyak in the Oval Office.

"I just fired the head of the FBI. He was crazy, a real nut job. I faced great pressure because of Russia. That's taken off. ... I'm not under investigation."

The president also told the Russian officials he wasn't concerned about Moscow's interference in the 2016 campaign. The United States does the same in other countries, Trump said.

Later that morning, Trump called Deputy FBI Director
Andrew McCabe. With Comey gone, McCabe was in charge.
Trump told him that he had received "hundreds" of messages
from FBI employees supporting his decision to fire Comey.

In a meeting at the White House that afternoon, Trump told
McCabe that at least 80 percent of the FBI had voted for
him in 2016. Then he asked a strange question: Whom had
McCabe voted for in the election?

McCabe was stunned. FBI directors are supposed to be
nonpartisan. He dodged the question, responding that he
always played it right down the middle.

When deputy press secretary Sarah Sanders briefed reporters that same afternoon, she echoed Trump's assertions about FBI support for Comey's firing, suggesting the views of rank-and-file agents contributed to the decision.

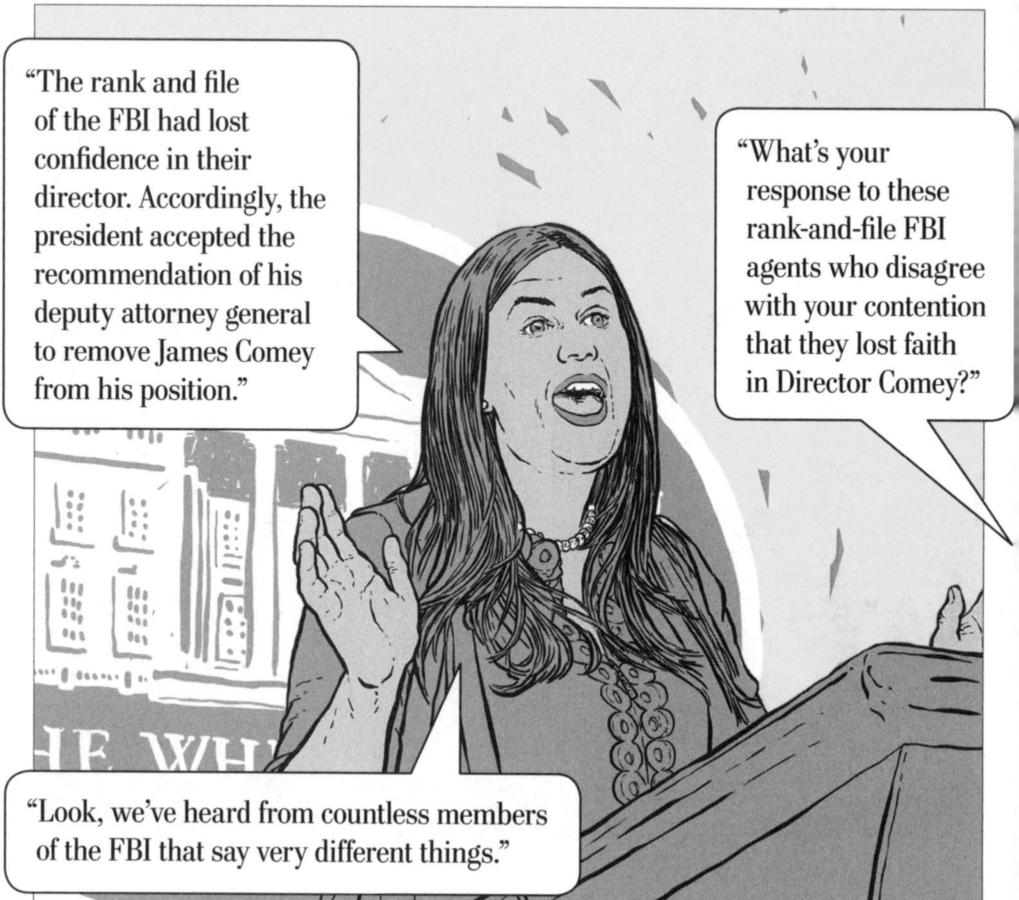
"The rank and file of the FBI had lost confidence in their director. Accordingly, the president accepted the recommendation of his deputy attorney general to remove James Comey from his position."
"What's your response to these rank-and-file FBI agents who disagree with your contention that they lost faith in Director Comey?"
"Look, we've heard from countless members of the FBI that say very different things."

It wasn't true. Sanders would later tell the special counsel's office that the statements about rank-and-file FBI agents losing confidence in Comey were made "in the heat of the moment" and were not based on fact.

Sessions and Rosenstein each spoke to McGahn and expressed concern that the White House was promoting a false narrative that Rosenstein had initiated Comey's firing. Inside the White House counsel's office, attorneys agreed it was a problem. They decided to work with the press office to get out a correct account.

Before they could, however, the president himself explained his real reasons for firing Comey. The next day, in a May 11 interview with NBC's Lester Holt, Trump said he had the Russia investigation in mind.

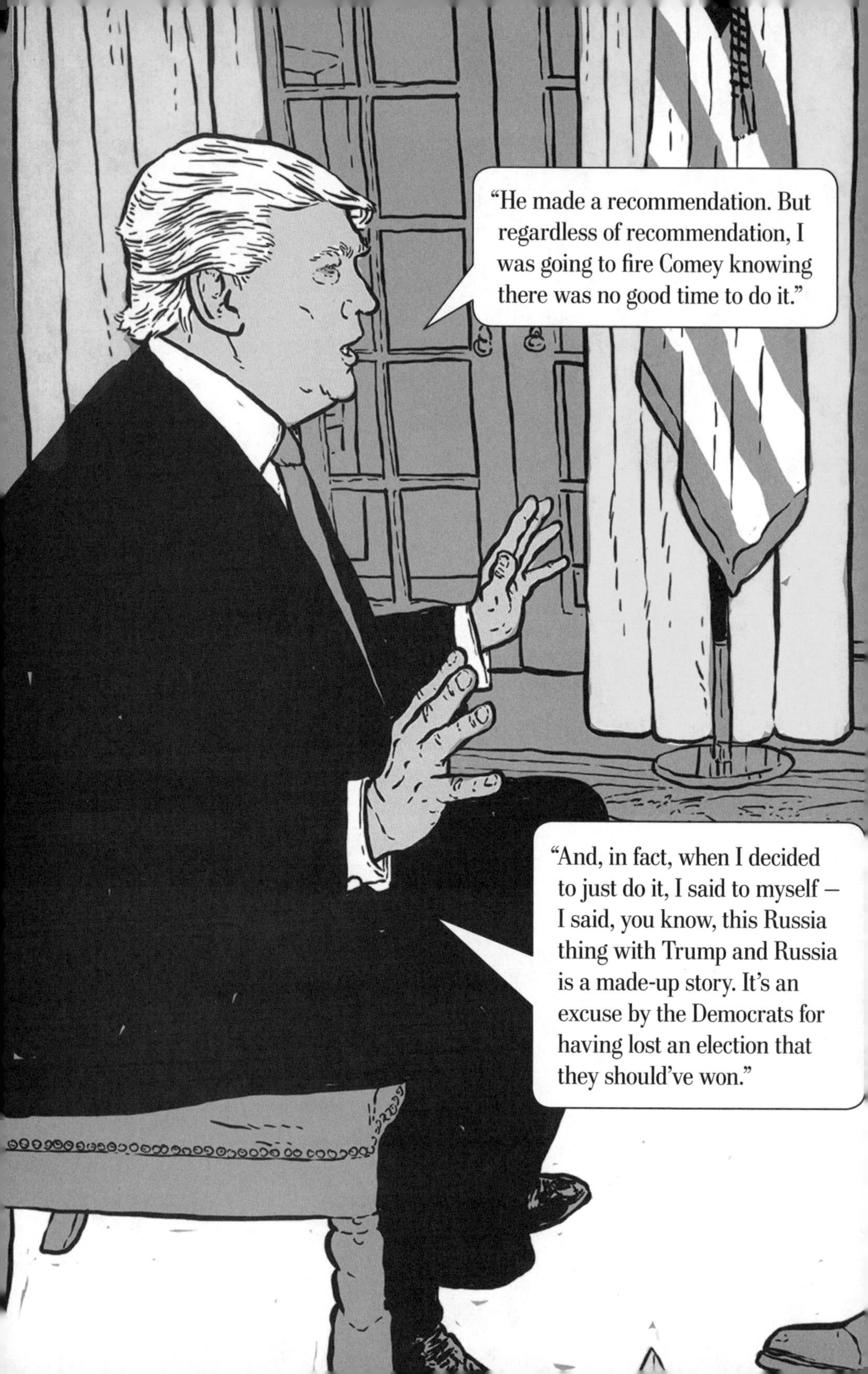
"He made a recommendation. But regardless of recommendation, I was going to fire Comey knowing there was no good time to do it."
"And, in fact, when I decided to just do it, I said to myself – I said, you know, this Russia thing with Trump and Russia is a made-up story. It's an excuse by the Democrats for having lost an election that they should've won."

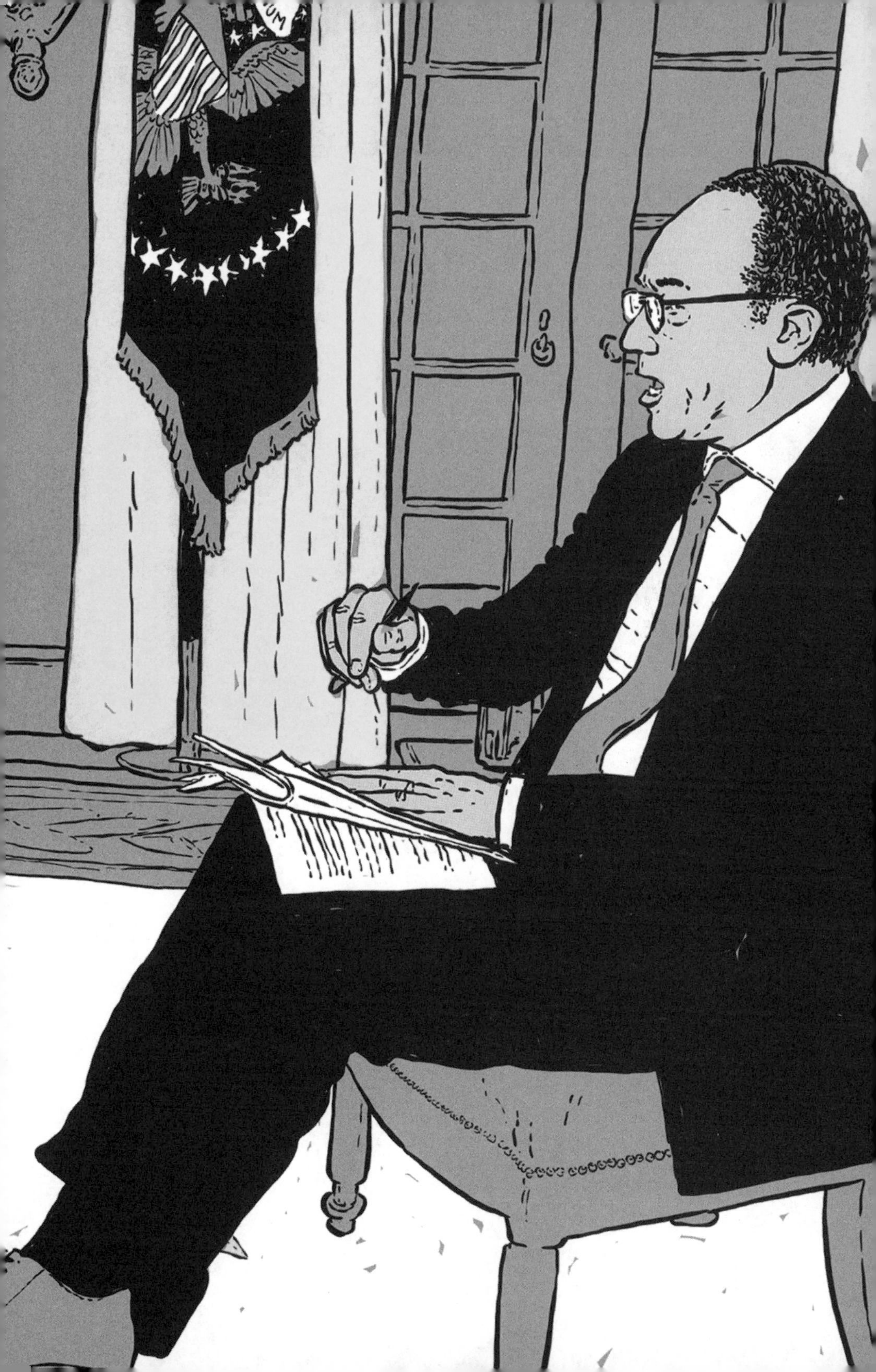

For good measure, the president later tweeted an attack on the Russia investigation.

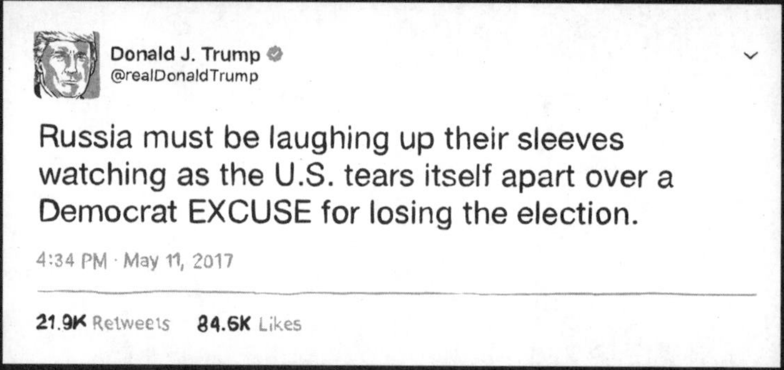

> **Donald J. Trump** ✔
> @realDonaldTrump
>
> Russia must be laughing up their sleeves watching as the U.S. tears itself apart over a Democrat EXCUSE for losing the election.
>
> 4:34 PM · May 11, 2017
>
> ───────────────────────
>
> **21.9K** Retweets   **84.6K** Likes

Meanwhile, the New York Times broke the news that Trump had tried to get Comey to pledge him his loyalty. Now it looked like the president might have fired the FBI director because he rebuffed Trump's efforts to control the investigation.

The New York Times

In a Private Dinner, Trump Demanded Loyalty. Comey Demurred.

Trump, again, was furious.

Donald J. Trump @realDonaldTrump

James Comey better hope that there are no "tapes" of our conversations before he starts leaking to the press!

8:26 AM · May 12, 2017

23.1K Retweets   **70K** Likes

The FBI director was gone. But the president's troubles were just beginning.

3

Mueller's arrival pushes Trump to the brink

President Trump's decision to fire FBI Director James B. Comey in May 2017 sparked a firestorm. Days later, the Russia investigation took a new and more dire turn for the president.

Deputy Attorney General Rod J. Rosenstein, who had been in charge of the probe since Attorney General Jeff Sessions recused himself, was unnerved by how the president pushed out Comey, and the criticism he and the Justice Department faced in the aftermath. He decided to appoint a special counsel to take over the investigation — putting it at arm's length from the Justice Department and Trump's control.

For the job, Rosenstein selected Robert S. Mueller III, a former FBI director who had served presidents of both parties and was widely respected on both sides of the aisle.

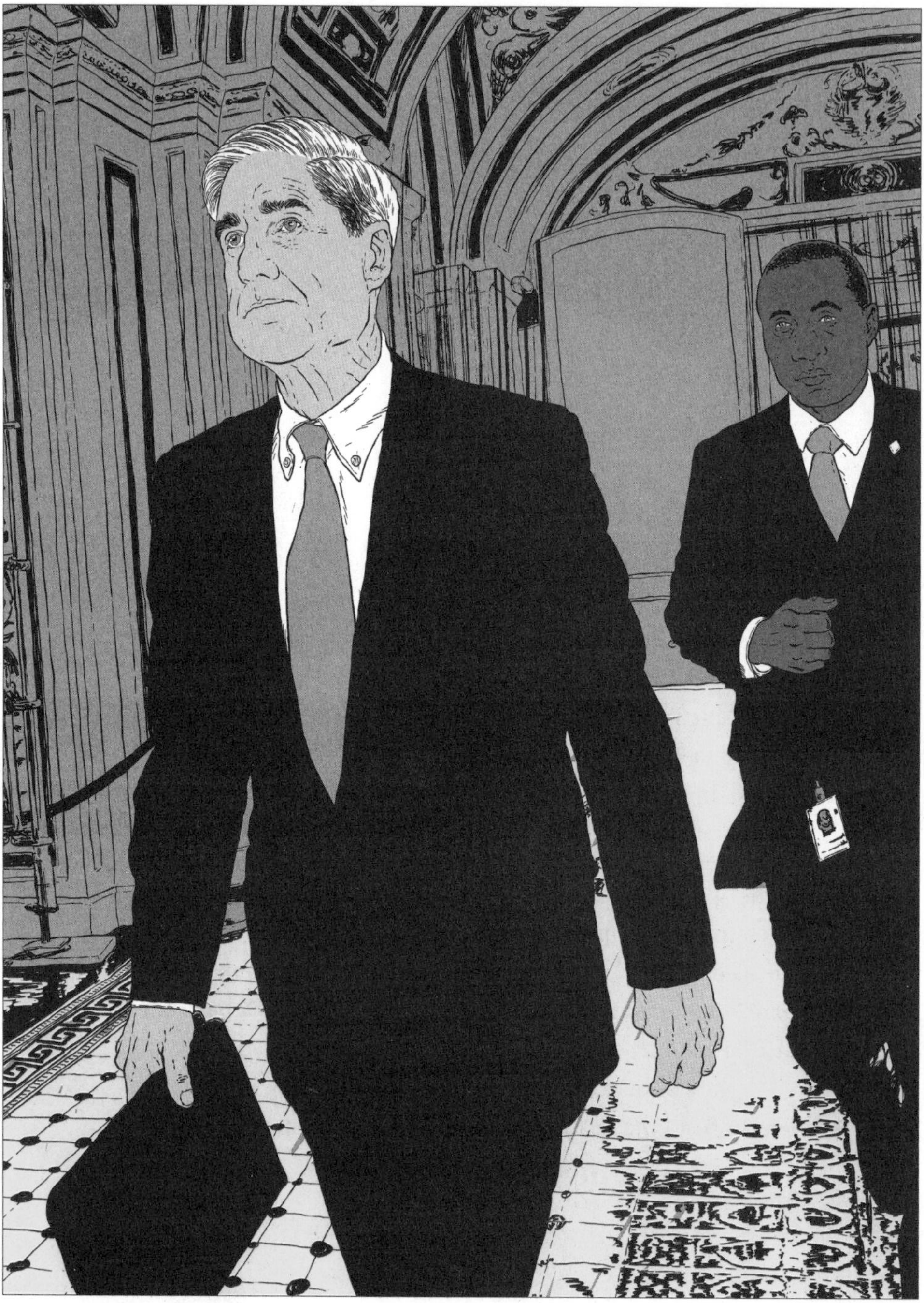

Trump learned the news on May 17, 2017, while meeting with Sessions, Sessions's chief of staff, Jody Hunt, and White House Counsel Donald McGahn.

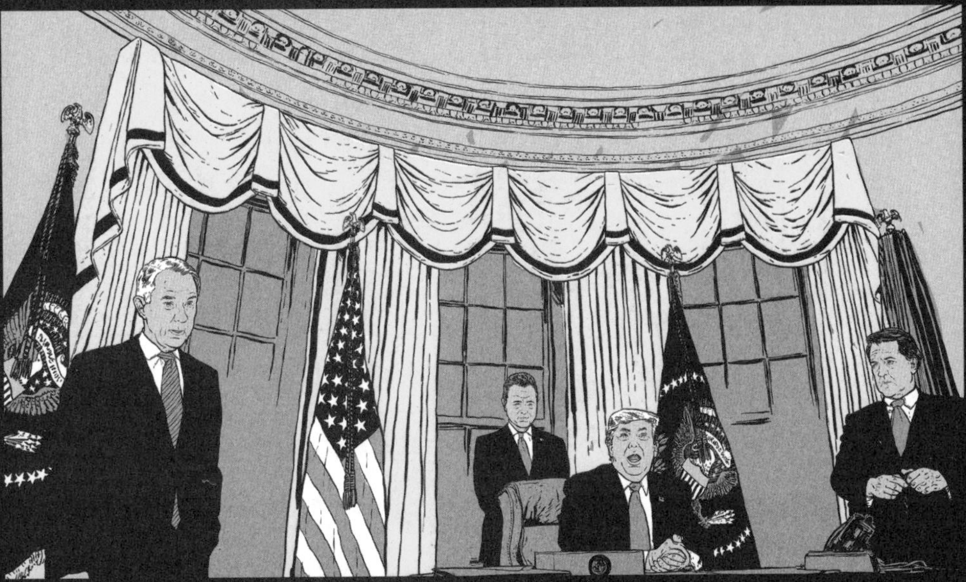

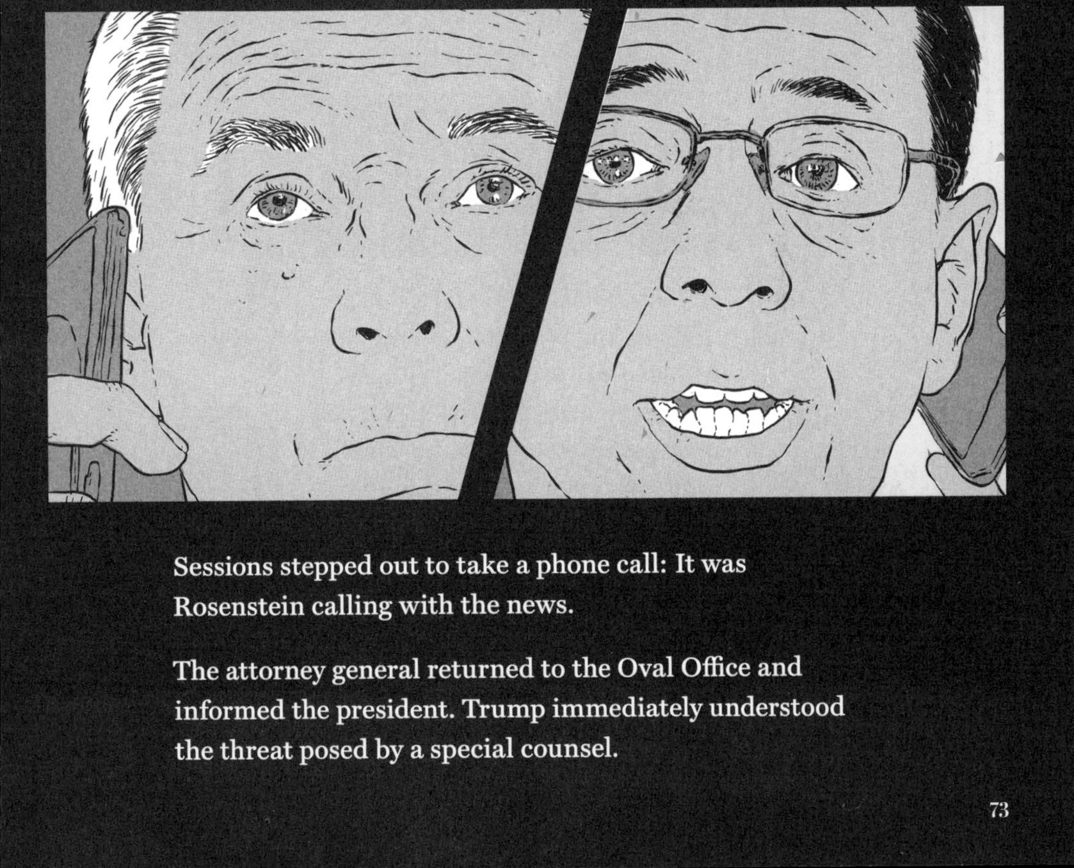

Sessions stepped out to take a phone call: It was Rosenstein calling with the news.

The attorney general returned to the Oval Office and informed the president. Trump immediately understood the threat posed by a special counsel.

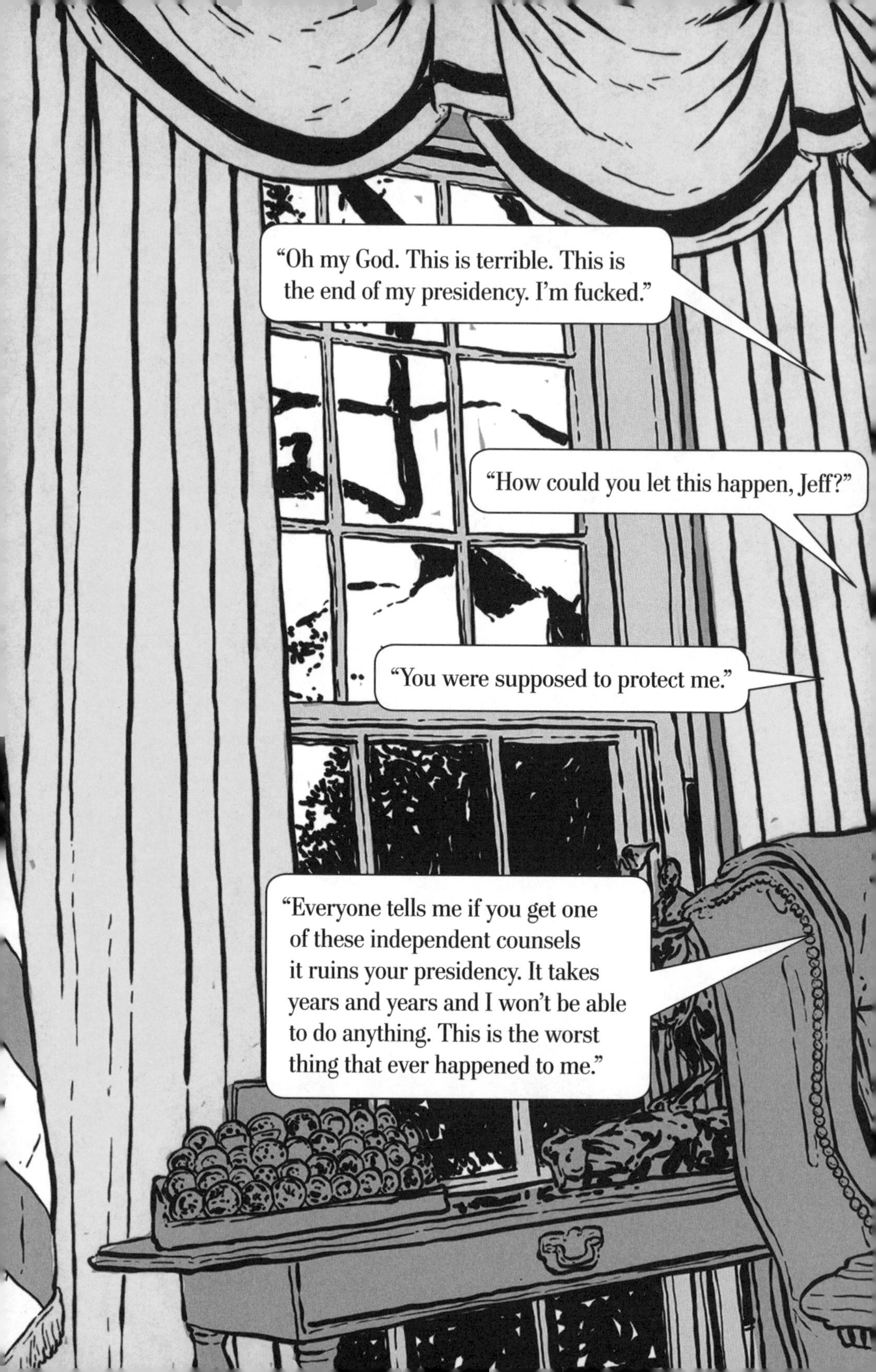
"Oh my God. This is terrible. This is the end of my presidency. I'm fucked."
"How could you let this happen, Jeff?"
"You were supposed to protect me."
"Everyone tells me if you get one of these independent counsels it ruins your presidency. It takes years and years and I won't be able to do anything. This is the worst thing that ever happened to me."

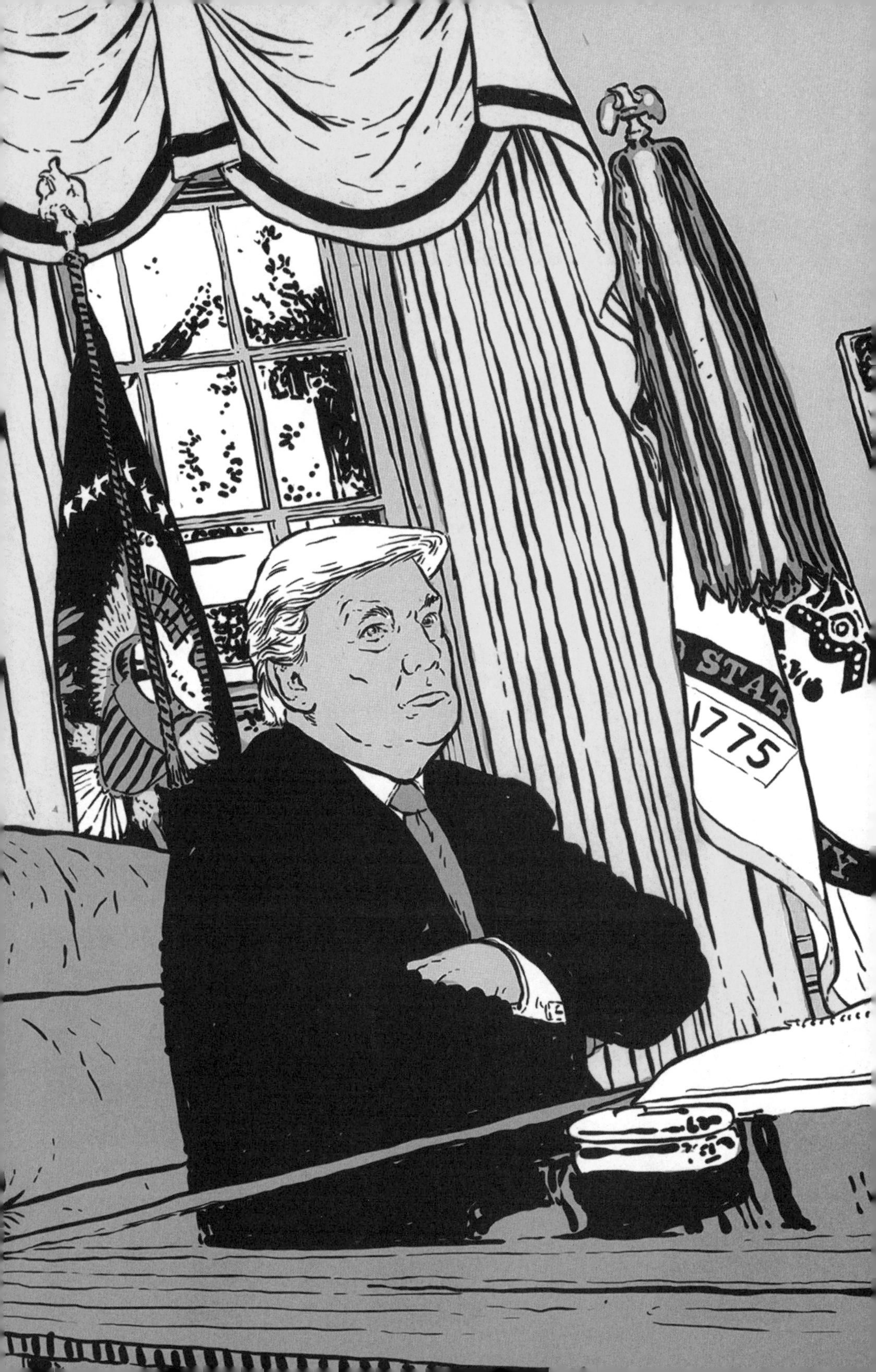
1775

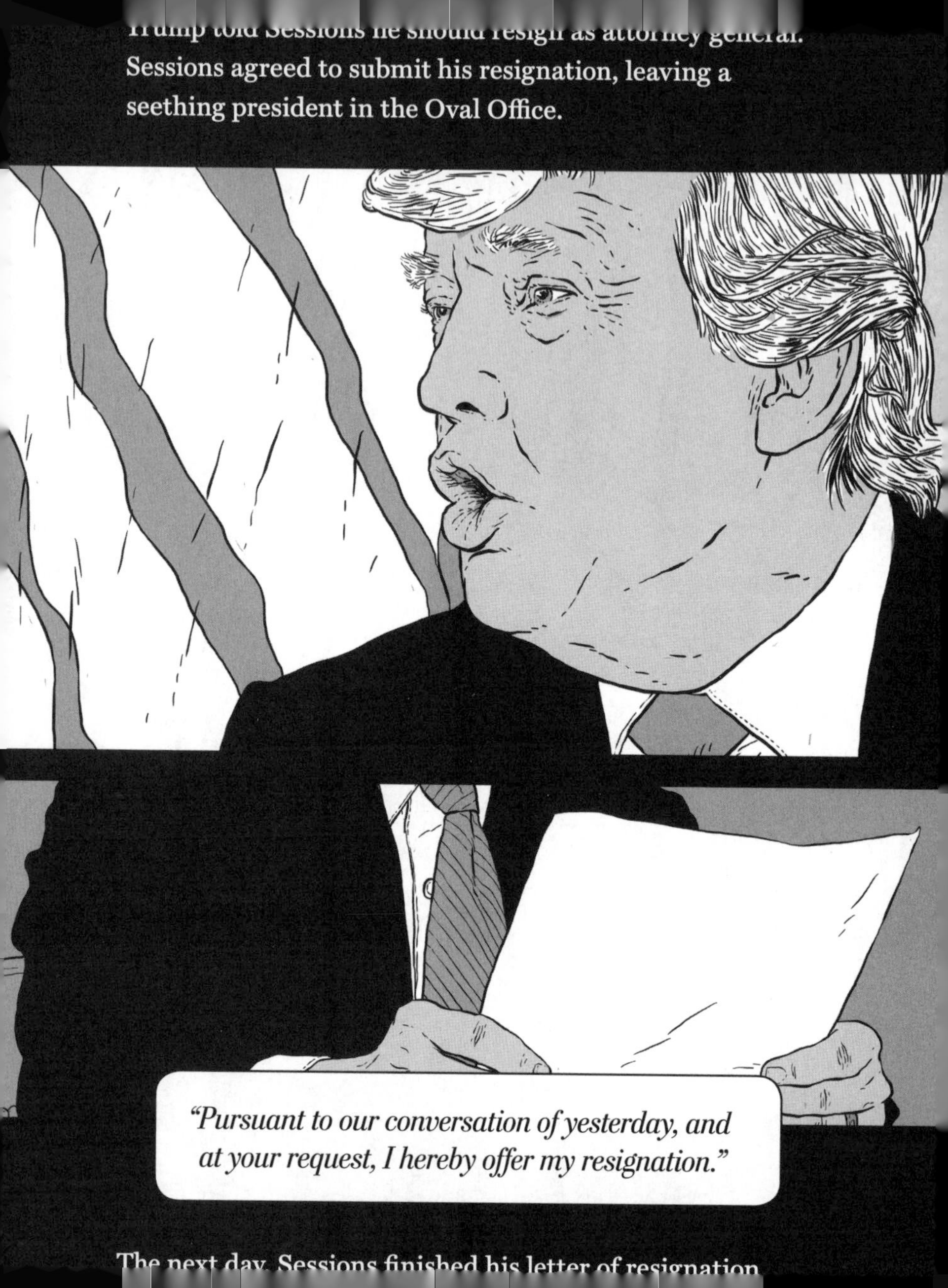
Trump told Sessions he should resign as attorney general.
Sessions agreed to submit his resignation, leaving a seething president in the Oval Office.
"Pursuant to our conversation of yesterday, and at your request, I hereby offer my resignation."
The next day, Sessions finished his letter of resignation.

Sessions went to the White House and gave Trump the letter. Instead of accepting the resignation, Trump asked his attorney general several times whether he wanted to leave his job. Sessions said he preferred to remain, but that the decision was up to the president. Trump said he wanted the attorney general to stay on.

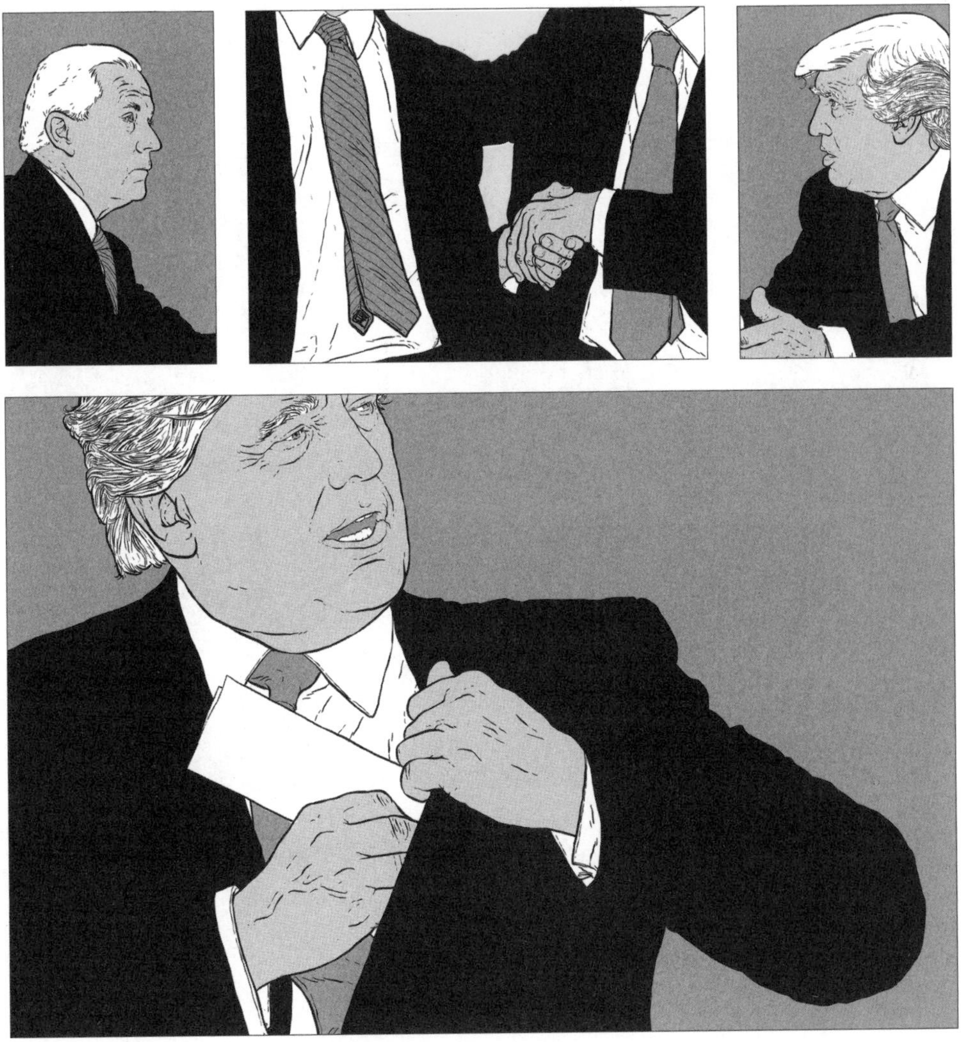

But the president did not return Sessions's resignation letter.

White House Chief of Staff Reince Priebus and senior
adviser Stephen K. Bannon learned that Trump had kept
Sessions's letter. They grew worried the president could use
it as leverage over the Justice Department. Priebus told
Sessions that the letter was a "shock collar" that Trump
could use whenever he wanted.

Trump has "DOJ by the throat."

Priebus and Bannon agreed they would try to get the letter
back from the president.

The following day, Trump left for the Middle East.

Aboard Air Force One, the president took Sessions's letter out of his pocket and showed it to adviser Hope Hicks and other senior aides, asking what he should do about it.

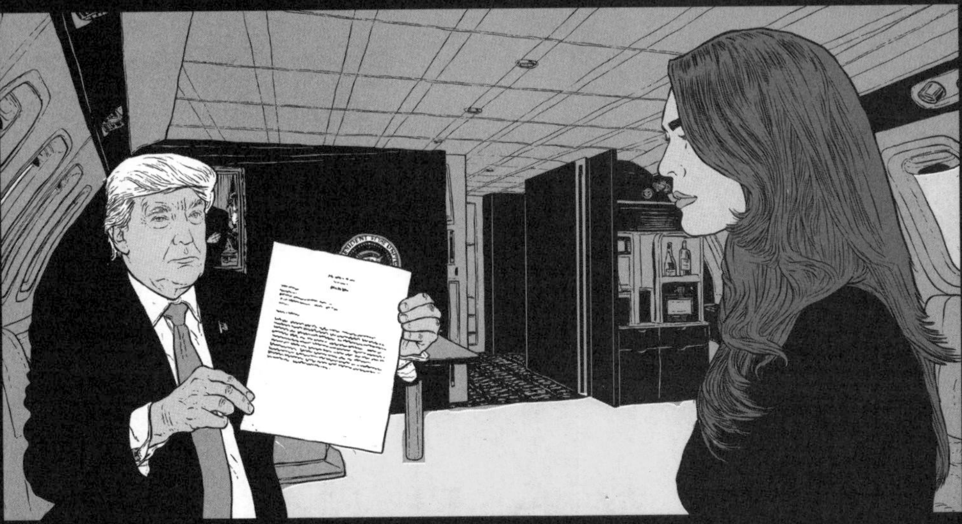

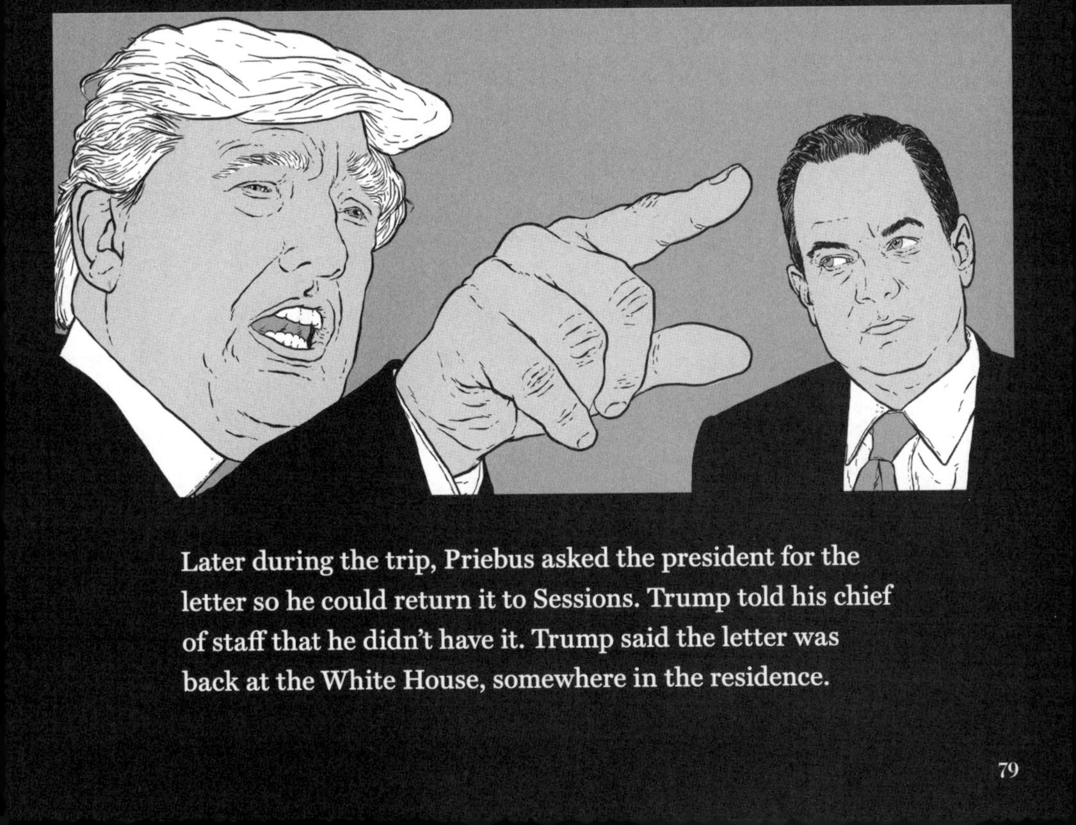

Later during the trip, Priebus asked the president for the letter so he could return it to Sessions. Trump told his chief of staff that he didn't have it. Trump said the letter was back at the White House, somewhere in the residence.

Finally, three days after returning from the Middle East, Trump gave the letter back to Sessions.

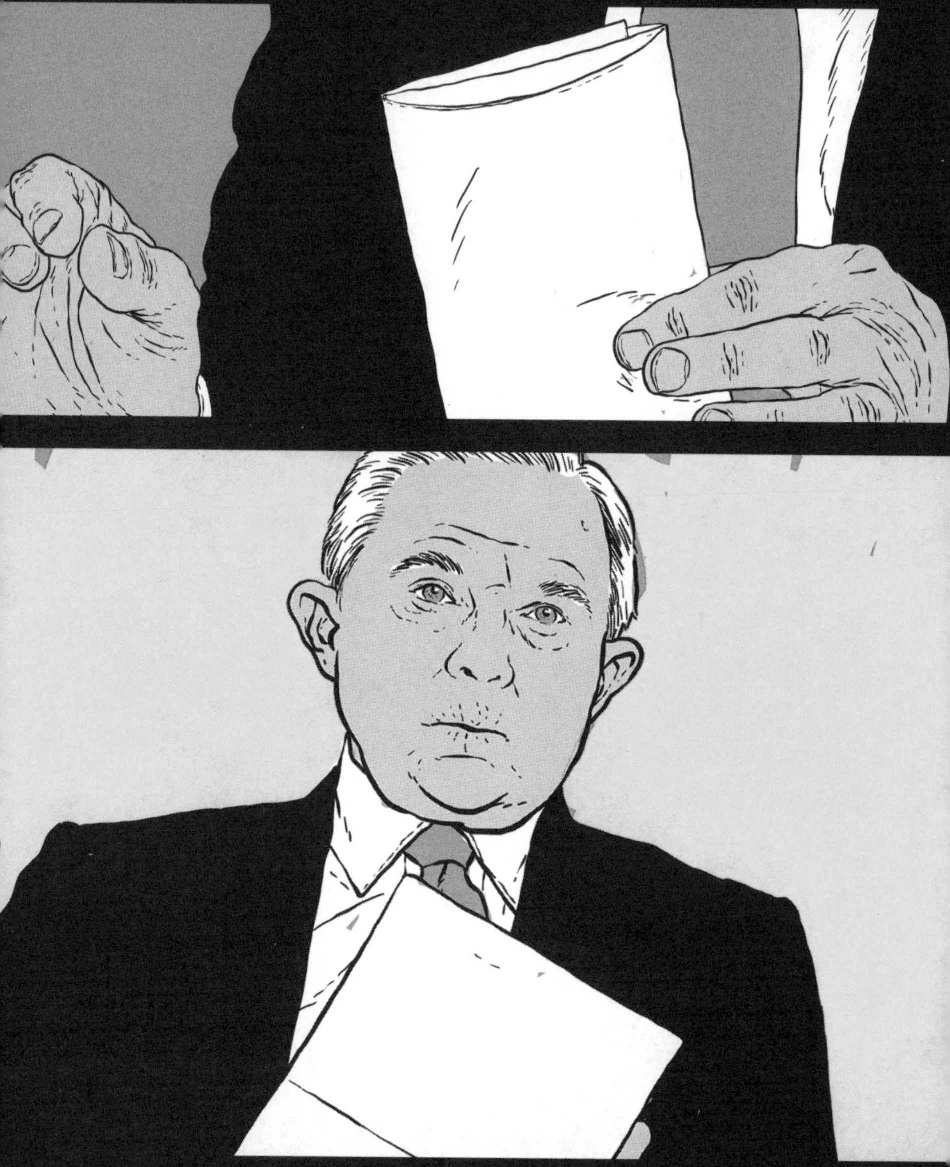

Trump had written across the paper: “Not accepted.”

The president continued to stew about Mueller's appointment. He repeatedly told aides that the new special counsel had conflicts of interest. Trump noted that attorneys at Mueller's former law firm had represented Trump associates. And he cited the fact that, six years earlier, Mueller tried to get a refund when his family resigned its membership at a Trump golf course in Northern Virginia.

Bannon and other Trump advisers pushed back, saying the issues he was raising were not serious.

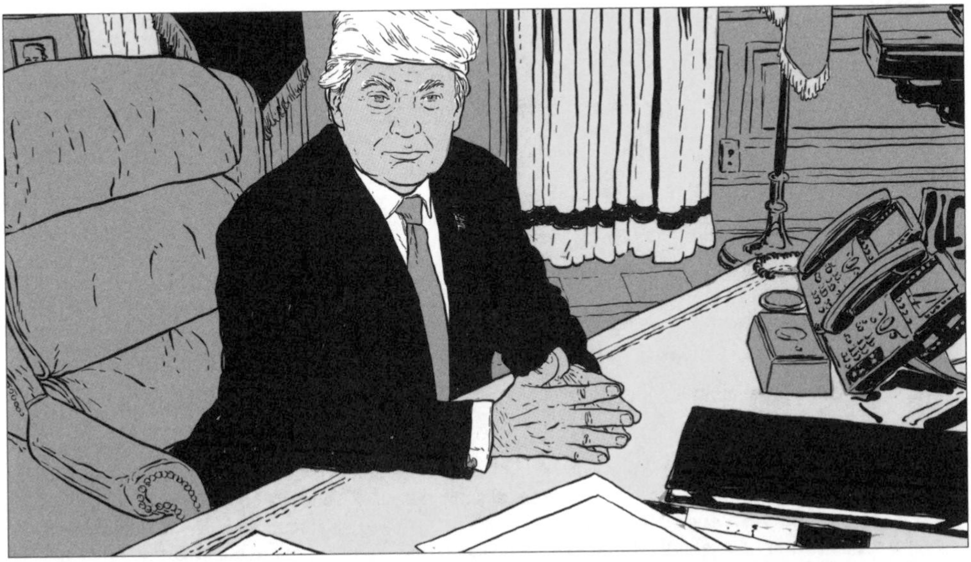

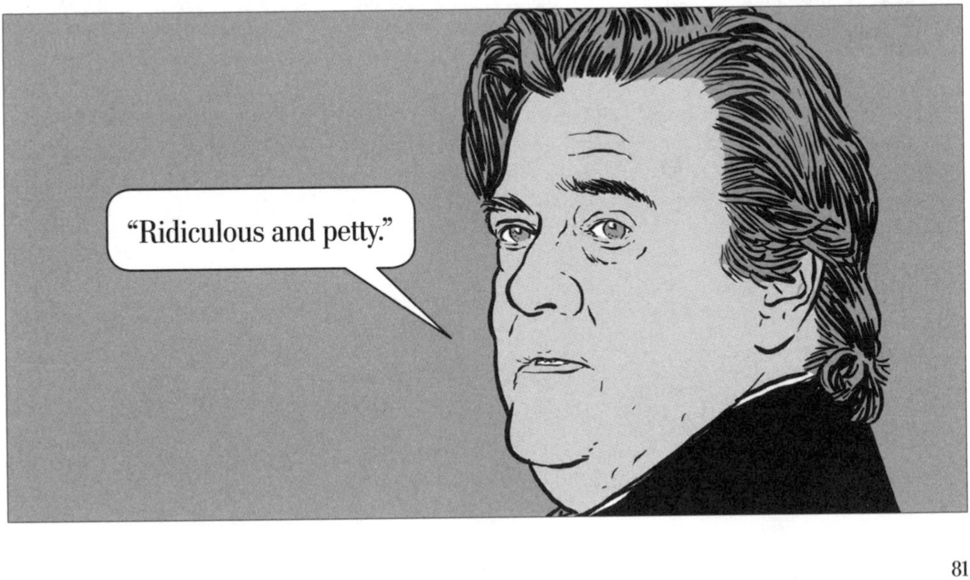
"Ridiculous and petty."

Five days after Mueller was appointed, the Justice Department announced that ethics officials had cleared him to serve as special counsel.

U.S. Department of Justice

Justice Management Division

Departmental Ethics Office

Washington, D.C. 20530

To: Scott Schools, Associate Deputy Attorney General

From: Cynthia K. Shaw. Director, Departmental Ethics Office   *CK.Shaw*

Date: May 18, 2017

Re: Robert Mueller authorization

You have asked if Robert Mueller, Special Counsel, requires authorization to participate in the investigation into Russia's role in the presidential campaign of 2016 and all matters arising from the investigation. Mr. Mueller's former law firm, WilmerHale, represents an individual and may represent other individuals in the future who may have some involvement in the investigation. I am not convinced that an authorization is needed, but unequivocally, if one is, the overwhelming need of the Government for Mr. Mueller's services greatly outweighs the concern that a reasonable person may question the integrity of the Department's programs and operations. 5 CFR 2635.502(d).

The Standards of Conduct apply to all federal employees. I assume for the purposes of this authorization that, having been appointed by the Acting Attorney General, Mr. Mueller is a federal employee pursuant to the regulations on the General Powers of Special Counsel. *See* 28 CFR Part 600.

Nevertheless, Trump urged McGahn to complain to Rosenstein about Mueller's possible conflicts.

McGahn refused, saying Trump could take up the matter with the president's personal attorney — but advised him against doing so.

"Knocking out Mueller" would "look like still trying to meddle in investigation."

"Biggest exposure" was the ask about Flynn.

McGahn told the president that pushing out the special counsel could be seen as obstruction. And Trump was already at risk because of his request to Comey to lay off national security adviser Michael Flynn, McGahn told him.

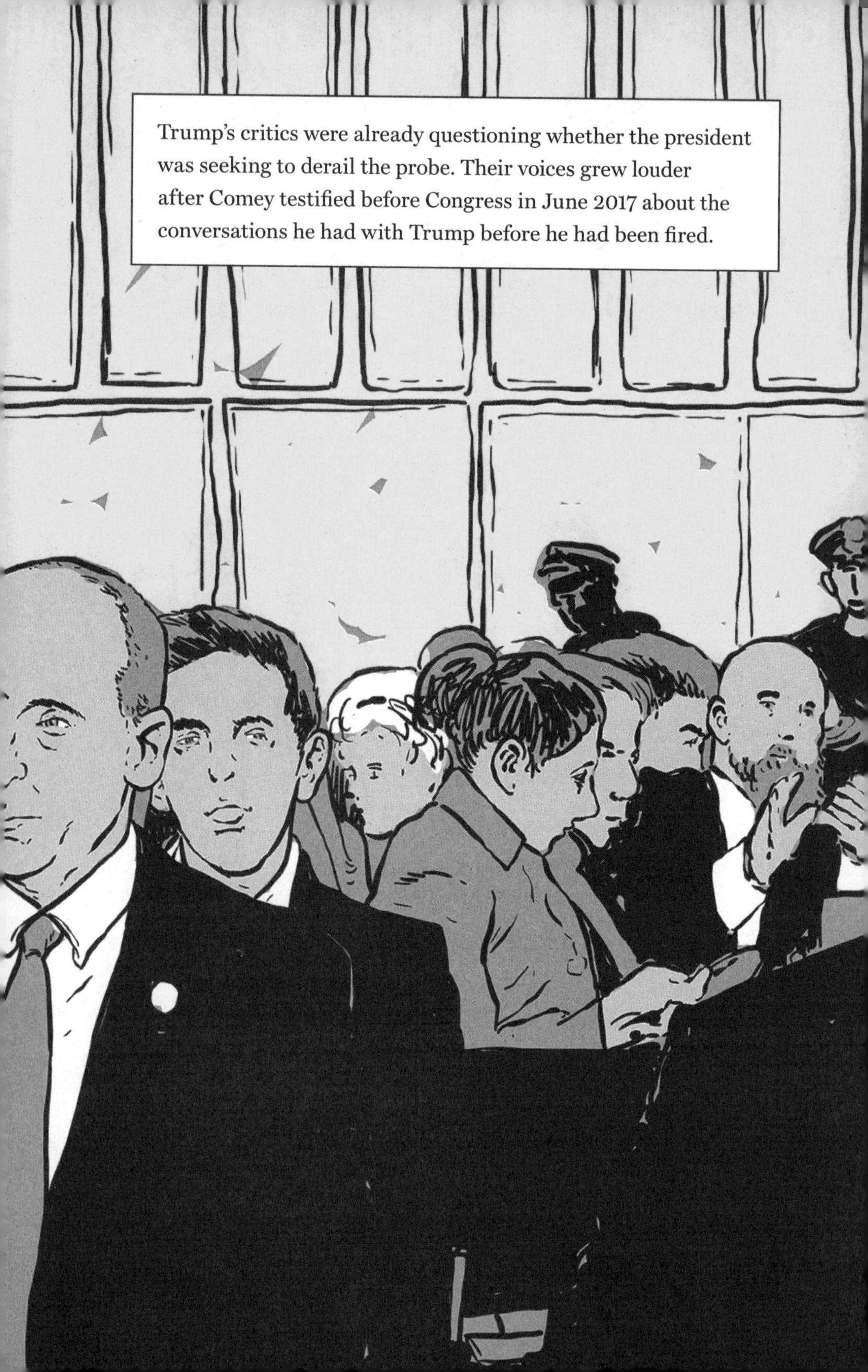
Trump's critics were already questioning whether the president was seeking to derail the probe. Their voices grew louder after Comey testified before Congress in June 2017 about the conversations he had with Trump before he had been fired.

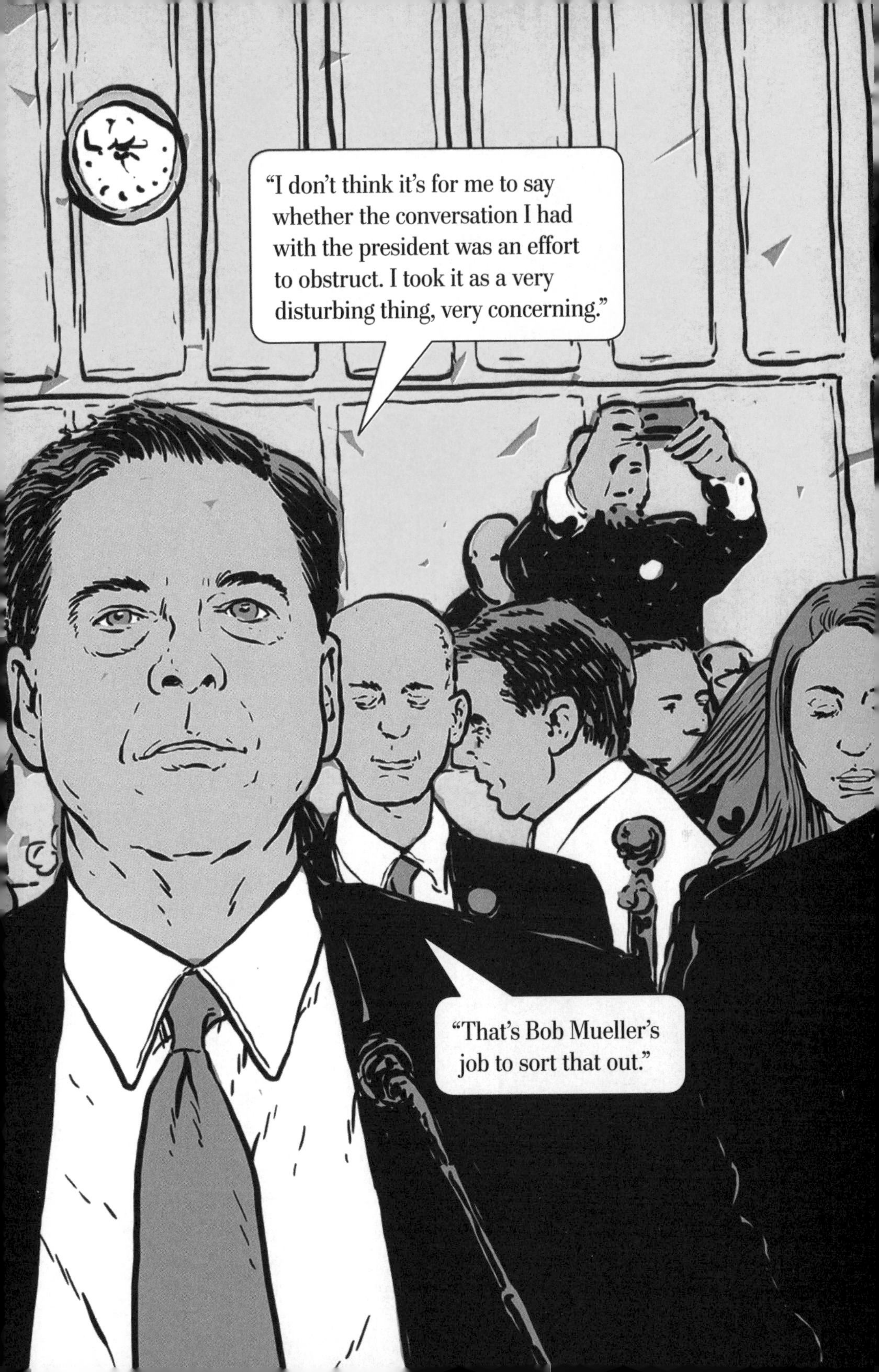
"I don't think it's for me to say whether the conversation I had with the president was an effort to obstruct. I took it as a very disturbing thing, very concerning."
"That's Bob Mueller's job to sort that out."

A few days later, Christopher Ruddy, Trump's friend and Newsmax Media's chief executive, met at the White House with Bannon and Priebus. They told him they were worried that the president was strongly considering firing Mueller — and could do so abruptly. Ruddy asked if he could talk about the issue publicly, and Priebus agreed.

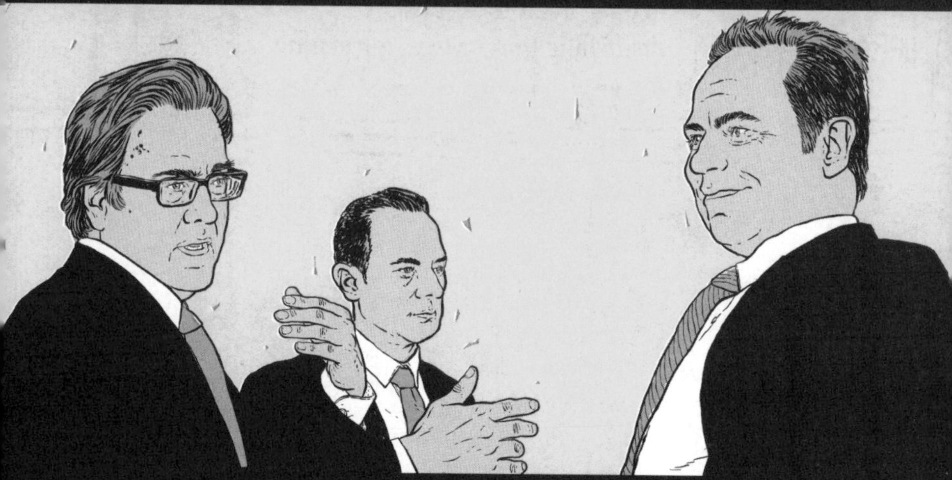

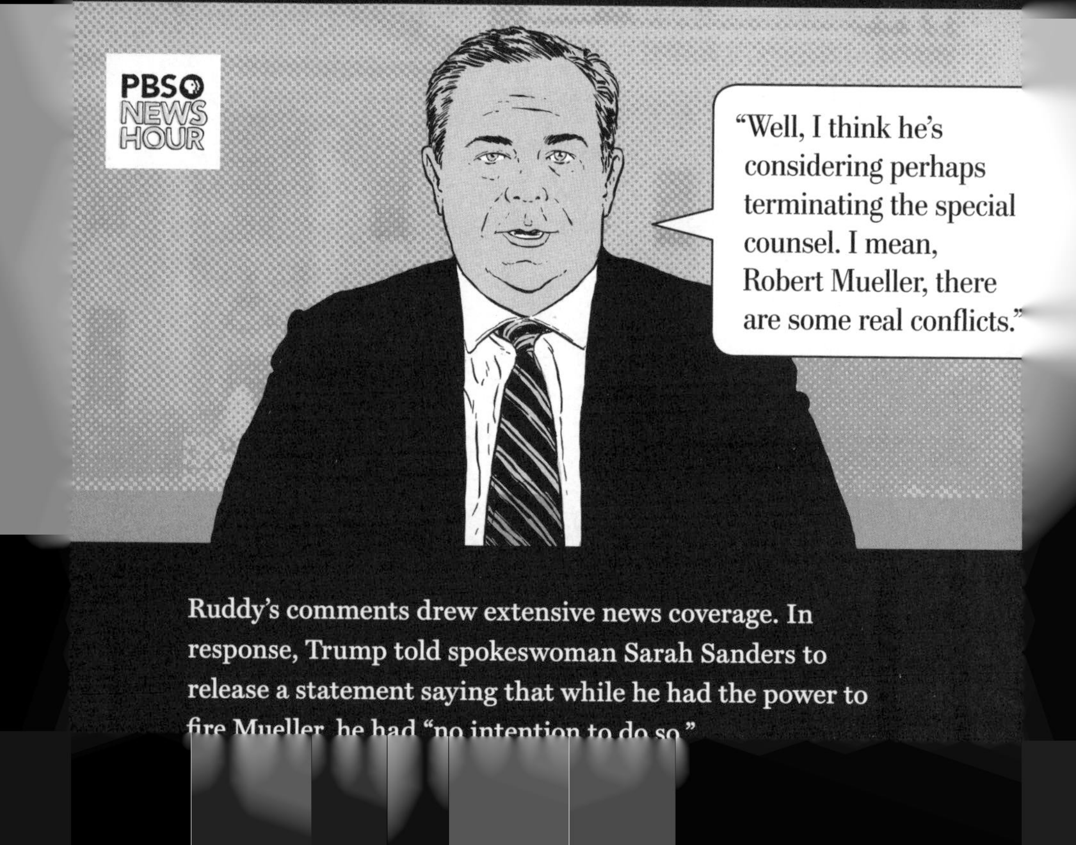
PBS NEWS HOUR
"Well, I think he's considering perhaps terminating the special counsel. I mean, Robert Mueller, there are some real conflicts."

Ruddy's comments drew extensive news coverage. In response, Trump told spokeswoman Sarah Sanders to release a statement saying that while he had the power to fire Mueller, he had "no intention to do so."

But privately, the next day, a personal attorney for Trump reached out to Mueller's office and expressed concerns that the special counsel had conflicts of interest, according to the prosecutors' internal notes. (A Trump lawyer would later deny that Mueller's possible conflicts were discussed.)

The president's pressure did not work. On June 13, as Rosenstein testified before Congress, Republican Sen. Lindsey O. Graham (S.C.), a Trump ally, quizzed him about Mueller's appointment.

"No, I do not."

"Do you know of any reason or cause to fire Mr. Mueller as of this date?"

On June 14, The Washington Post broke a bombshell story.

Trump's actions now a focus of Mueller inquiry

Officials: Counsel looking at whether president tried to obstruct justice

BY DEVLIN BARRETT,
ADAM ENTOUS,
ELLEN NAKASHIMA
AND SARI HORWITZ

The special counsel overseeing the investigation into Russia's role in the 2016 election is interviewing senior intelligence officials as part of a widening probe that now includes an examination of whether President Trump attempted to obstruct justice, officials said.

The move by special counsel Robert S. Mueller III to investigate Trump's conduct marks a major turning point in the nearly year-old FBI investigation, which until recently focused on Russian meddling during the presidential campaign and on whether there was any coordination between the Trump campaign and the Kremlin. Investigators have also been looking for any evidence of possible financial crimes among Trump associates, officials said.

Trump had received private assurances from then-FBI Director James B. Comey starting in January that he was not personally under investigation. Officials say that changed shortly after Comey's firing.

Five people briefed on the interview requests, speaking on the condition of anonymity because they were not authorized to discuss the matter publicly, said that Daniel Coats, the current director of national intelligence, Mike Rogers, head of the National Security Agency, and Rogers's recently departed deputy, Richard Ledgett, agreed to be interviewed by Mueller's investigators as early as this week. The investigation has been cloaked in secrecy, and it is unclear how many others have been questioned by the FBI.

The NSA said in a statement that it will "fully cooperate with the special counsel" and declined to comment further. The office of the director of national intelligence and Ledgett declined to comment.

The White House now refers all questions about the Russia investigation to Trump's personal attorney, Marc Kasowitz.

"The FBI leak of information regarding the president is outrageous, inexcusable and illegal," said Mark Corallo, a spokesman for Kasowitz.

The officials said Coats, Rogers and Ledgett would appear voluntarily, though it remains unclear whether they will describe in full their conversations with Trump and other top officials or will be directed by the White House to

MUELLER CONTINUED ON A17

Russia sanctions are protected
The Senate voted to curtail Trump's power to ease punishments. **A17**

In "a major turning point," The Post reported, the special counsel was investigating the president himself for possible obstruction of justice.

What Trump had feared most had come to pass: His own
actions were under scrutiny.

Early the next day, the president began tweeting.

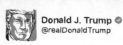

Donald J. Trump ✔
@realDonaldTrump

They made up a phony collusion with the Russians story, found zero proof, so now they go for obstruction of justice on the phony story. Nice

6:55 AM · Jun 15, 2017

35.9K Retweets   **127.5K** Likes

Donald J. Trump ✔
@realDonaldTrump

You are witnessing the single greatest WITCH HUNT in American political history - led by some very bad and conflicted people! #MAGA

7:57 AM · Jun 15, 2017

30.9K Retweets   **108.4K** Likes

Donald J. Trump ✔
@realDonaldTrump

Crooked H destroyed phones w/ hammer, 'bleached' emails, & had husband meet w/AG days before she was cleared- & they talk about obstruction?

3:56 PM · Jun 15, 2017

47.3K Retweets   **137.5K** Likes

Trump's anger continued unabated the following day.

Donald J. Trump ✔
@realDonaldTrump

After 7 months of investigations & committee hearings about my "collusion with the Russians," nobody has been able to show any proof. Sad!

7:53 AM · Jun 16, 2017

22.1K Retweets **98.5K** Likes

Donald J. Trump ✔
@realDonaldTrump

I am being investigated for firing the FBI Director by the man who told me to fire the FBI Director! Witch Hunt

9:07 AM · Jun 16, 2017

42.6K Retweets **138.2K** Likes

This was it. Mueller had to go, the president had decided.

On Saturday, June 17, Trump traveled to the presidential retreat at Camp David.

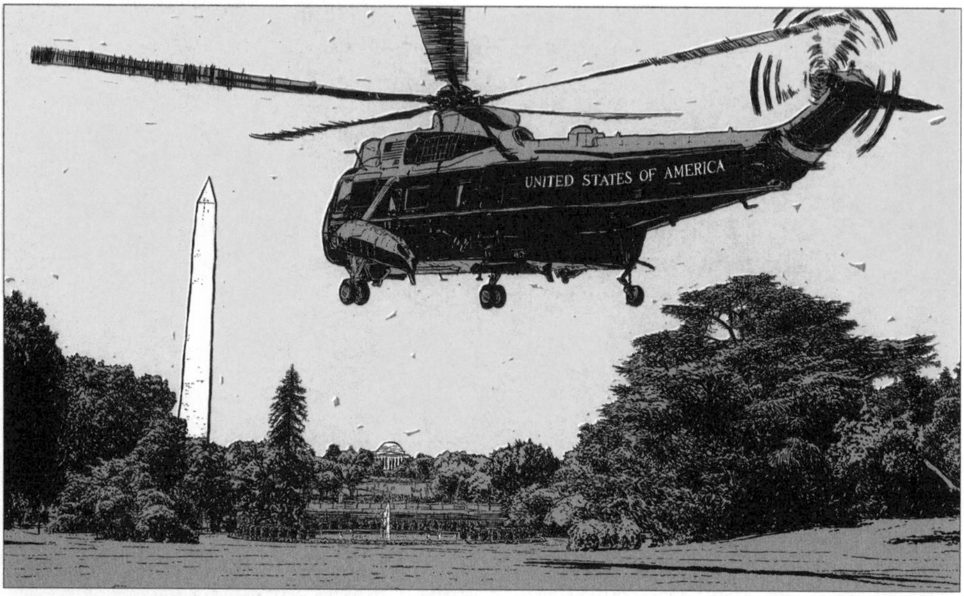
UNITED STATES OF AMERICA

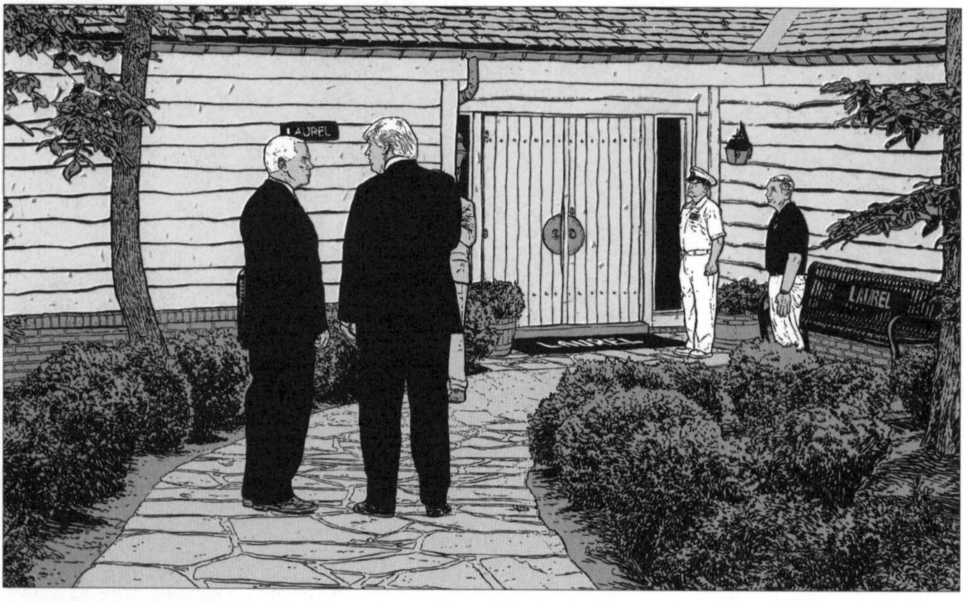
LAUREL
LAUREL
LAUREL

From there, he called McGahn at home and directed him to have the special counsel removed.

"You gotta do this. You gotta call Rod."

"Call Rod, tell Rod that Mueller has conflicts and can't be the special counsel."

"Mueller has to go."

"Call me back when you do it."

McGahn tried to put off the president, telling him he would see what he could do. To get Trump off the phone, he left him with the impression he would call Rosenstein. But he had no intention of doing so.

The White House counsel felt trapped. He didn't know what he would say if the president called again.

He decided he had to resign.

McGahn called his personal attorney, William Burck, to tell him of his difficult decision. He also told his chief of staff, Annie Donaldson.

To try to keep her out of the investigation, McGahn did not want to tell Donaldson exactly what Trump had asked of him. But he said that the president had asked him to call the Justice Department and do something he did not want to do. In one call, he told her, Trump asked him, "Have you done it?"

Donaldson guessed that Trump's request had something to do with Russia. She decided to resign along with her boss.

That evening, McGahn called Bannon and Priebus and told them he planned to quit.

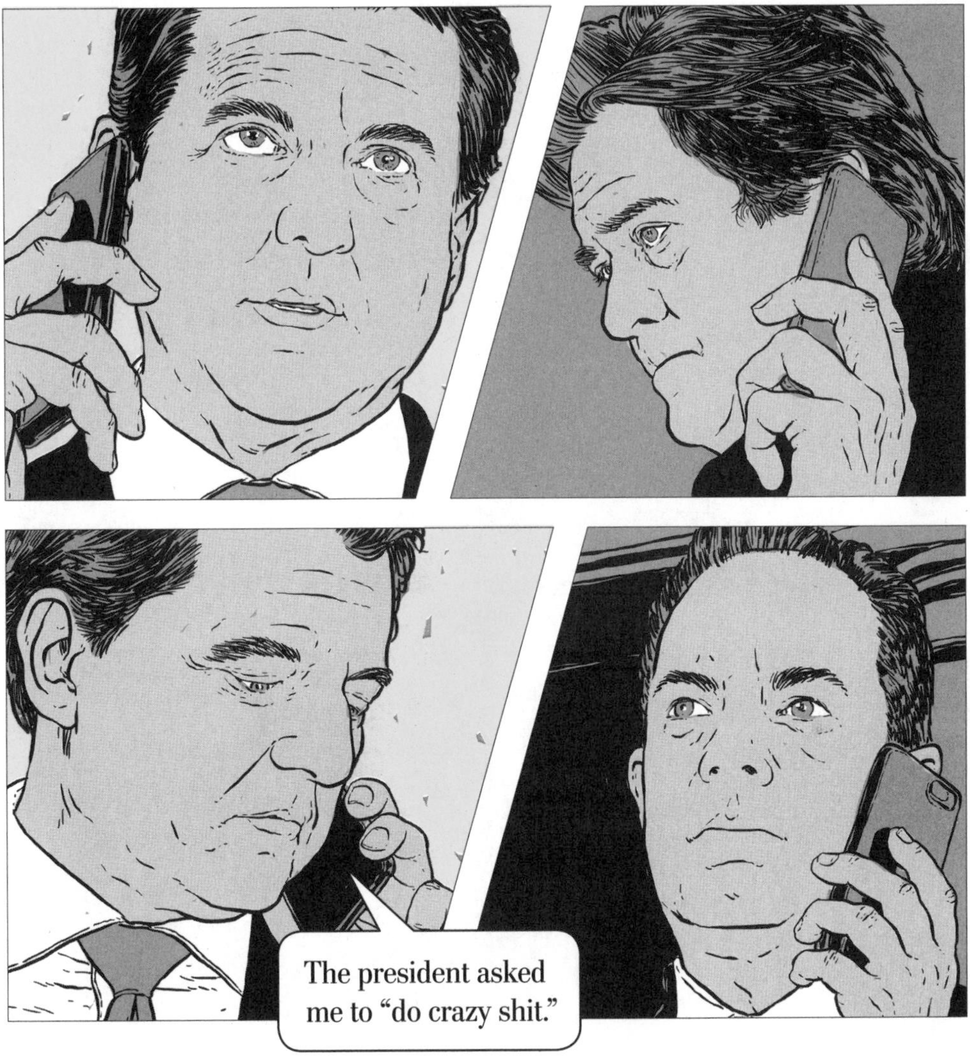
The president asked me to "do crazy shit."

Bannon and Priebus urged him to reconsider.

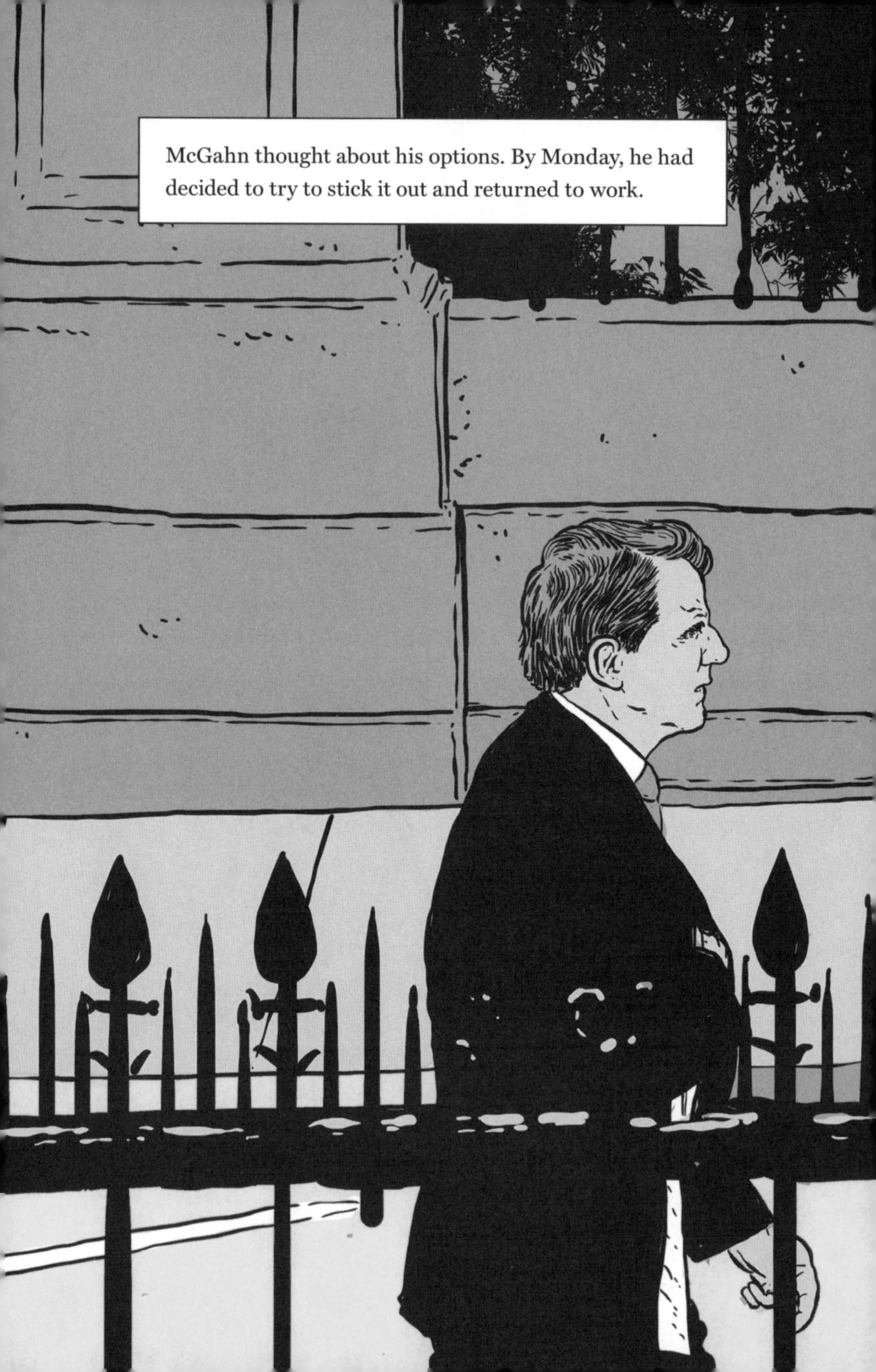
McGahn thought about his options. By Monday, he had decided to try to stick it out and returned to work.

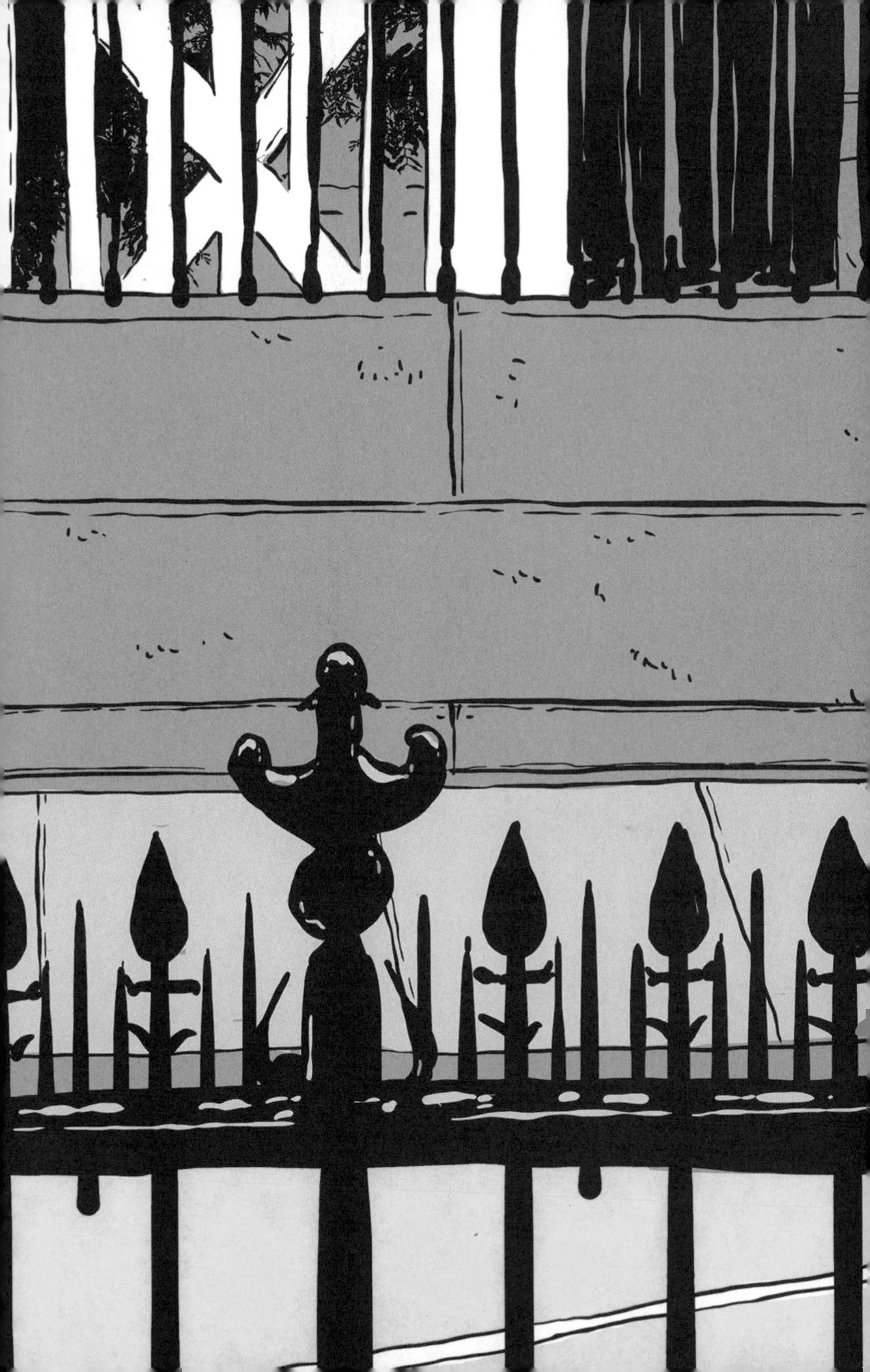

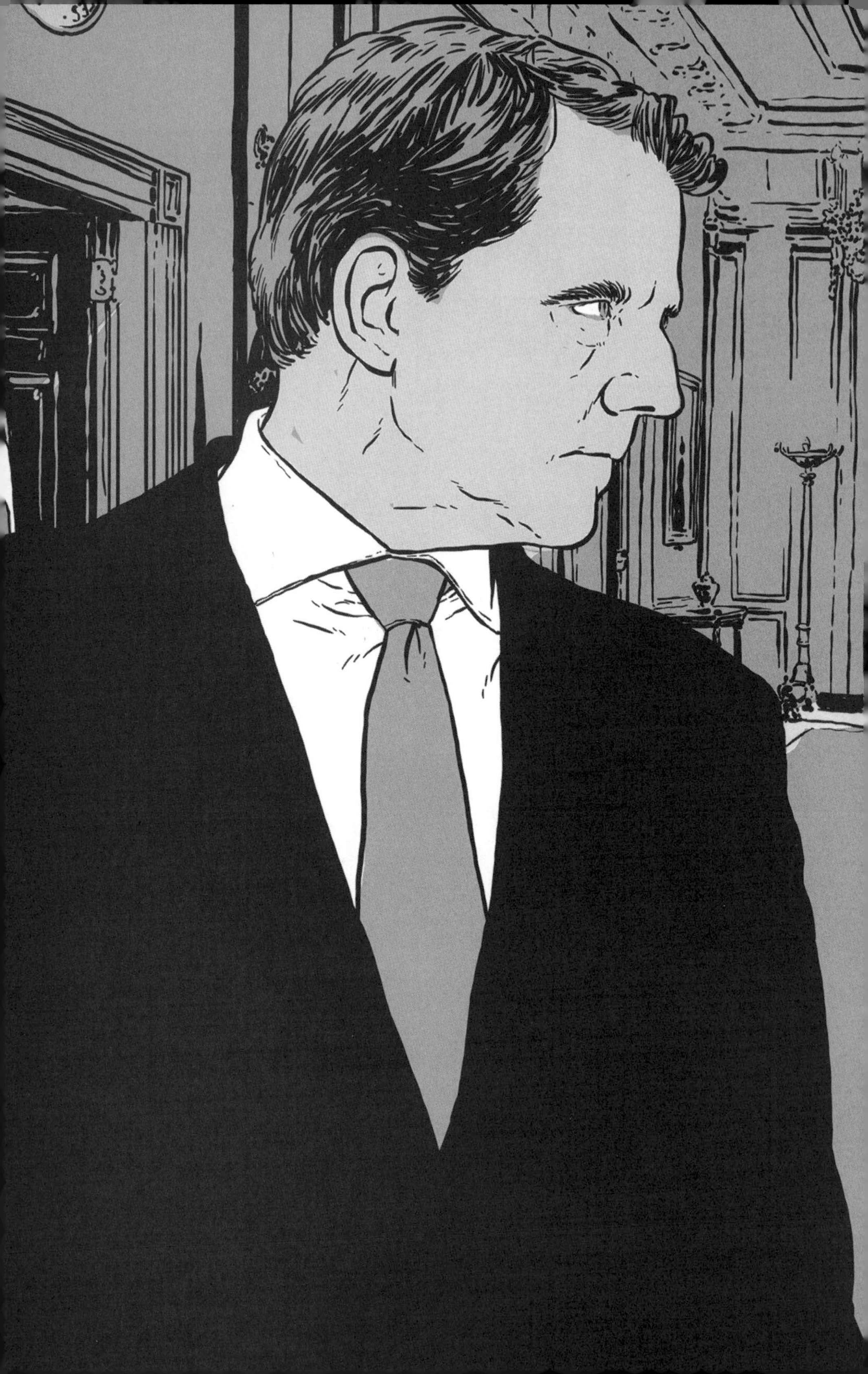

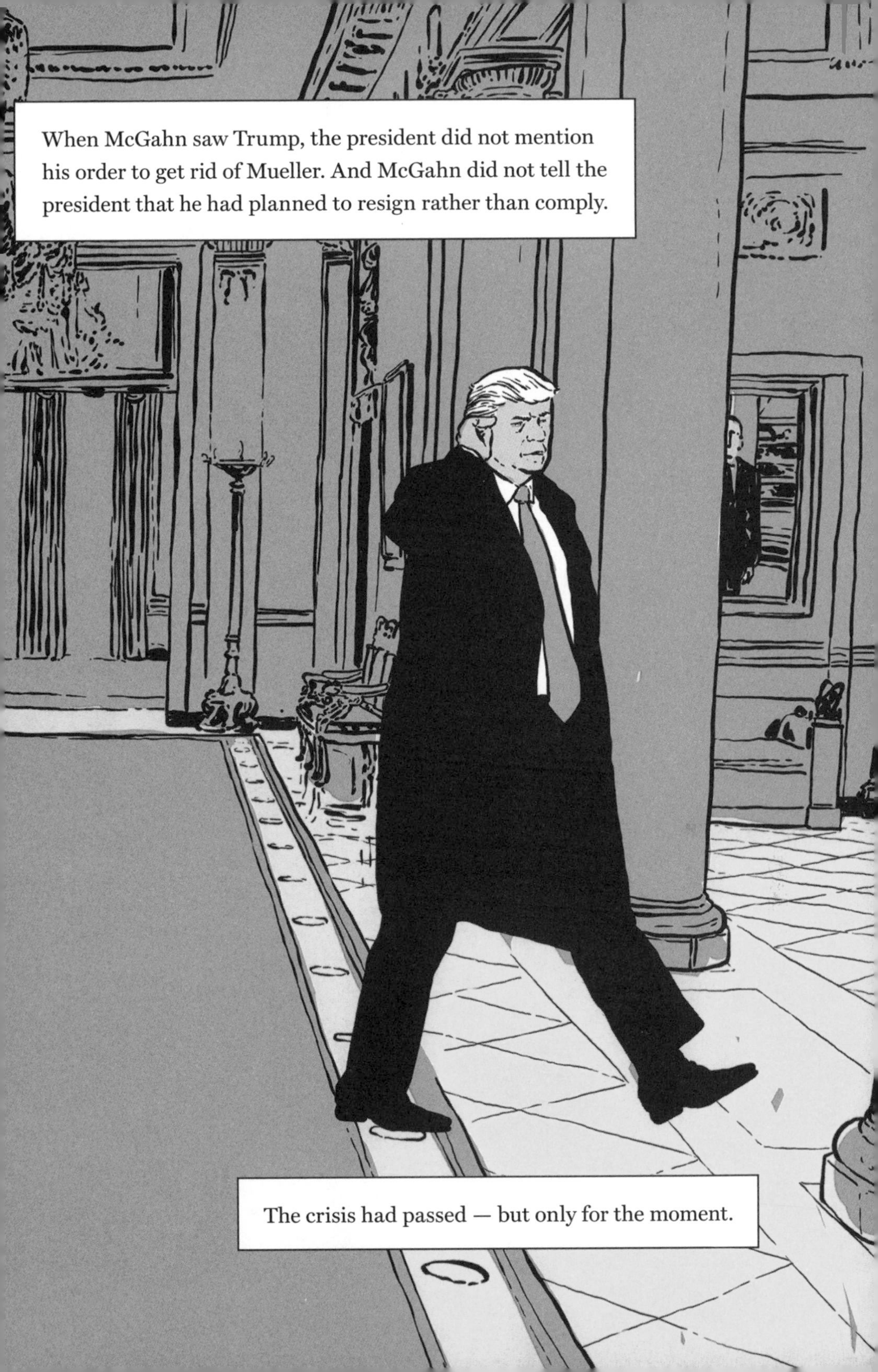
When McGahn saw Trump, the president did not mention his order to get rid of Mueller. And McGahn did not tell the president that he had planned to resign rather than comply.
The crisis had passed — but only for the moment.

Trump turns to
a loyal ally for help

President Trump had just learned in June 2017 that he was
under investigation by Robert S. Mueller III. He had tried
and failed to get his White House counsel to order Mueller's
removal. Two days later, he sought another way to rein in the
special counsel.

On June 19, Trump met alone in the Oval Office with his former campaign manager, Corey Lewandowski.

After some small talk, Trump turned the conversation to Attorney General Jeff Sessions. He told Lewandowski that Sessions was weak. The president said Sessions should not have recused himself from overseeing the Russia investigation, a decision the attorney general had announced a few months earlier.

"Write this down."

Trump said he never would have appointed Sessions if he'd known he would take that step. The president then told his former campaign manager to deliver a message to Sessions: The attorney general should give a speech. Trump dictated what it should say.

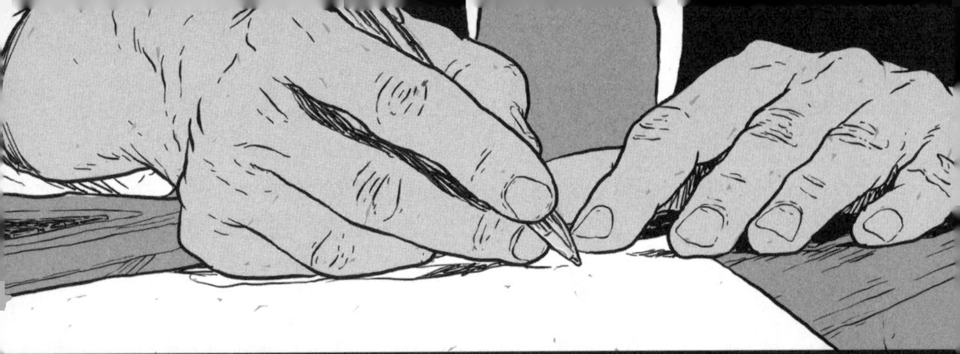

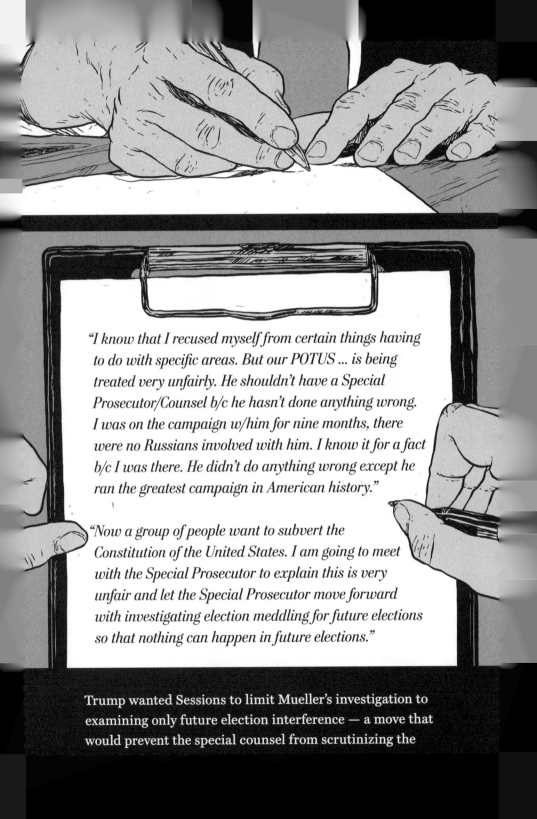

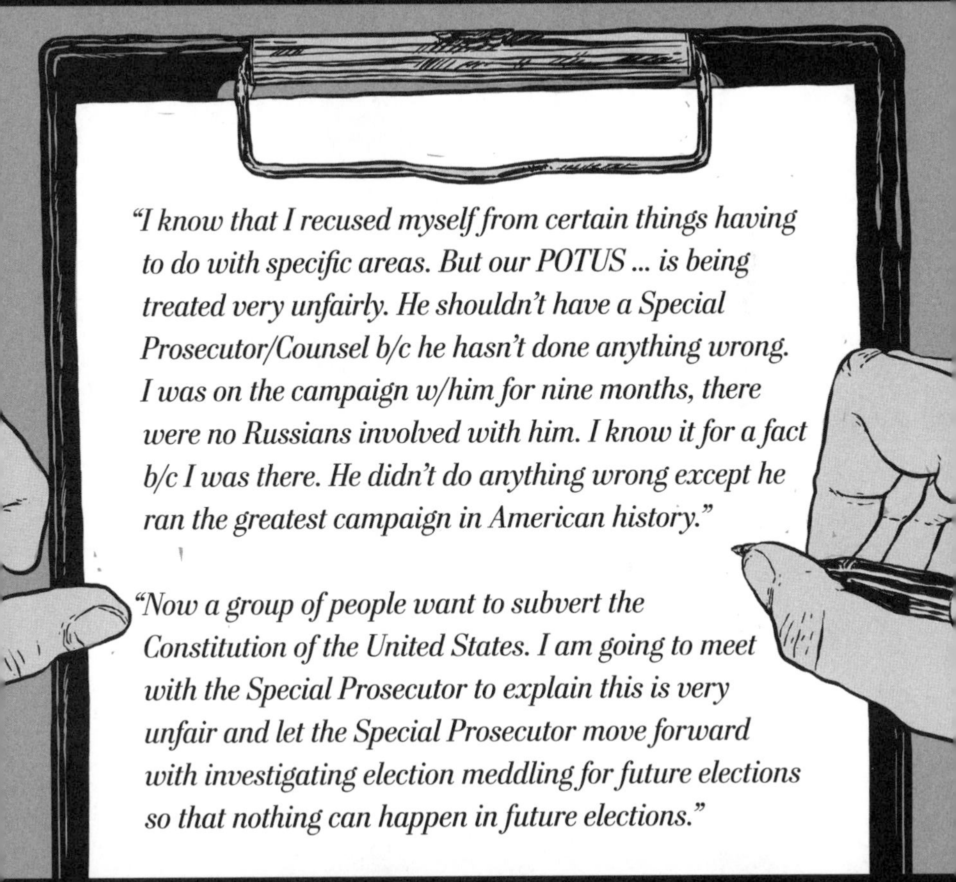
"I know that I recused myself from certain things having to do with specific areas. But our POTUS ... is being treated very unfairly. He shouldn't have a Special Prosecutor/Counsel b/c he hasn't done anything wrong. I was on the campaign w/him for nine months, there were no Russians involved with him. I know it for a fact b/c I was there. He didn't do anything wrong except he ran the greatest campaign in American history."
"Now a group of people want to subvert the Constitution of the United States. I am going to meet with the Special Prosecutor to explain this is very unfair and let the Special Prosecutor move forward with investigating election meddling for future elections so that nothing can happen in future elections."

Trump wanted Sessions to limit Mueller's investigation to examining only future election interference — a move that would prevent the special counsel from scrutinizing the

Trump told Lewandowski that it would be good for Sessions if he gave such a speech.

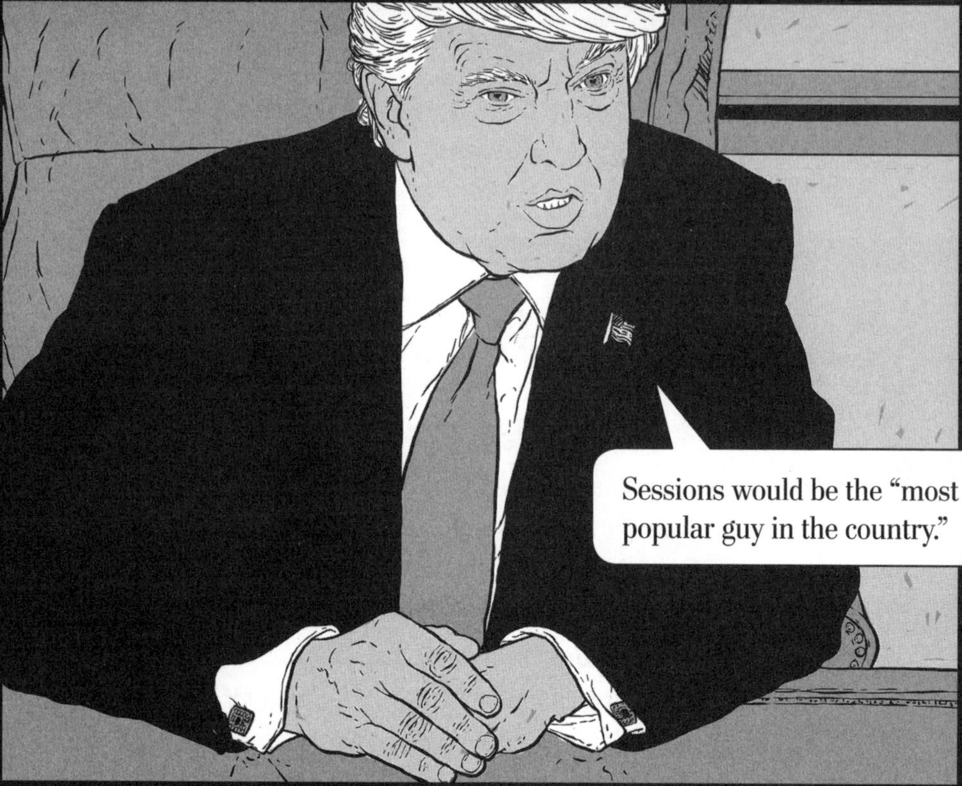
Sessions would be the "most popular guy in the country."

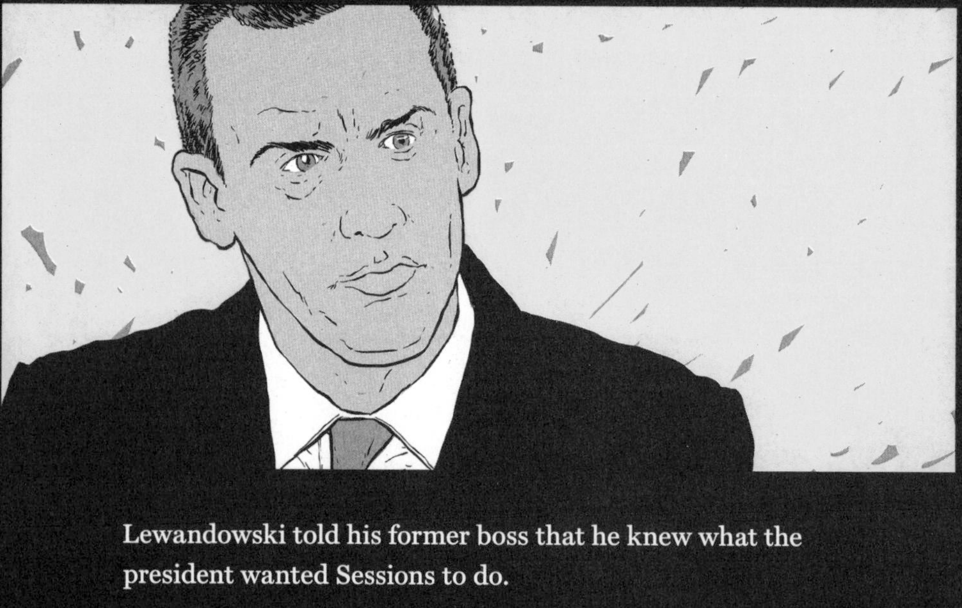

Lewandowski told his former boss that he knew what the president wanted Sessions to do.

The request was extraordinary. The president wanted his attorney general to interfere in an investigation — one examining Trump's own conduct and that of his campaign.

Lewandowski decided he wanted to give Sessions the message in person, but he didn't want to meet at the Justice Department. That was Sessions's home turf and would give the attorney general an advantage. Lewandowski also didn't want to sign in to enter the government building, which would leave a record of his meeting.

He called Sessions and the two men agreed to meet the following evening at Lewandowki's office.

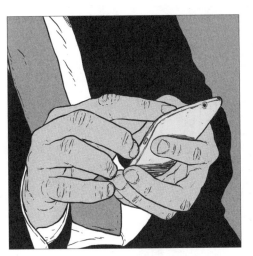 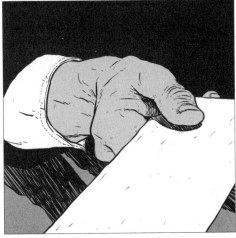

At the last minute, Sessions canceled the meeting. Lewandowski left Washington, having failed to deliver the president's message.

Lewandowski knew the notes he had taken in the Oval Office were sensitive. He placed them in a safe at his home.

Lewandowski came up with another plan: He called Rick Dearborn, a senior White House official, and asked if he could pass a message to the attorney general. Lewandowski figured the message would be better coming from Dearborn, who had been Sessions's chief of staff and — unlike Lewandowski — worked in the White House.

Dearborn agreed — without knowing what the message said. He planned to give it to Sessions at a dinner in late July.

On July 19, Lewandowski was back at the White House. The Russia investigation was heating up. A few days earlier, the media had reported for the first time that Trump's son, Donald Trump Jr., had met during the campaign with a Russian lawyer who he was told would help his father's presidential bid.

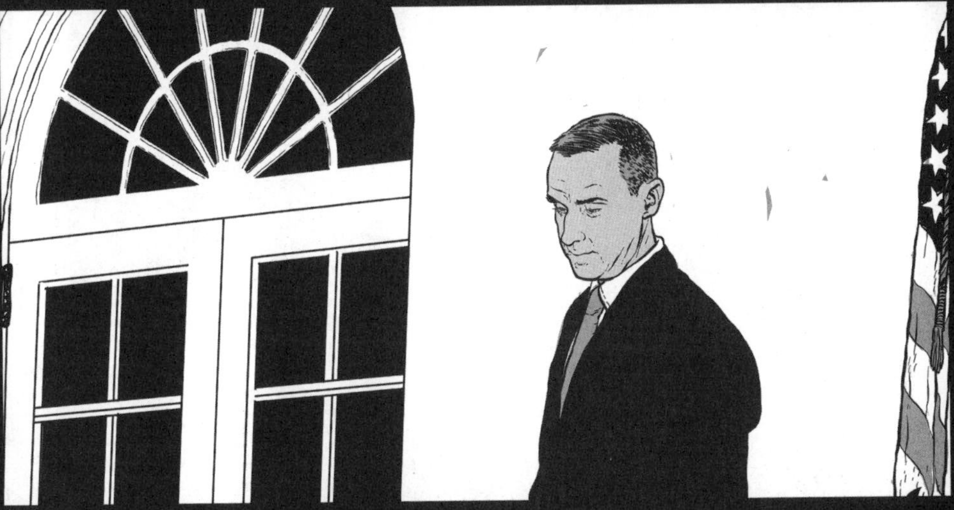

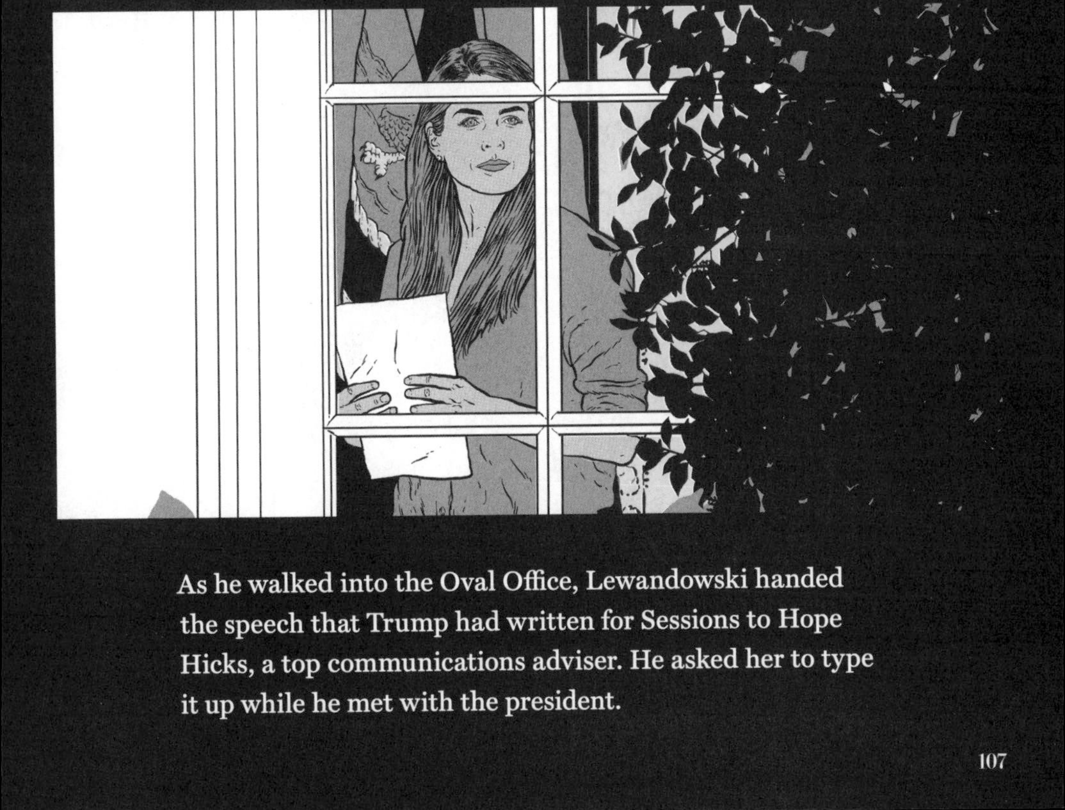

As he walked into the Oval Office, Lewandowski handed the speech that Trump had written for Sessions to Hope Hicks, a top communications adviser. He asked her to type it up while he met with the president.

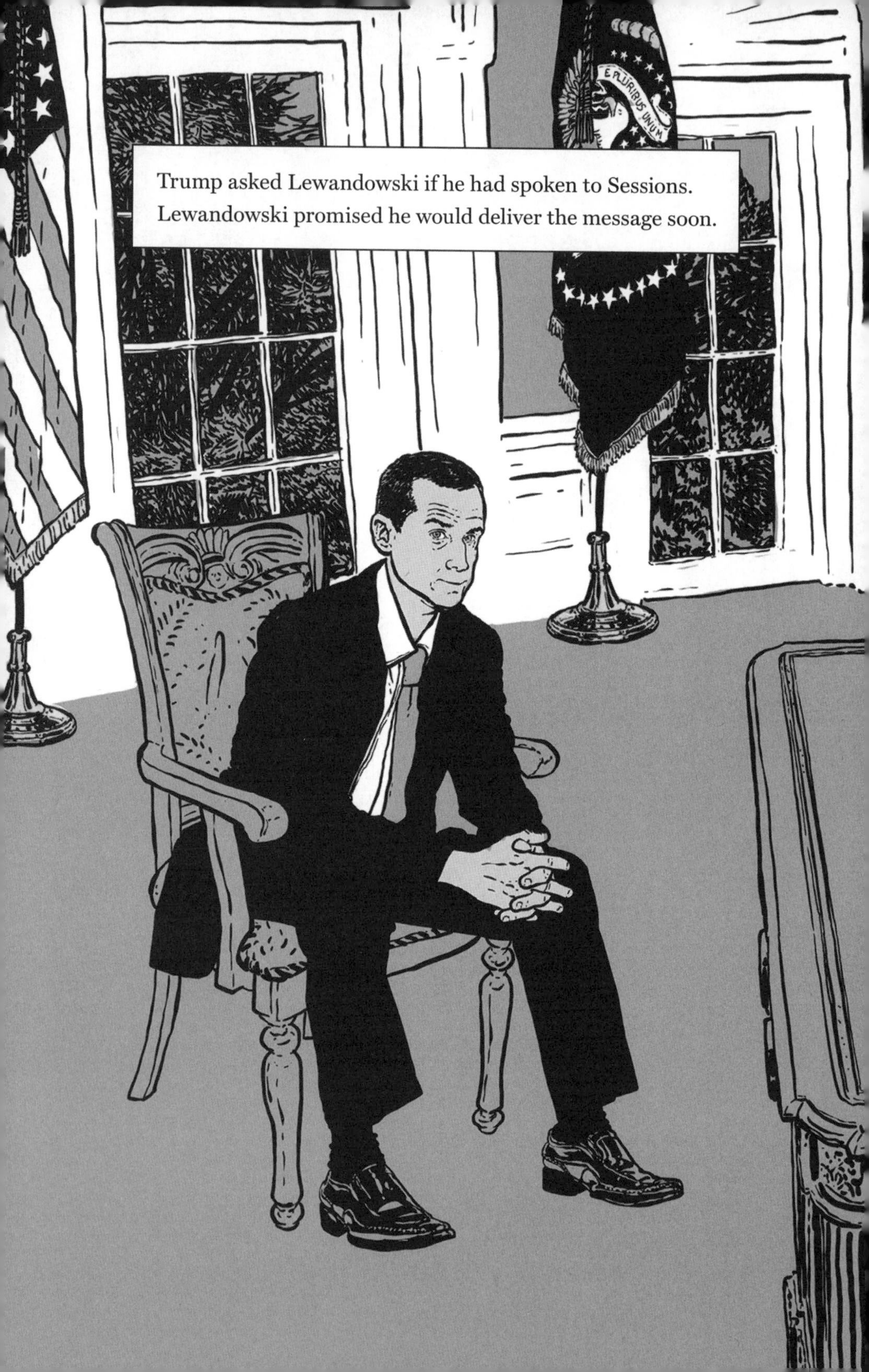
E PLURIBUS UNUM
Trump asked Lewandowski if he had spoken to Sessions. Lewandowski promised he would deliver the message soon.

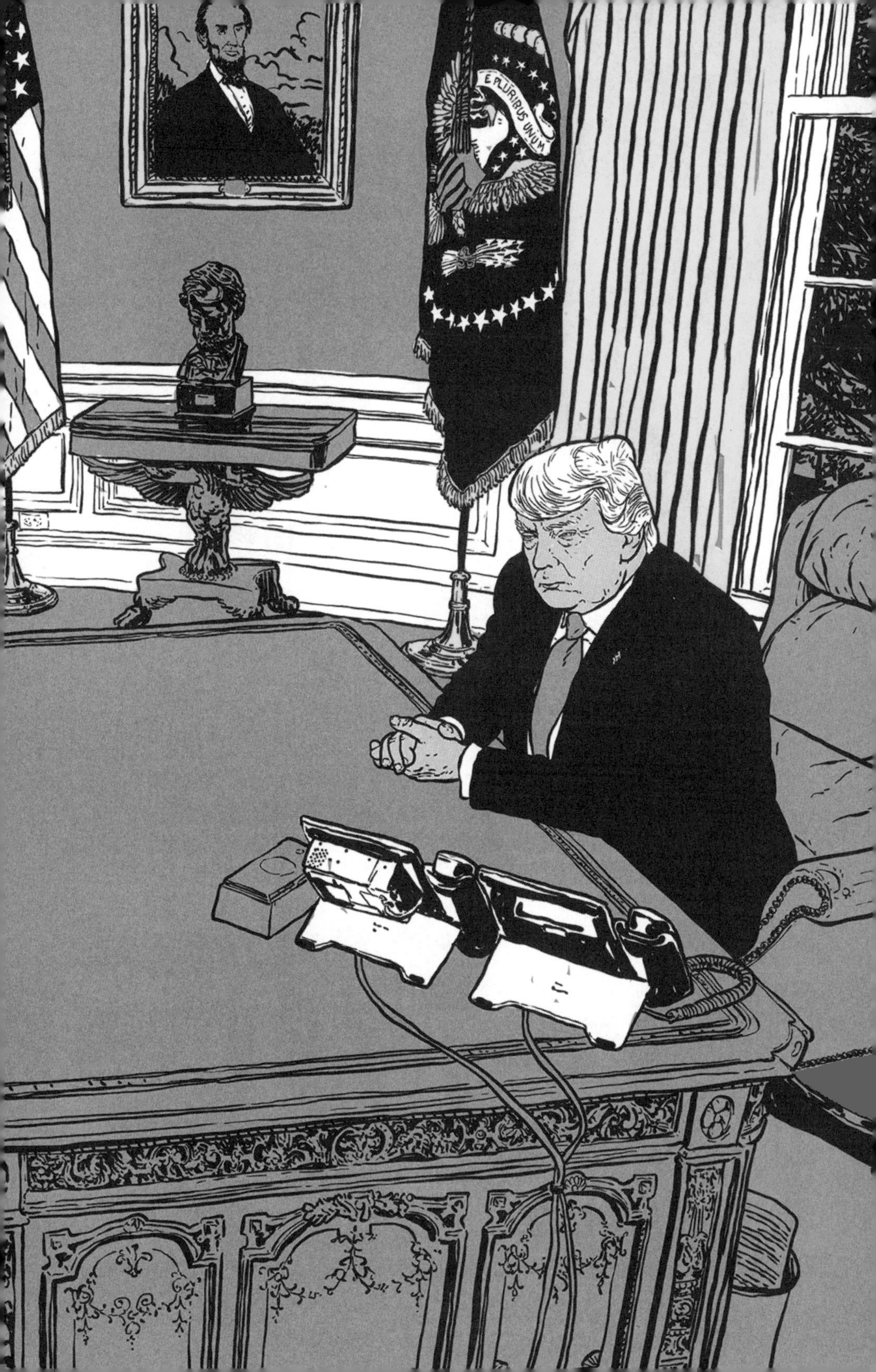
E PLURIBUS UNUM

The president told his former campaign manager that if
Sessions did not meet with him, Lewandowski should tell
Sessions he was fired.

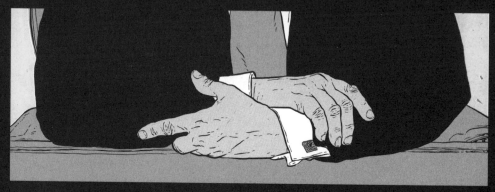

It was an odd request for Lewandowksi. He was not
the attorney general's boss. He didn't even work for the
government.

Leaving the meeting, Lewandowski ran into Dearborn in the anteroom of the Oval Office and gave him the notes that Hicks had typed. Lewandowksi explained this was the message for Sessions they had discussed.

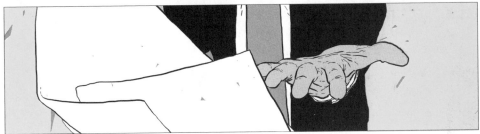

Dearborn was wary and did not feel comfortable carrying a message to Sessions. He decided he didn't want to know any more and threw away the notes without ever speaking to the attorney general.

Dearborn told Lewandowski he had handled the situation.

Lewandowski would later be asked about the episode on Capitol Hill. He told members of Congress in September 2019 that he did not believe the president had asked him to do anything illegal or improper by proposing that he speak with the attorney general about Mueller's investigation.

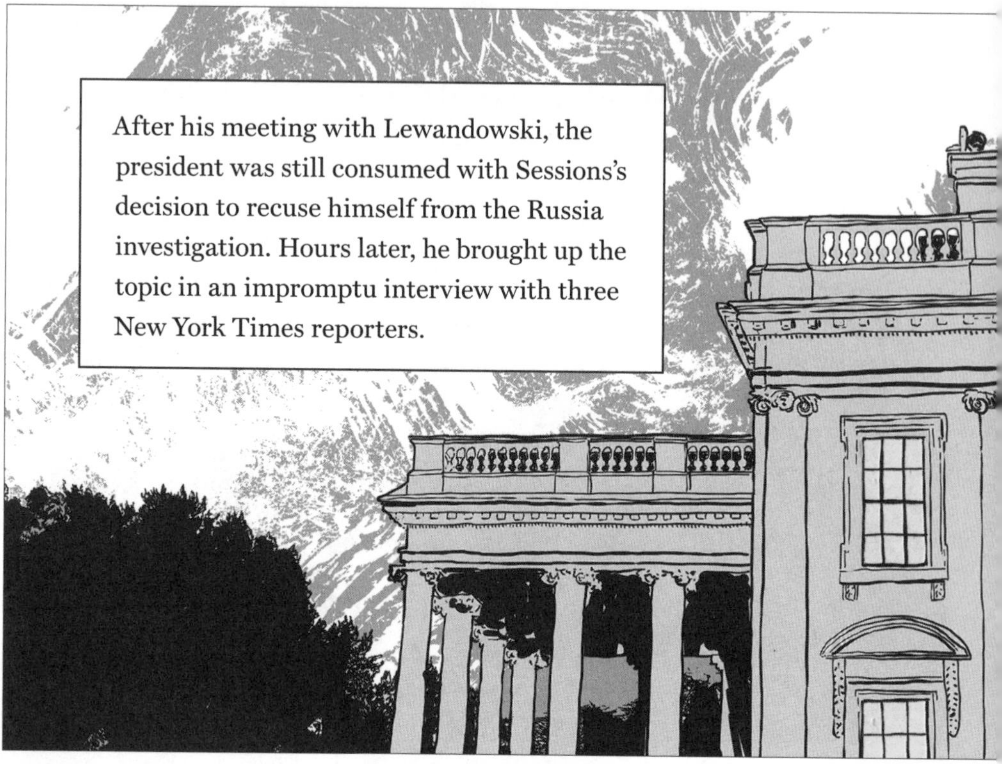
After his meeting with Lewandowski, the president was still consumed with Sessions's decision to recuse himself from the Russia investigation. Hours later, he brought up the topic in an impromptu interview with three New York Times reporters.

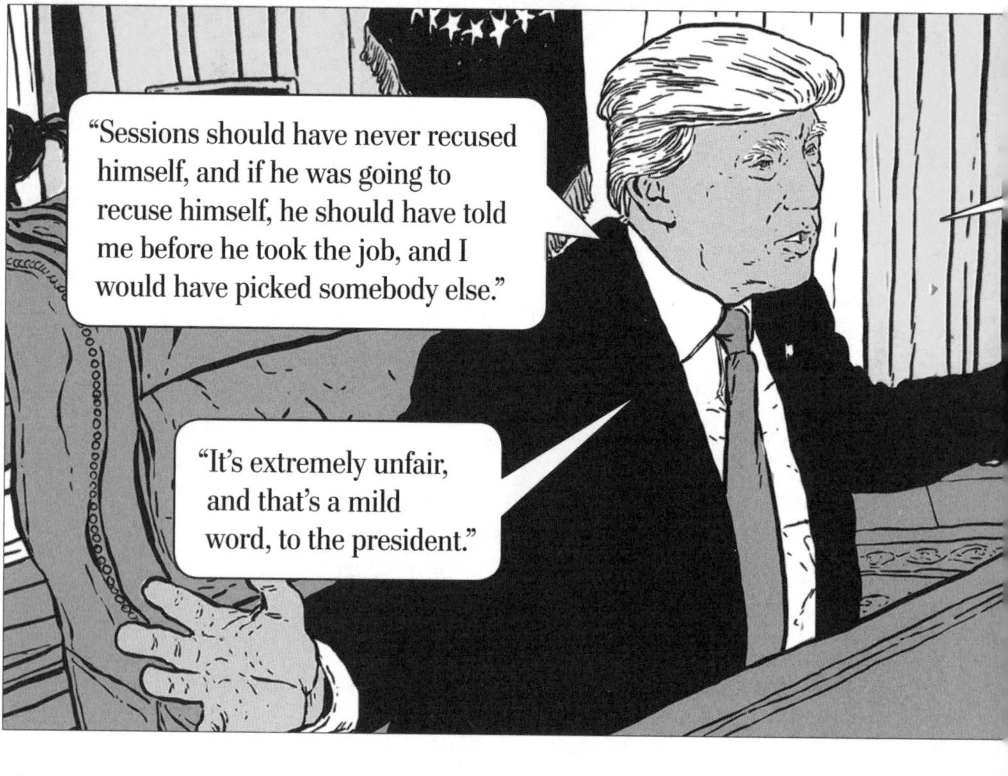
"Sessions should have never recused himself, and if he was going to recuse himself, he should have told me before he took the job, and I would have picked somebody else."
"It's extremely unfair, and that's a mild word, to the president."

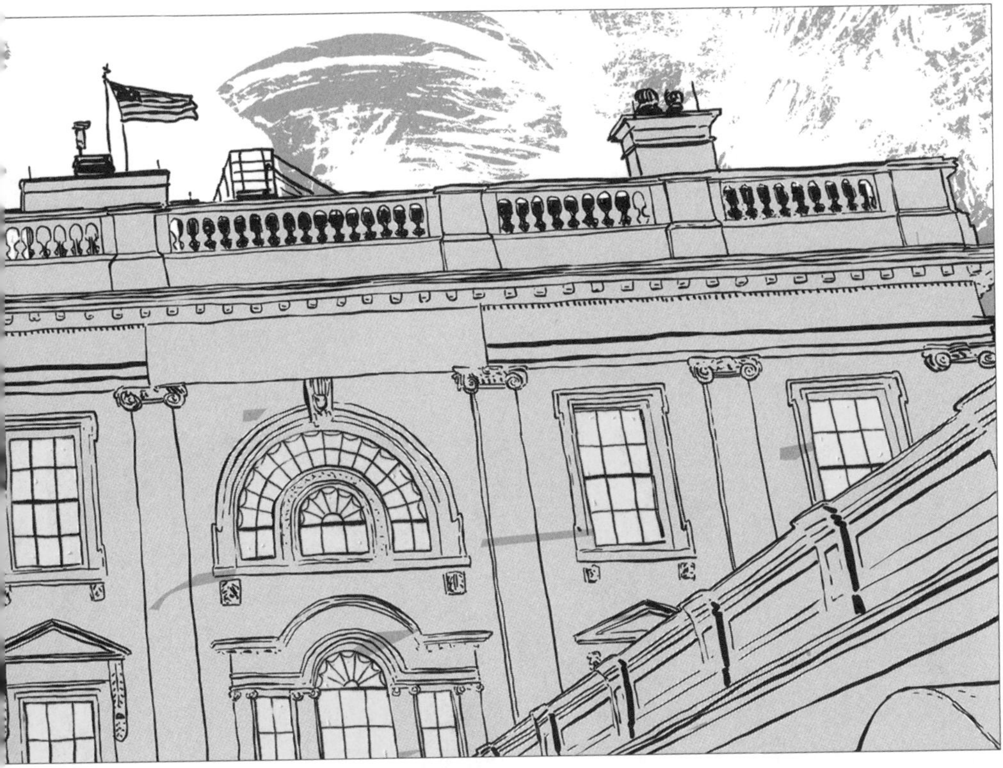

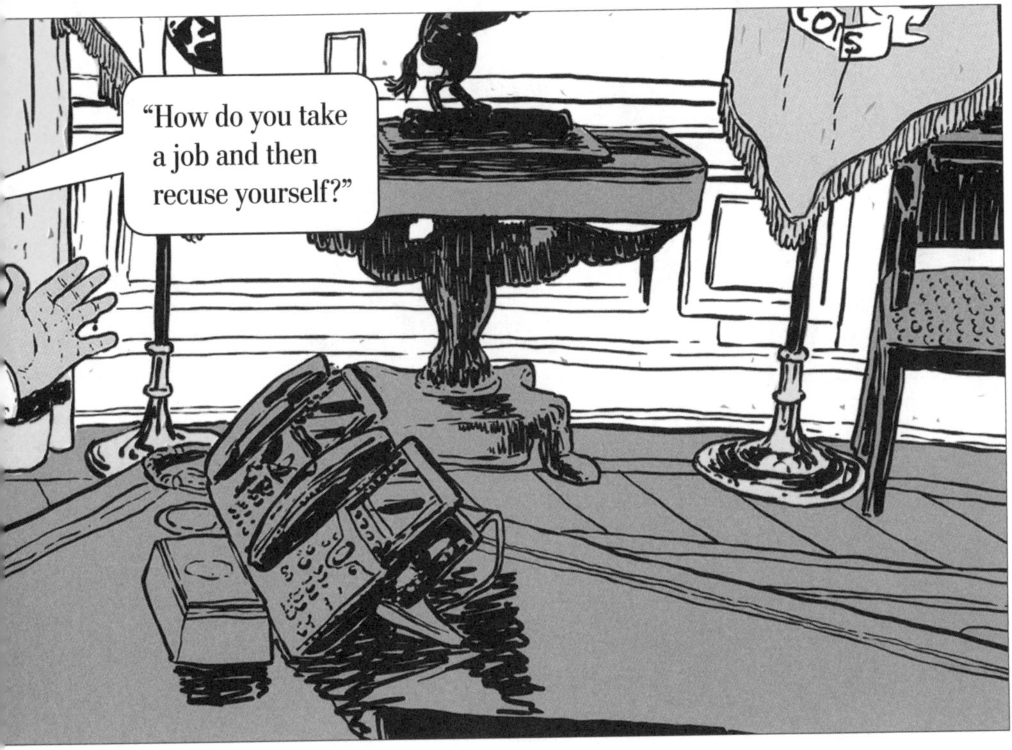
"How do you take a job and then recuse yourself?"

Hicks was deeply worried about the president's critical comments about Sessions, which immediately spurred public questions about whether he was trying to bully his attorney general into interfering with the Russia investigation. But later that day, Trump called her to say how happy he was with the coverage.

Three days later, on July 21, The Washington Post reported that Sessions had discussed campaign-related matters with Russian Ambassador Sergey Kislyak during the 2016 presidential race, contrary to what Sessions had said publicly.

The Washington Post

Prices may vary in areas outside metropolitan Washington.

K RE V1 V2 V3 V

Thunderstorm 93/76 • Tomorrow: Thunderstorm 90/77 B6   *Democracy Dies in Darkness*   SATURDAY, JULY 22, 2017 · $2

Kislyak's reports implicate Sessions

Envoy is said to have told Kremlin they discussed Trump, Russia's desires

BY ADAM ENTOUS,
ELLEN NAKASHIMA
AND GREG MILLER

Russia's ambassador to Washington told his superiors in Moscow that he discussed campaign-related matters, including policy issues important to Moscow, with Jeff Sessions during the 2016 presidential race, contrary to public assertions by the embattled attorney general, according to current and former U.S. officials.

Ambassador Sergey Kislyak's accounts of two conversations with Sessions — then a top foreign policy adviser to Republican candidate Donald Trump — were intercepted by U.S. spy agencies, which monitor the communications of senior Russian officials in the United States and in Russia. Sessions initially failed to disclose his contacts with Kislyak and then said that the meetings were not about the Trump campaign.

One U.S. official said that Sessions — who testified that he had no recollection of an April encounter — has provided "misleading" statements that are "contradicted by other evidence." A former official said that the intelligence indicates that Sessions and Kislyak had "substantive" discussions on matters including

SESSIONS CONTINUED ON A8

Battered ISIS shifts to simple, solo plots

Trump's chain reaction of chaos

PHOTOS BY JABIN BOTSFORD/THE WASHINGTON POST

Former White House press secretary Sean Spicer, above left, walks into the West Wing on Friday after abruptly resigning his position in protest of President Trump's decision to install Anthony Scaramucci, below, as communications director.

Scaramucci is cut from same cloth as his new boss

BY RENAE MERLE,
DAMIAN PALETTA
AND HEATHER LONG

NEW YORK — To avoid the pitfalls of politics, Anthony Scaramucci, the talkative Wall Street financier picked by President Trump on Friday to lead his communications strategy, often advises those close to him to have thick skin.

It is a lesson he learned years ago from Trump. The two were seated at the same table during a Lupus Foundation luncheon, and a dispirited Scaramucci told Trump that he was being "ripped apart" by the media.

"Look, it comes with the terri-

PRESIDENT SHAKES UP SENIOR TEAM

Protesting financier's rise press secretary resigns

BY ASHLEY PARKER,
ABBY PHILLIP
AND DAMIAN PALETTA

President Trump overhauled his White House on Friday in a dramatic shake-up of his senior team at the six-month mark of his presidency, which so far has been beset by a special counsel's widening Russia investigation, a floundering legislative agenda and seemingly constant chaos and infighting within his West Wing.

Trump's decision Friday morning to install wealthy financier Anthony Scaramucci as White House communications director set off an unexpected chain reaction, with White House press secretary Sean Spicer resigning in protest, according to people familiar with the departures. By afternoon, Spicer's deputy, Sarah Huckabee Sanders, had been named to replace him.

As the reorganization unfolded throughout the day, Trump's communications shop — not known for finely tuned messaging — offered its best attempt at a display of unity, a Kabuki-theater performance

CHAOS CONTINUED ON A6

Spicer was caught in the crossfire from the start

BY DAVID NAKAMURA

Sean Spicer had not fully moved into his West Wing office in January when he interrupted an informal chat with reporters to show off a prized new possession: the ceremonial White House press secretary flak jacket passed down by his predecessors.

It was meant to symbolize the incoming blasts from reporters. But for Spicer, who announced his resignation Friday after six tumultuous months on the job, it was the crossfire from inside the West Wing that brought him down.

To a degree unseen before a

The focus on his interactions with Kislyak made the embattled attorney general even more vulnerable.

That evening, White House Chief of Staff Reince Priebus called Sessions's chief of staff, Jody Hunt, to talk about whether Sessions might be fired or resign.

Hunt told him that Sessions had no intention of resigning — and noted that even if Trump fired Sessions, the special counsel investigation would continue.

The next day was Saturday. Aboard Marine One bound for Norfolk, Va., that morning, Trump told Priebus that the country had lost confidence in Sessions and the negative publicity surrounding the attorney general was intolerable. The president wanted Sessions out.

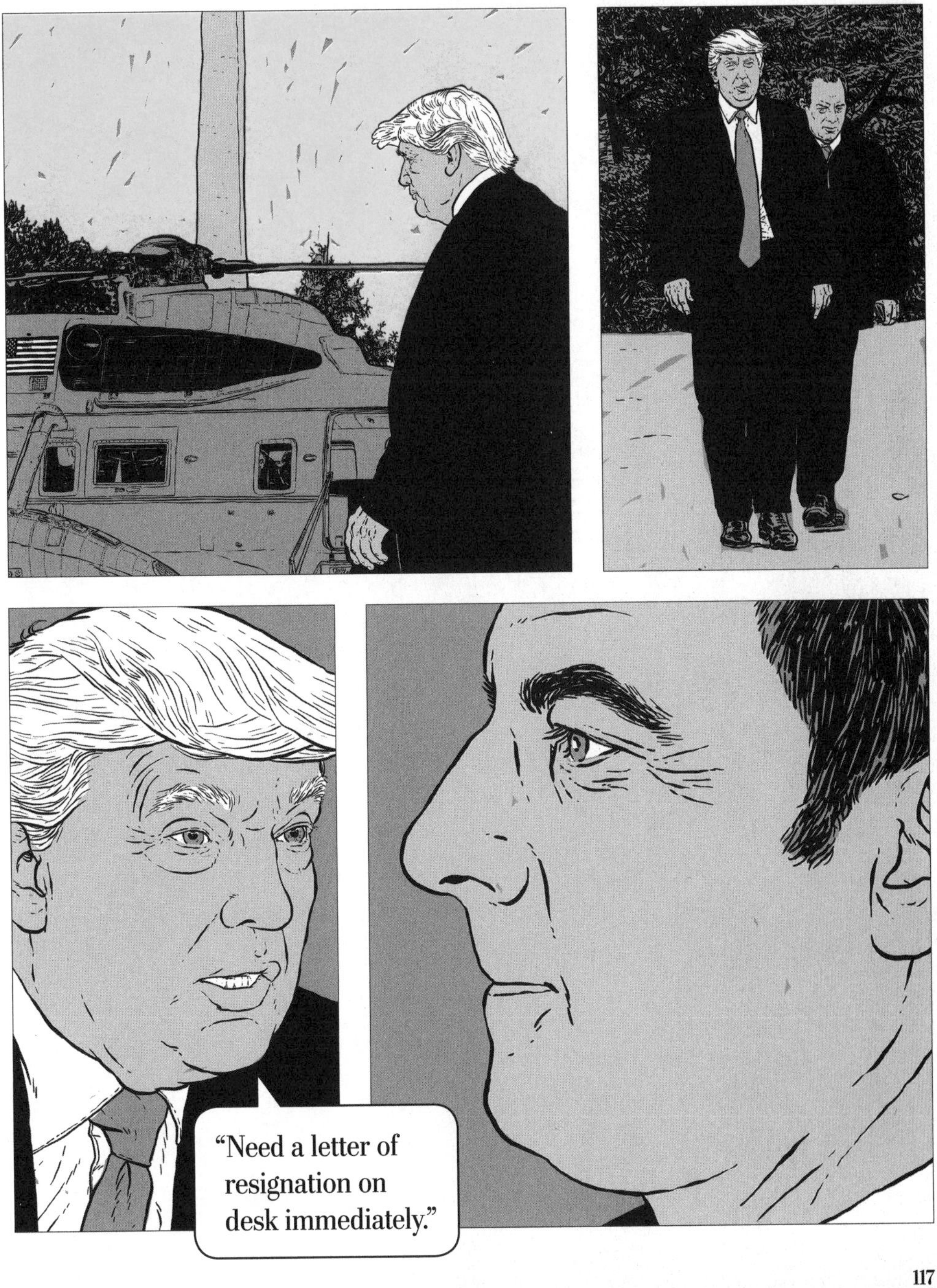
"Need a letter of resignation on desk immediately."

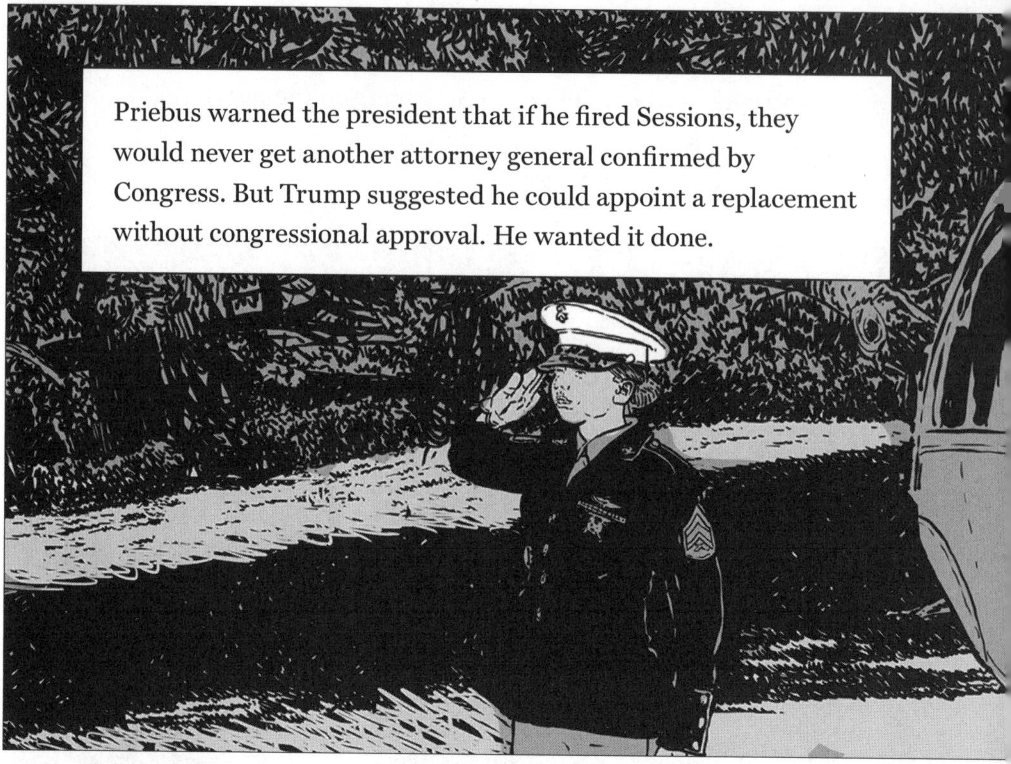
Priebus warned the president that if he fired Sessions, they would never get another attorney general confirmed by Congress. But Trump suggested he could appoint a replacement without congressional approval. He wanted it done.

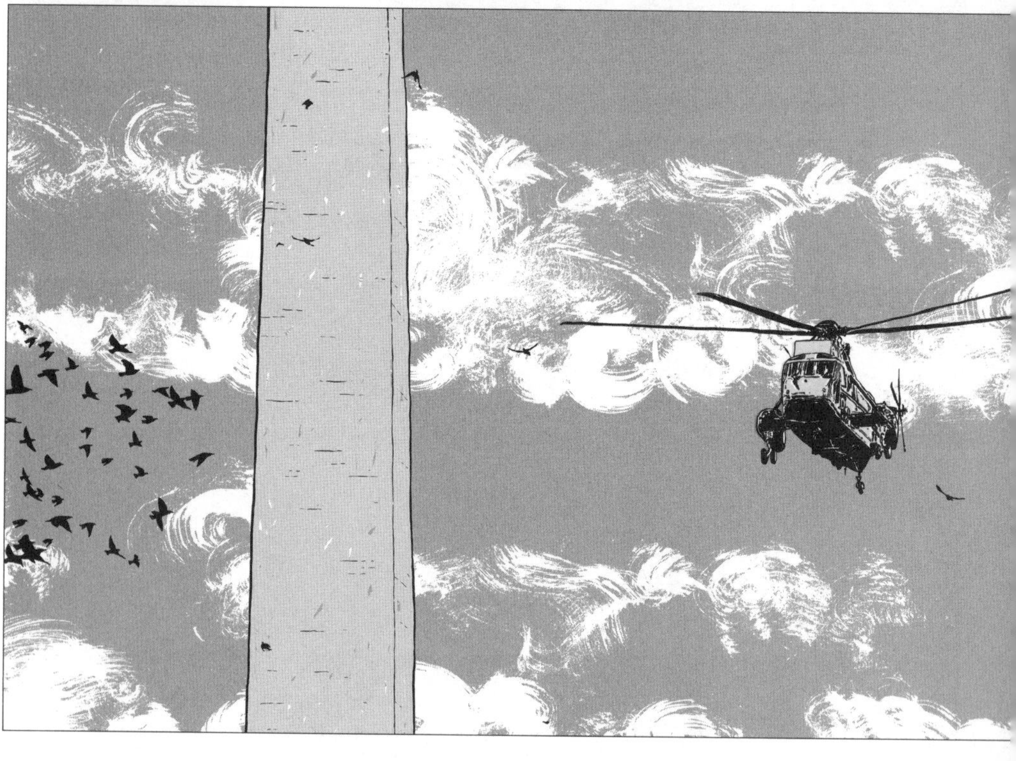

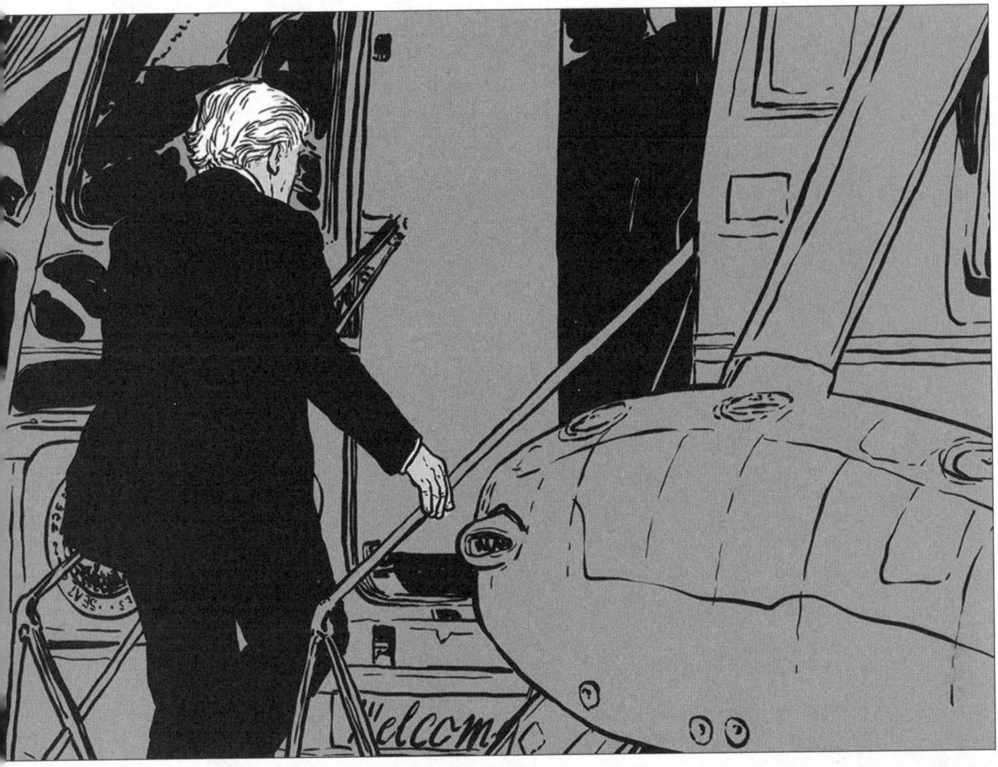

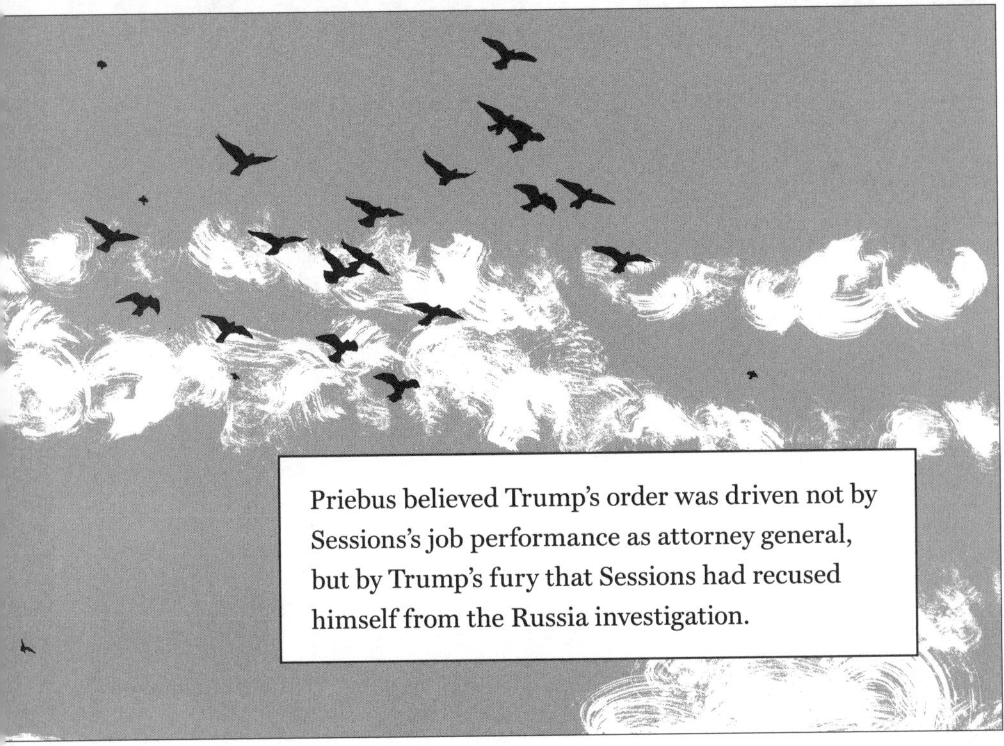
Priebus believed Trump's order was driven not by Sessions's job performance as attorney general, but by Trump's fury that Sessions had recused himself from the Russia investigation.

Priebus thought Trump's order was a problem. He called White House Counsel Donald McGahn for advice. McGahn told Priebus he should not follow the order.

The two men discussed possibly resigning together rather than carry out the president's demand to fire the attorney general.

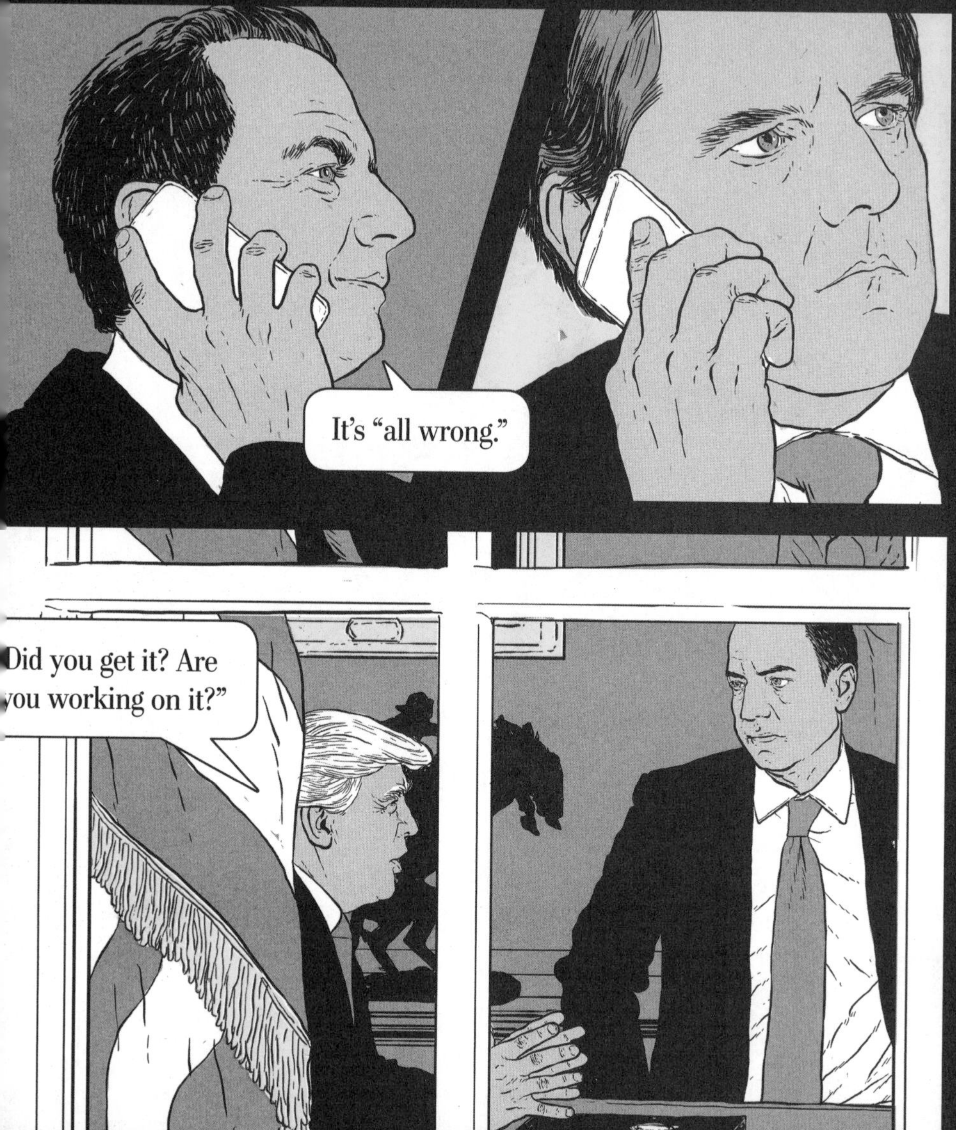
It's "all wrong."
Did you get it? Are you working on it?"

That afternoon, Trump met with Priebus again and pressed him for Sessions's resignation.

Priebus believed his own job depended on securing Sessions's resignation. He told the president he would get Sessions to step down, even though he did not plan on following the directive.

Later that day, Priebus called the president and told him that firing Sessions would be a calamity.

Other Justice Department officials would also resign, he told Trump. Trump would not be able to get anyone else confirmed.

Trump relented — slightly. He agreed to put off his demand for Sessions's resignation until after the Sunday news shows aired the following day, to prevent them from focusing on the firing.

By the end of the weekend, Trump had backed down and allowed the attorney general to remain in his job. But he kept up the pressure on Sessions in a series of tweets.

Donald J. Trump ✓
@realDonaldTrump

So why aren't the Committees and investigators, and of course our beleaguered A.G., looking into Crooked Hillarys crimes & Russia relations?

8:49 AM · Jul 24, 2017

21.9K Retweets   79.2K Likes

Donald J. Trump ✓
@realDonaldTrump

Attorney General Jeff Sessions has taken a VERY weak position on Hillary Clinton crimes (where are E-mails & DNC server) & Intel leakers!

6:12 AM · Jul 25, 2017

17.3K Retweets   63.7K Likes

Donald J. Trump ✓
@realDonaldTrump

Why didn't A.G. Sessions replace Acting FBI Director Andrew McCabe, a Comey friend who was in charge of Clinton investigation but got....

9:48 AM · Jul 26, 2017

14.5K Retweets   57.5K Likes

Donald J. Trump ✓
@realDonaldTrump

...big dollars ($700,000) for his wife's political run from Hillary Clinton and her representatives. Drain the Swamp!

9:52 AM · Jul 26, 2017

15.3K Retweets   67.3K Likes

For the second time, Sessions prepared a resignation letter.

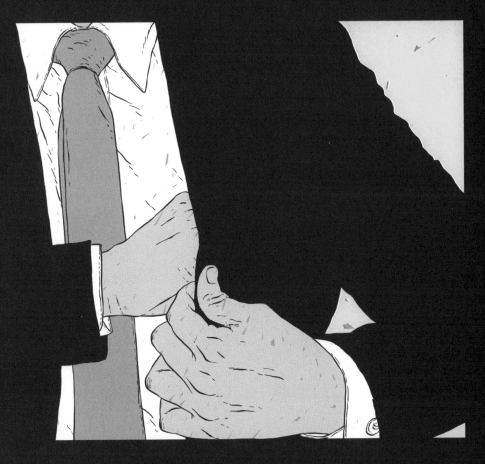

For the rest of the year, he carried it in his pocket every time he visited the White House — just in case.

5

"Maybe I'll have to get rid of him"

By the winter of 2018, President Trump had been in office a full year, dogged by the Russia investigation virtually from the start. His staff repeatedly warned him that his attacks on the probe would only prolong it. But the president would not listen.

On Jan. 25, 2018, the New York Times broke the news that, during the previous summer, Trump had ordered White House Counsel Donald McGahn to get the Justice Department to fire special counsel Robert S. Mueller III. The Times said McGahn threatened to quit rather than follow the order.

The New York Times

Trump Ordered Mueller Fired, but Backed Off When White House Counsel Threatened to Quit

The Washington Post
Democracy Dies in Darkness

Trump moved to fire Mueller in June, bringing White House counsel to the brink of leaving

The Washington Post quickly followed with its own report, clarifying that while McGahn had told colleagues he planned to resign rather than follow Trump's orders, he had never informed the president that he was going to walk. Trump had dropped the idea, The Post reported, and McGahn had stayed in his job.

The news stories were a problem: They indicated that if not for the reluctance of one of his top advisers, the president would have fired the special counsel — a move that would have been seen as an attempt to impede the investigation.

Publicly, the president denied he had called for Mueller's firing.

"Fake news, folks. Fake news."

Privately, Trump began an aggressive campaign to get McGahn to dispute the reports.

The next day, Trump's personal lawyer John Dowd called William Burck, McGahn's attorney, and told him that the president wanted McGahn to put out a statement denying he had been asked to fire the special counsel.

After consulting with McGahn, Burck told Dowd that the stories were correct in reporting that Trump had wanted Mueller removed. McGahn would not put out a statement.

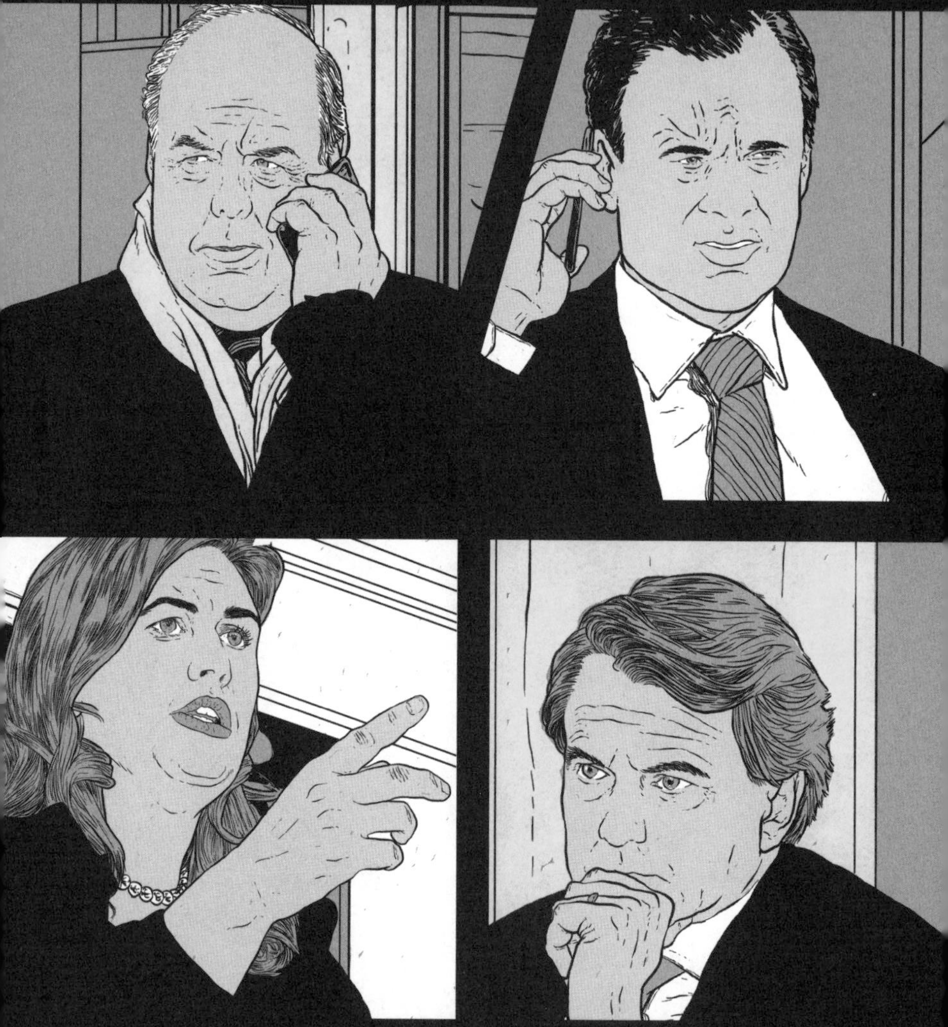

Trump also asked press secretary Sarah Sanders to contact McGahn about the story. McGahn repeated to Sanders that

Trump knew the special counsel was already focused on whether the president was trying to block the inquiry. Trump also knew Mueller was interviewing White House staffers like McGahn. Pressing a key witness to change his story could look like an attempt to tamper with the investigation once again. But the president wouldn't let it go.

In early February, Trump complained to White House staff secretary Rob Porter that he had never tried to fire Mueller and that McGahn had leaked the information to make himself look good.

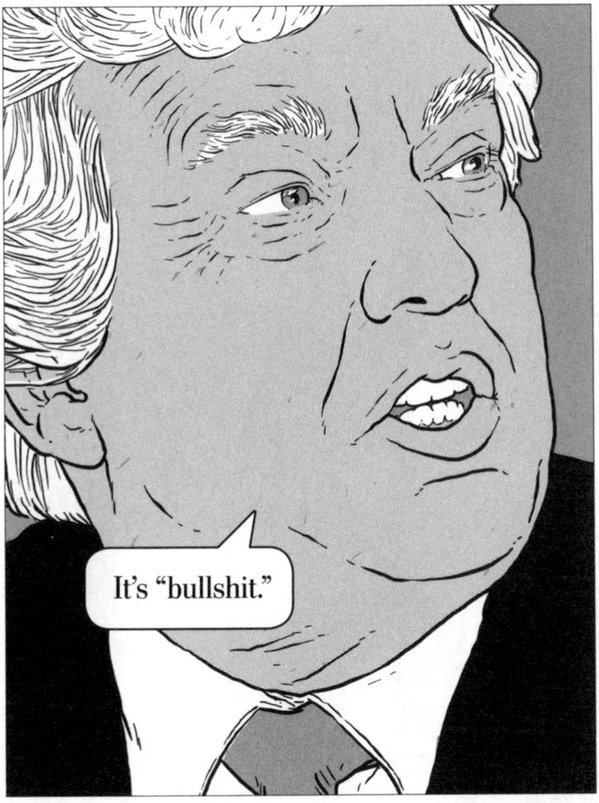
It's "bullshit."

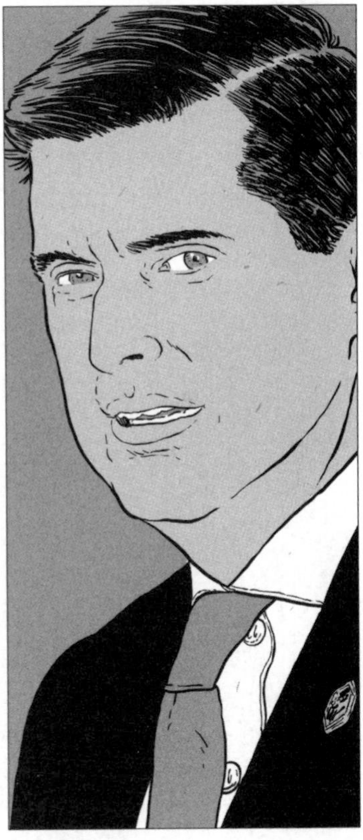

The president then gave Porter a job: He needed to get McGahn to write a letter "for our records" stating that the president never directed him to fire Mueller. The letter would prove the reporting was inaccurate, Trump said.

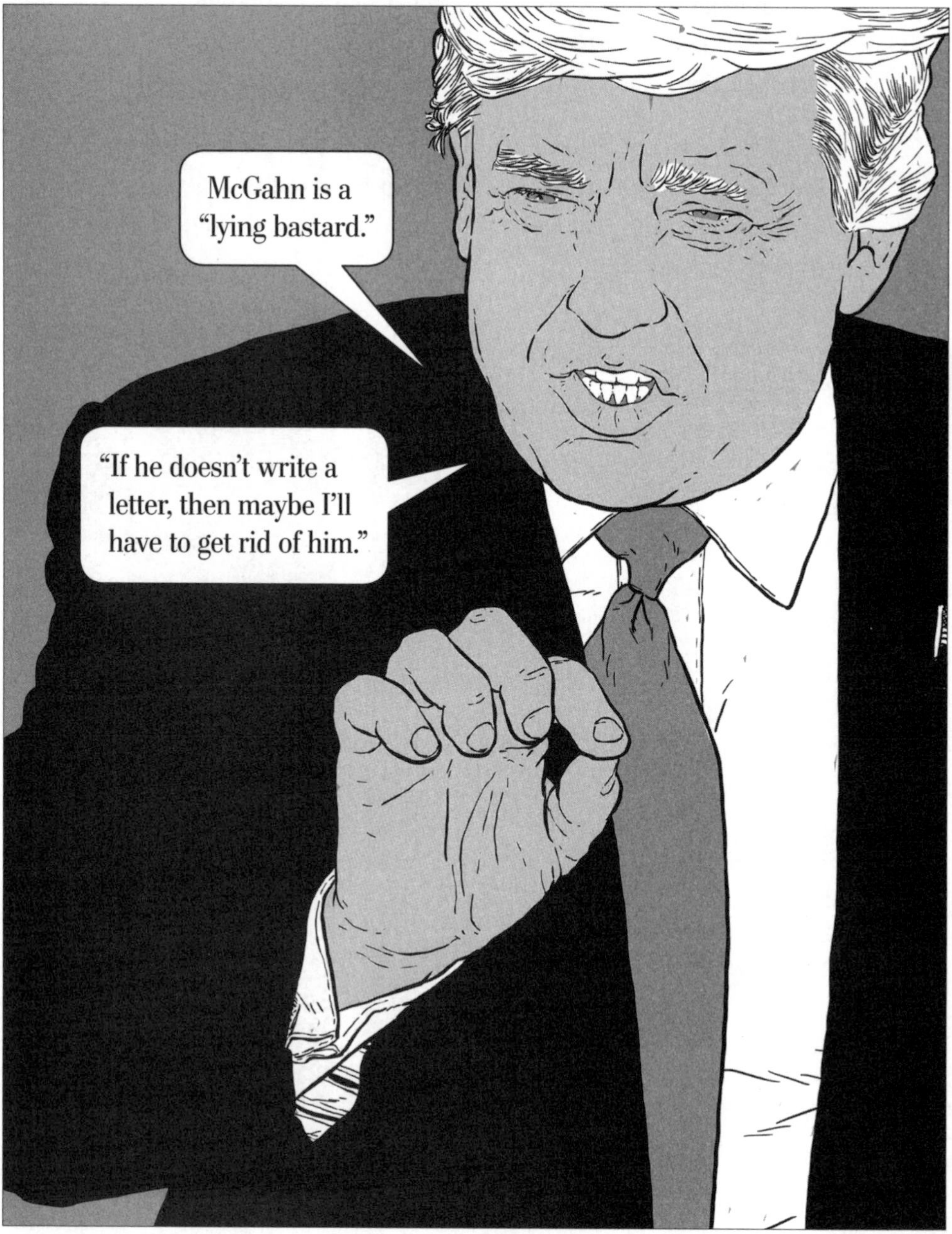
McGahn is a "lying bastard."
"If he doesn't write a letter, then maybe I'll have to get rid of him."

Later that day, Porter delivered the message to McGahn. But the White House counsel refused to write the letter Trump wanted. The news reports were accurate, he told the staff secretary. Trump had indeed wanted him to fire Mueller, and McGahn had in fact planned to resign instead of carrying out the order.

Porter said the president might fire him if he didn't write the letter. McGahn dismissed the threat. He knew the optics of such a move would be terrible.

Trump kept pressing the matter.

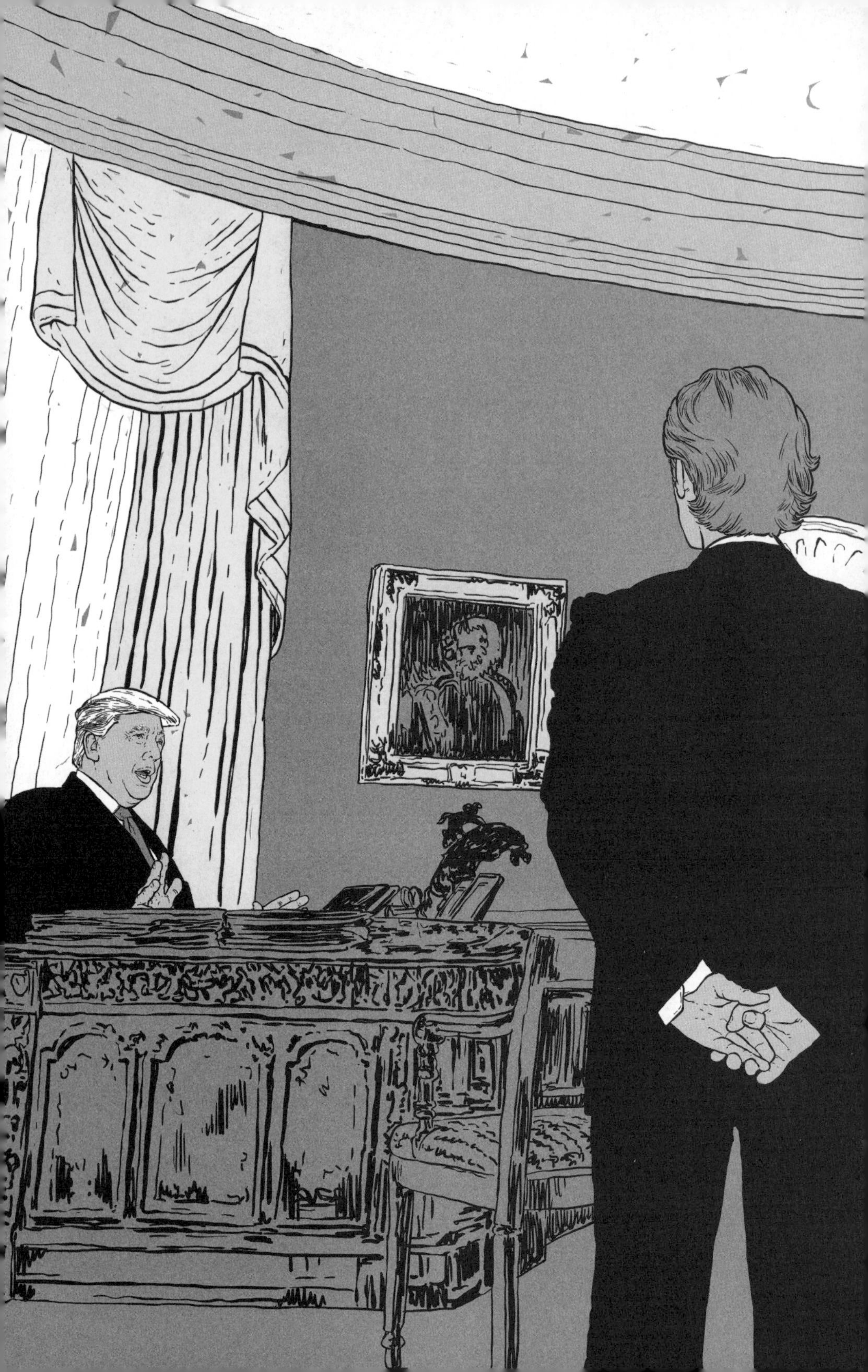

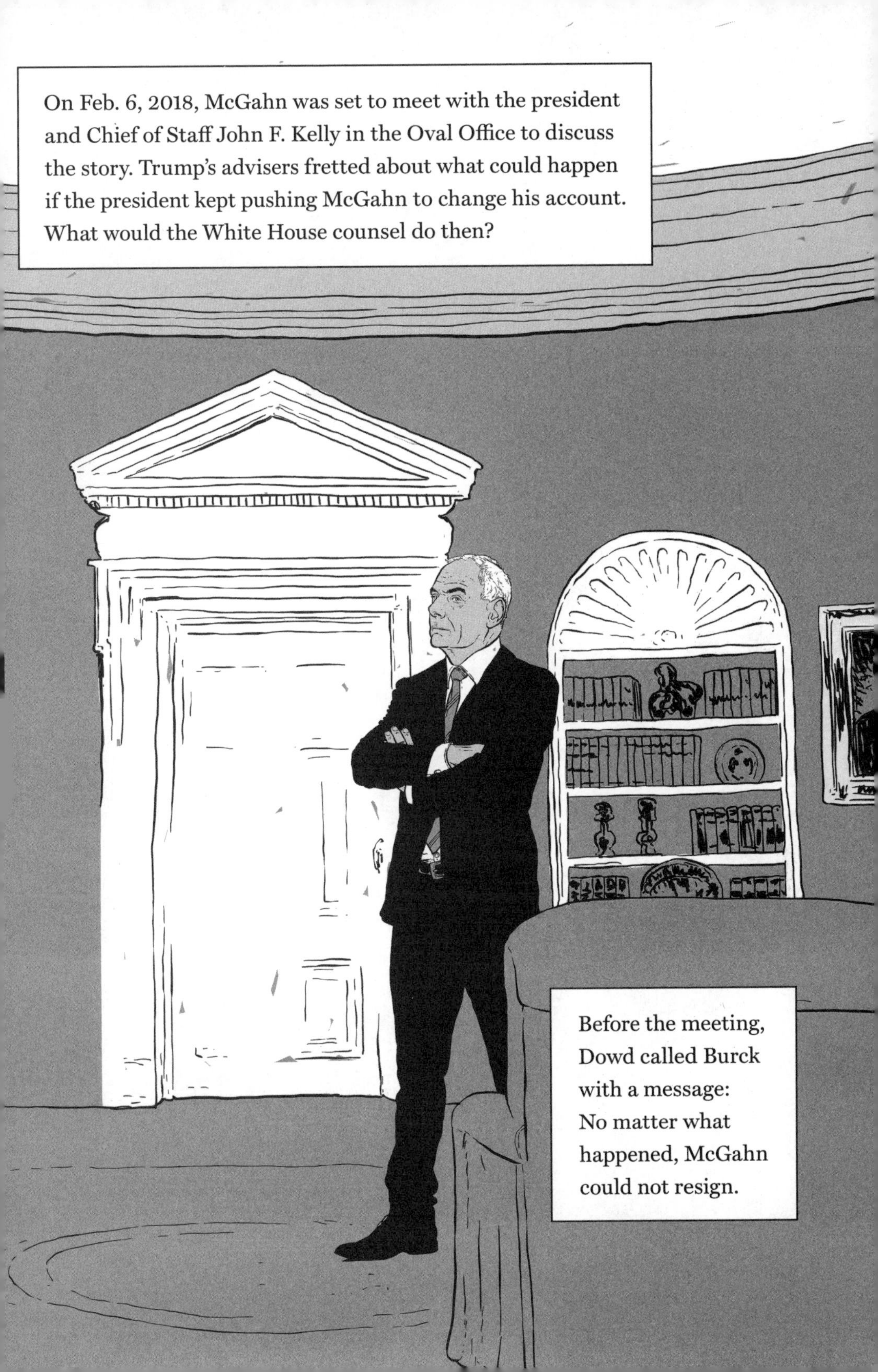
On Feb. 6, 2018, McGahn was set to meet with the president and Chief of Staff John F. Kelly in the Oval Office to discuss the story. Trump's advisers fretted about what could happen if the president kept pushing McGahn to change his account. What would the White House counsel do then?
Before the meeting, Dowd called Burck with a message: No matter what happened, McGahn could not resign.

The president began the meeting by complaining about the New York Times story.

"I never said to fire Mueller. I never said 'fire.' This story doesn't look good. You need to correct this. You're the White House counsel."

McGahn responded that while he had not told the president directly that he planned to resign, the New York Times story was otherwise accurate.

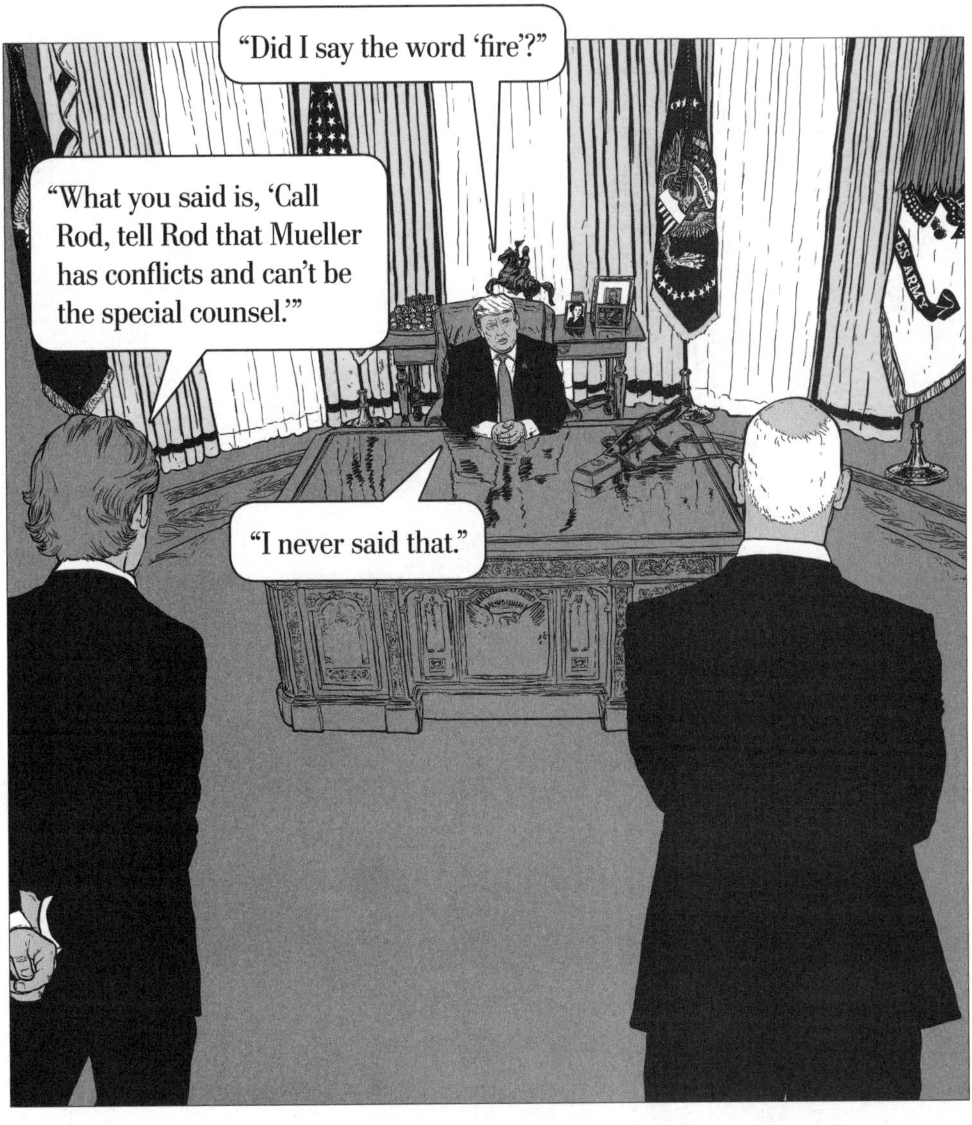
"Did I say the word 'fire'?"
"What you said is, 'Call Rod, tell Rod that Mueller has conflicts and can't be the special counsel.'"
"I never said that."

Trump insisted that he had just wanted McGahn to raise the issue of Mueller's conflicts of interest with Deputy Attorney General Rod J. Rosenstein and let him decide what to do.

McGahn said he heard it differently — that the president said: "Call Rod. There are conflicts. Mueller has to go."

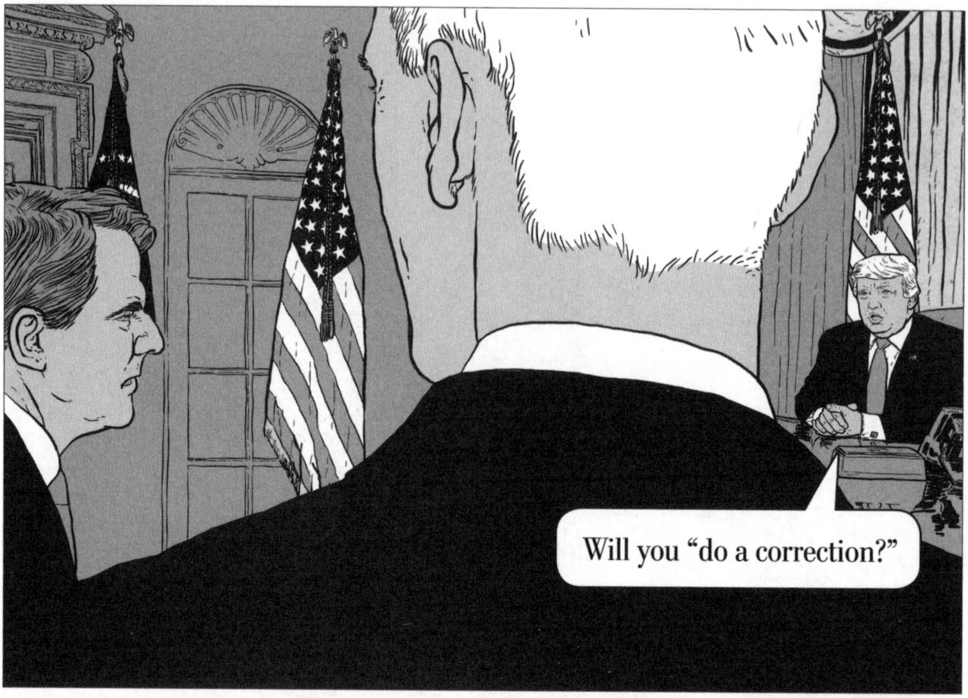
Will you "do a correction?"

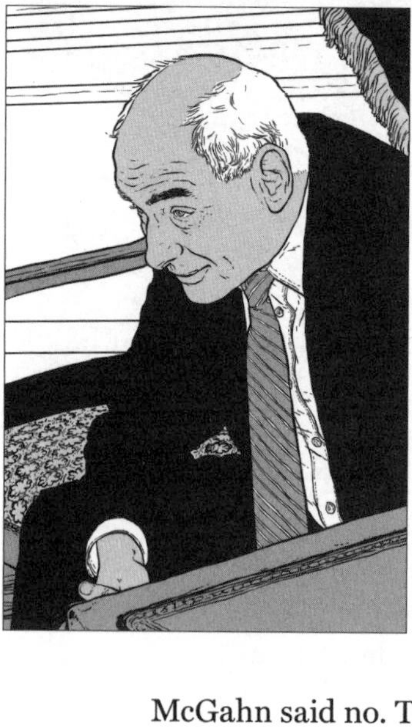

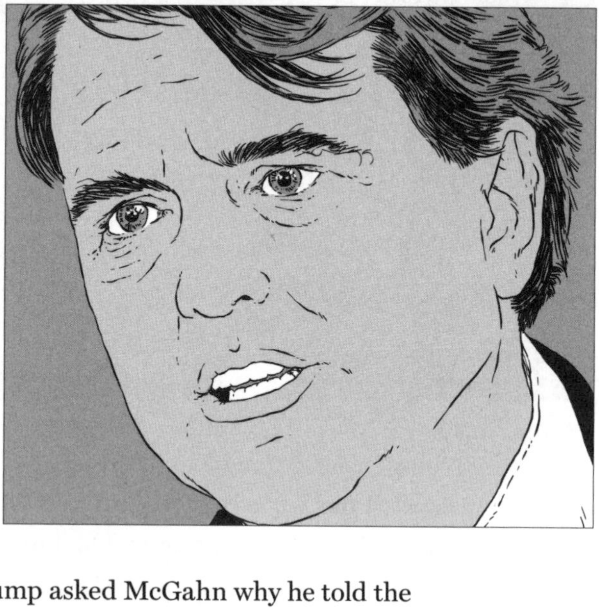

McGahn said no. Trump asked McGahn why he told the special counsel's office about the incident. McGahn said he had no choice.

He was the White House counsel, not the president's personal lawyer, so their conversations were not protected by attorney-client privilege, he explained. That meant that when federal investigators asked McGahn about it, he was required by law to answer truthfully.

Then Trump asked why McGahn took notes in meetings, creating a record of what went on in the White House that Mueller could review.

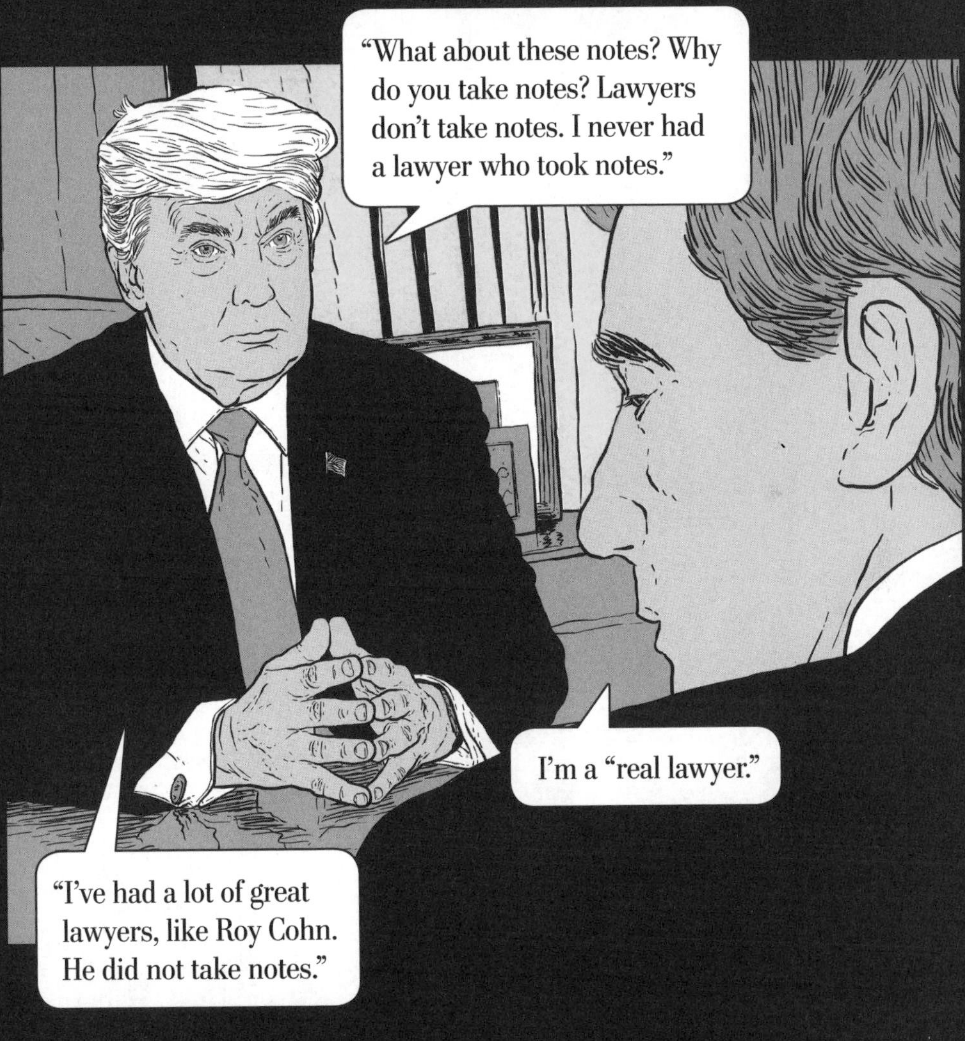
"What about these notes? Why do you take notes? Lawyers don't take notes. I never had a lawyer who took notes."
I'm a "real lawyer."
"I've had a lot of great lawyers, like Roy Cohn. He did not take notes."

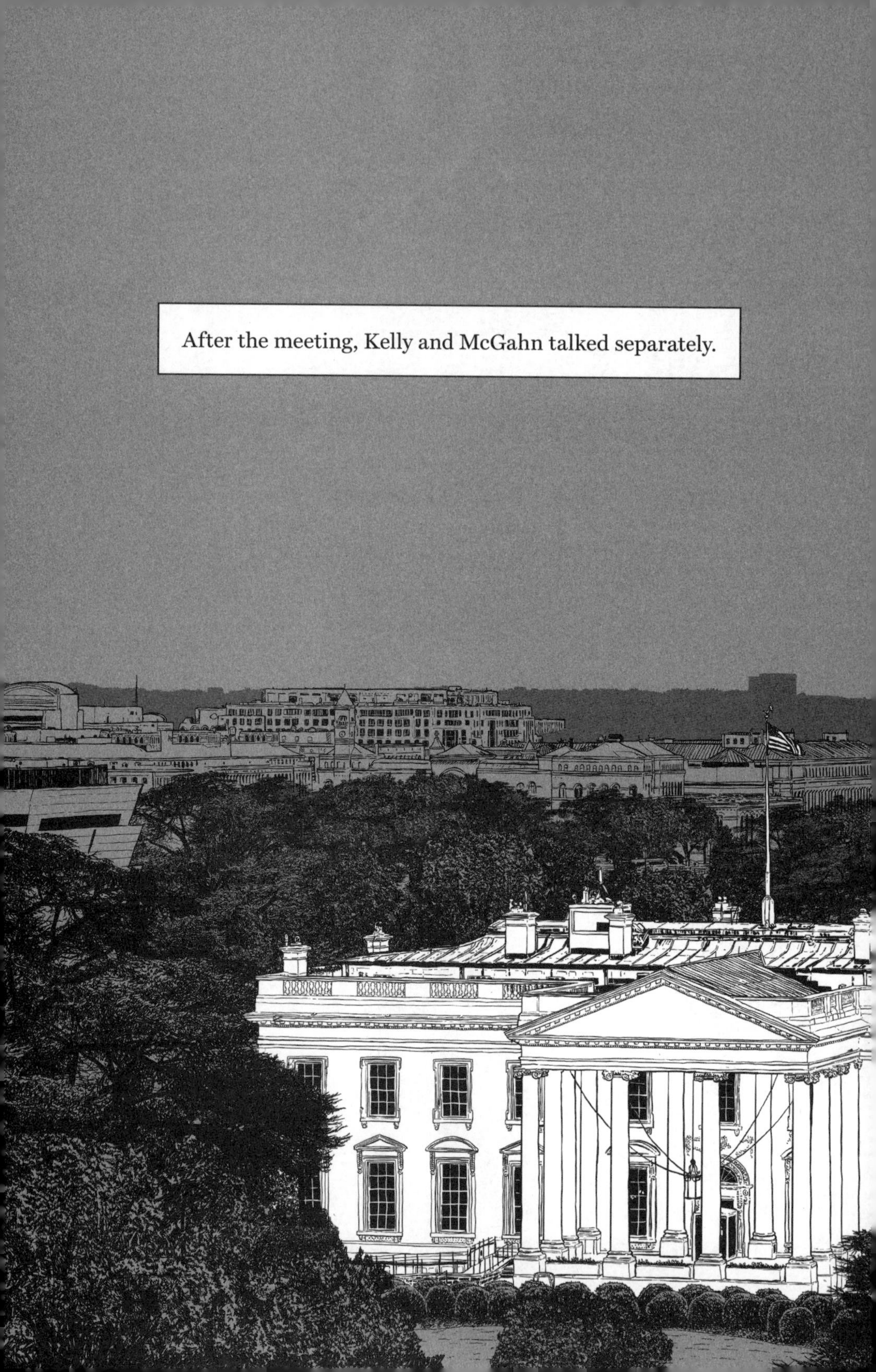
After the meeting, Kelly and McGahn talked separately.

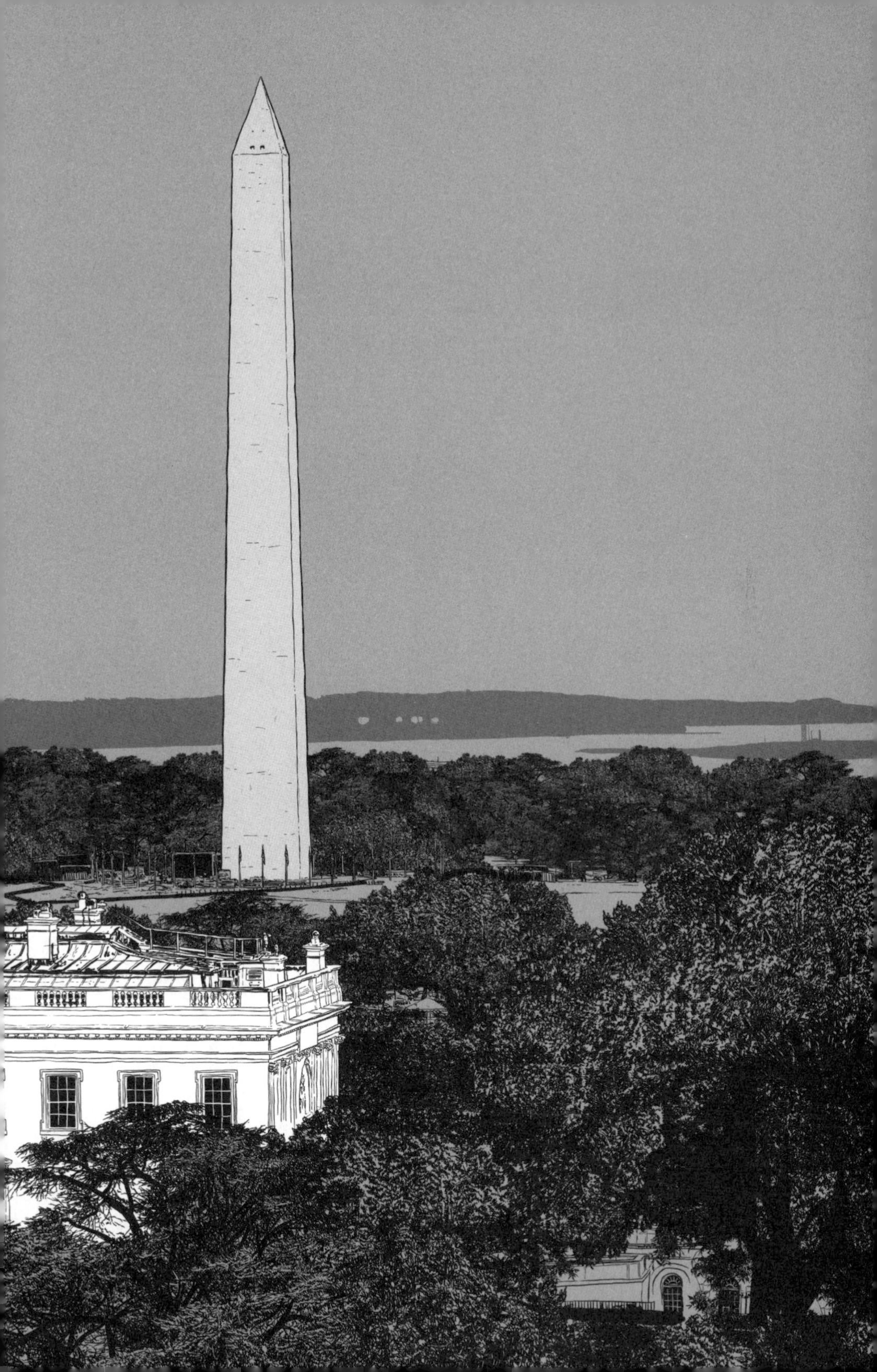

McGahn told Kelly that he and Trump "did have that conversation" about removing Mueller. Kelly responded that he had pointed out to the president that McGahn was not backing down.

Trump had pushed and pushed, but he wasn't able to get McGahn to retract his account. Stymied, the president gave up.

His personal attorney, Dowd, called McGahn's lawyer, Burck,
with a new message: Trump was "fine" with McGahn.

Other witnesses in the special counsel investigation would
soon consume the president's attention.

6

The president goes after Mueller's witnesses

Even as President Trump railed against the investigation, special counsel Robert S. Mueller III and his team of prosecutors moved forward. Beginning in 2017, they quickly uncovered possible crimes committed by several of Trump's advisers, including some acts unrelated to the 2016 campaign.

With his own associates in jeopardy, the president blasted those who cooperated with Mueller and left open the possibility of pardons for those who did not — raising fears that he was trying to influence their testimony and tamper with witnesses.

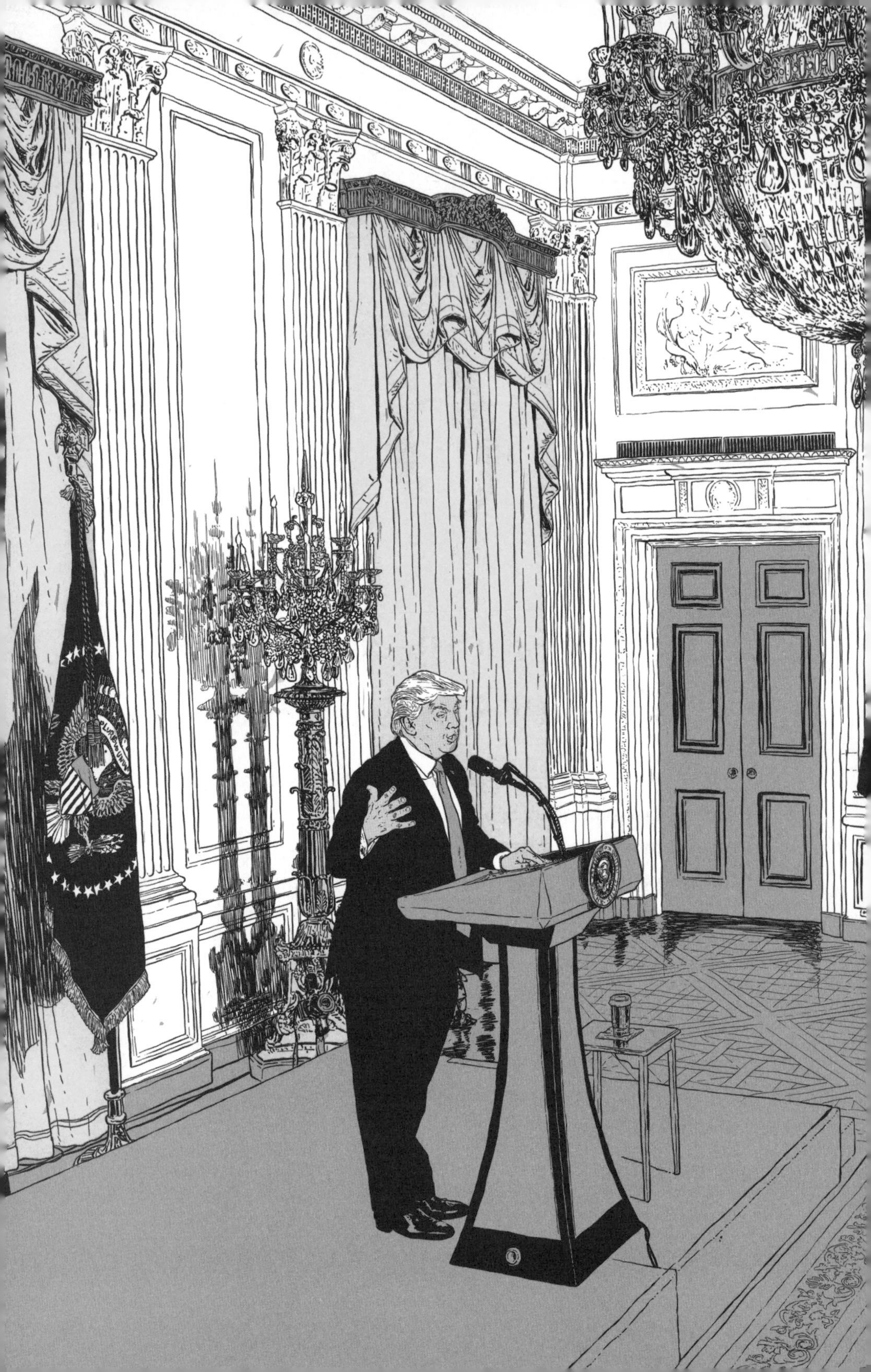

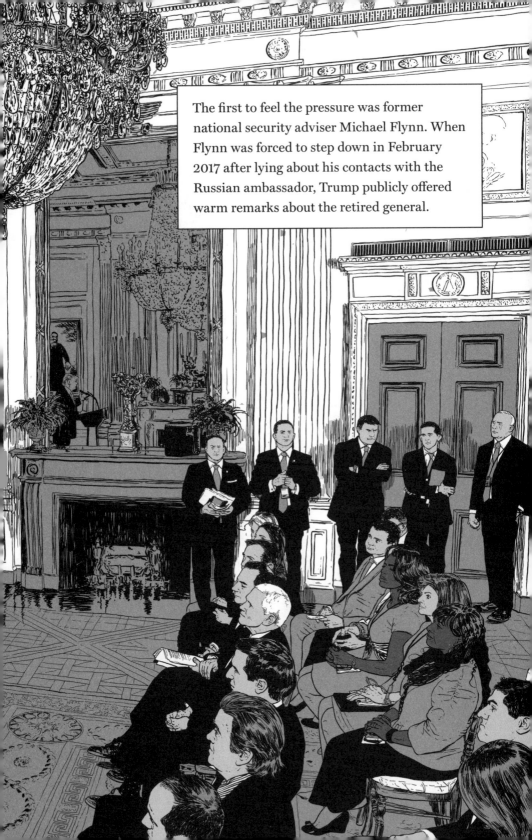

The first to feel the pressure was former national security adviser Michael Flynn. When Flynn was forced to step down in February 2017 after lying about his contacts with the Russian ambassador, Trump publicly offered warm remarks about the retired general.

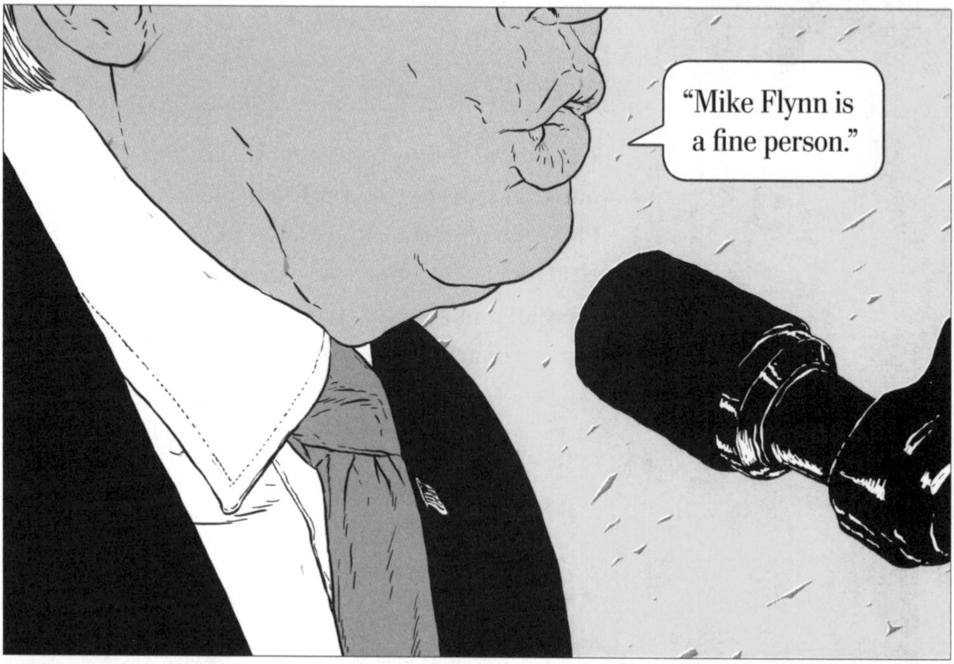
"Mike Flynn is a fine person."

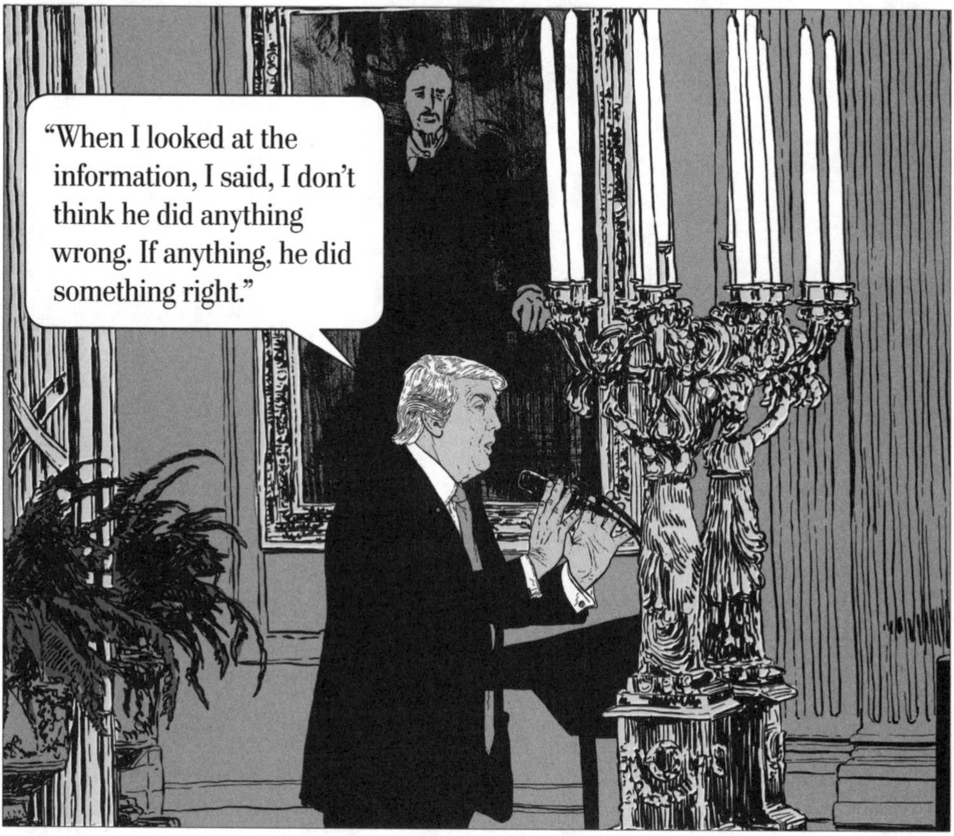
"When I looked at the information, I said, I don't think he did anything wrong. If anything, he did something right."

Nine months later, Flynn began cooperating with the special counsel's office. On Nov. 22, 2017, Flynn's attorney informed the president's lawyers that Flynn was withdrawing from an agreement to share information with the president's legal team. It was a sign that Flynn was switching sides and planned to help Mueller.

That night, Trump's lawyer John Dowd left a voicemail for Robert Kelner, an attorney for Flynn.

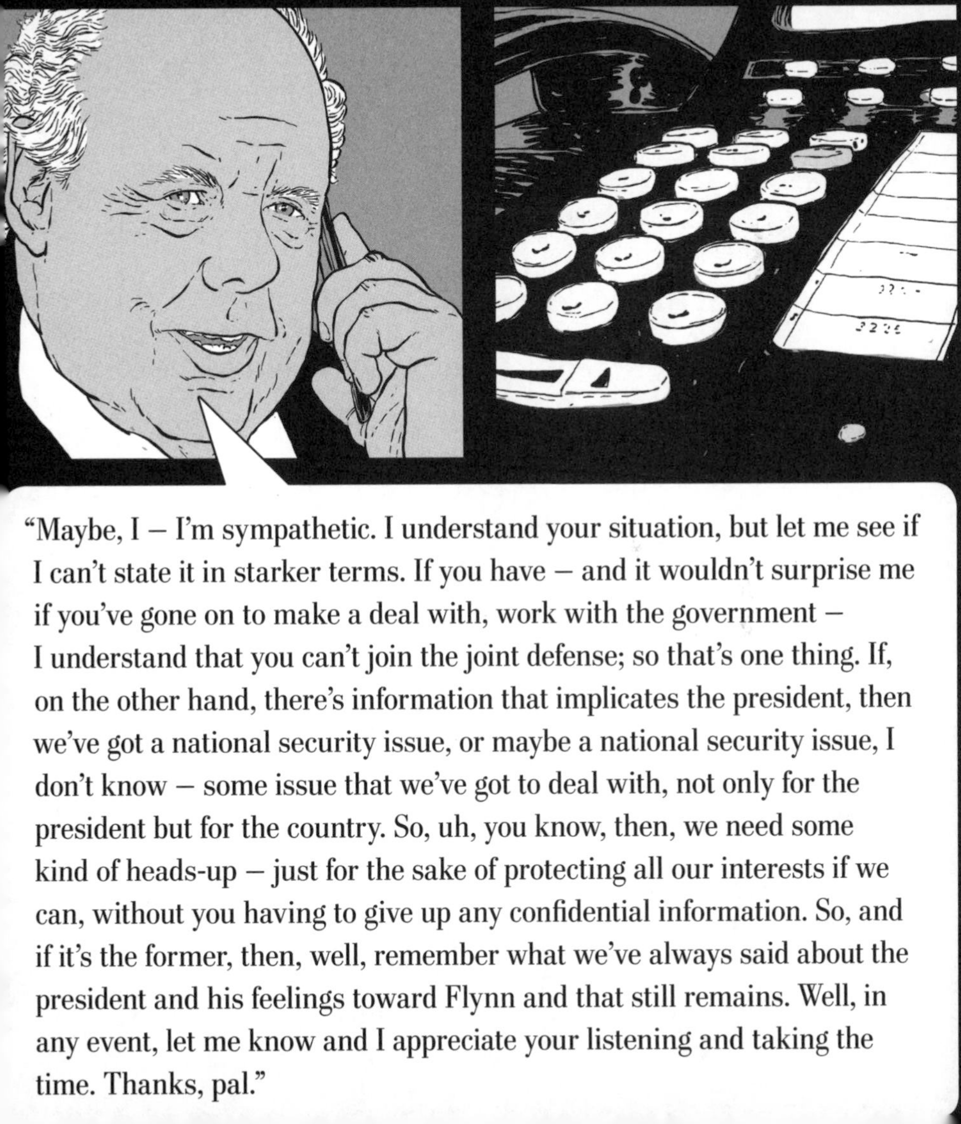
"Maybe, I – I'm sympathetic. I understand your situation, but let me see if I can't state it in starker terms. If you have – and it wouldn't surprise me if you've gone on to make a deal with, work with the government – I understand that you can't join the joint defense; so that's one thing. If, on the other hand, there's information that implicates the president, then we've got a national security issue, or maybe a national security issue, I don't know – some issue that we've got to deal with, not only for the president but for the country. So, uh, you know, then, we need some kind of heads-up – just for the sake of protecting all our interests if we can, without you having to give up any confidential information. So, and if it's the former, then, well, remember what we've always said about the president and his feelings toward Flynn and that still remains. Well, in any event, let me know and I appreciate your listening and taking the time. Thanks, pal."

The next day, Flynn's attorneys returned the call. They repeated that they could no longer have confidential communications with the president's team. Dowd was indignant. He told Flynn's lawyers that he planned to tell the president that Flynn was now hostile toward him.

Flynn's attorneys saw Dowd's call as an attempt to get Flynn to reconsider his cooperation.

Dowd later said the special counsel did not provide the full context of his message in his report and changed "the tenor and the contents" of what he said.

Flynn didn't buckle. Within days, on Dec. 1, he pleaded guilty to making false statements to the FBI.

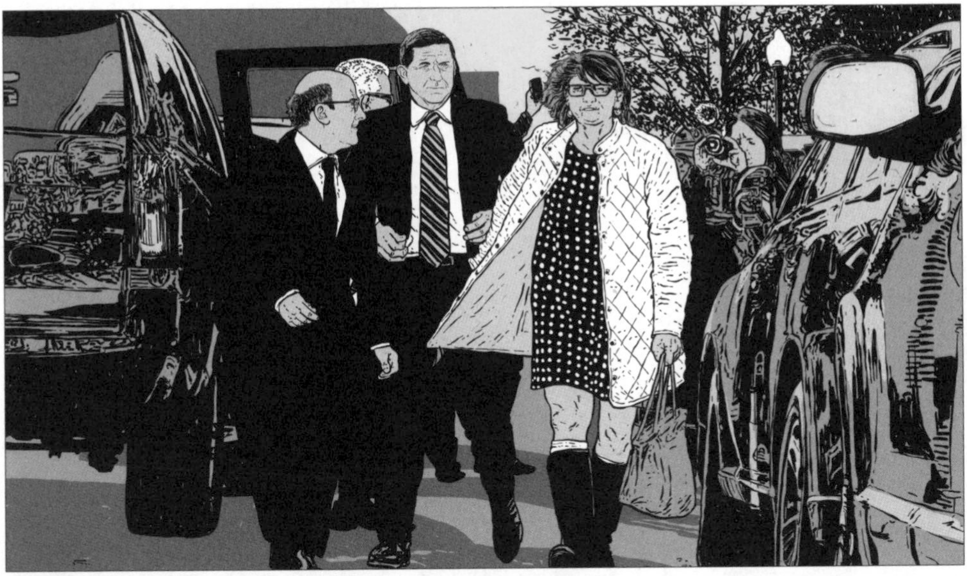

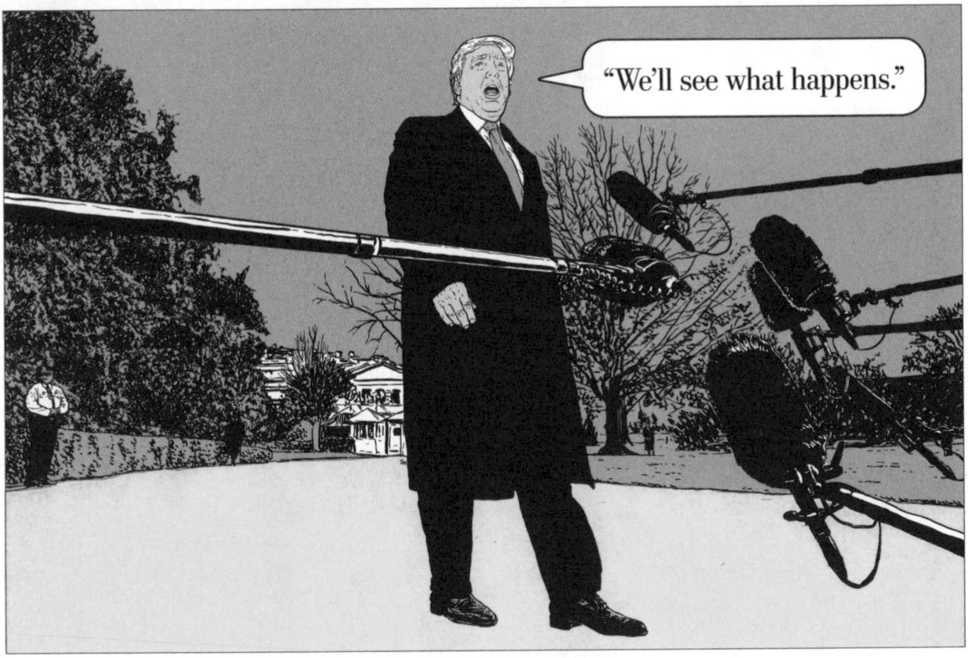
"We'll see what happens."

Trump expressed sympathy for Flynn. The president suggested he hadn't ruled out using the powers of his office to pardon him.

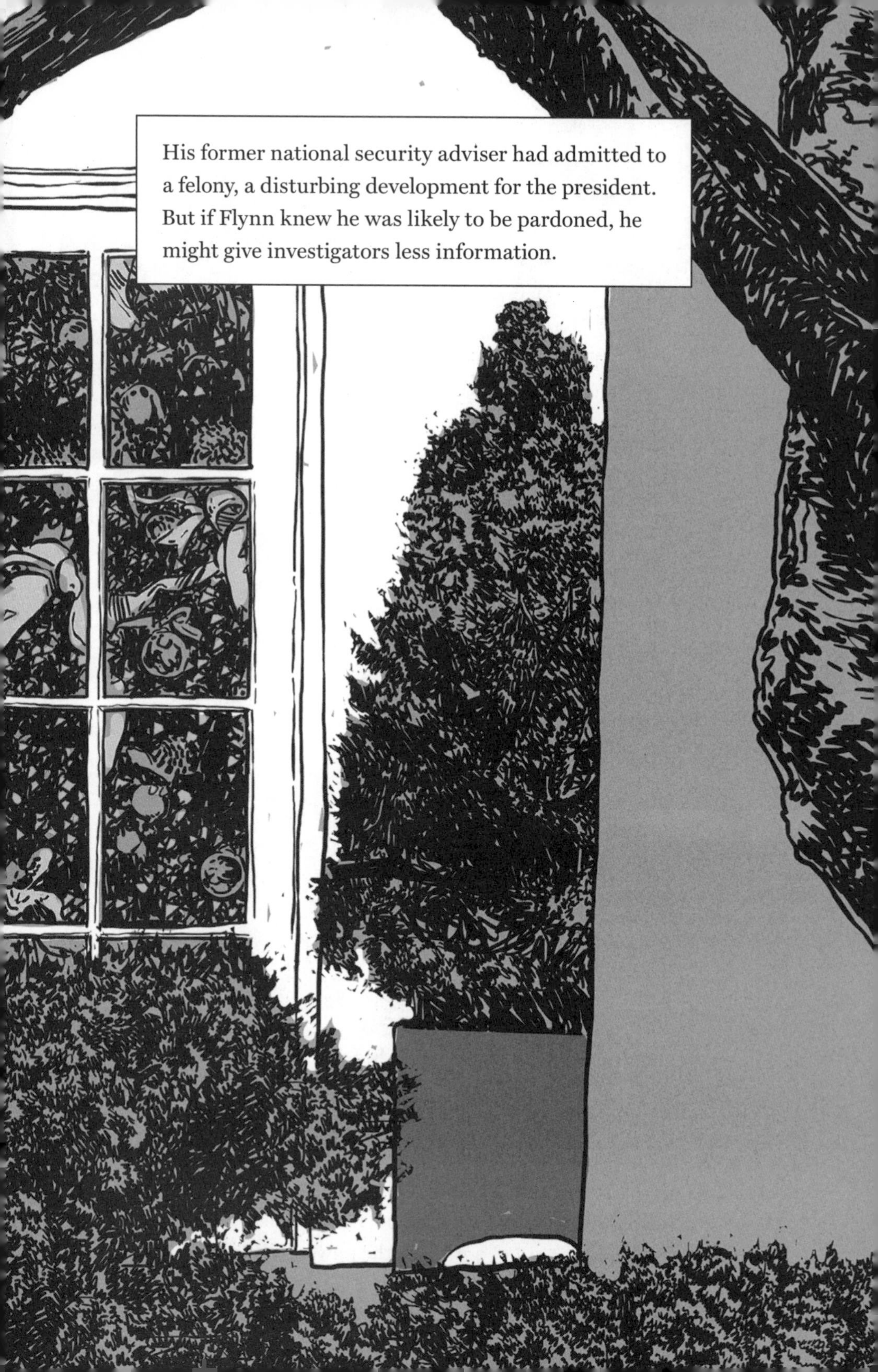
His former national security adviser had admitted to a felony, a disturbing development for the president. But if Flynn knew he was likely to be pardoned, he might give investigators less information.

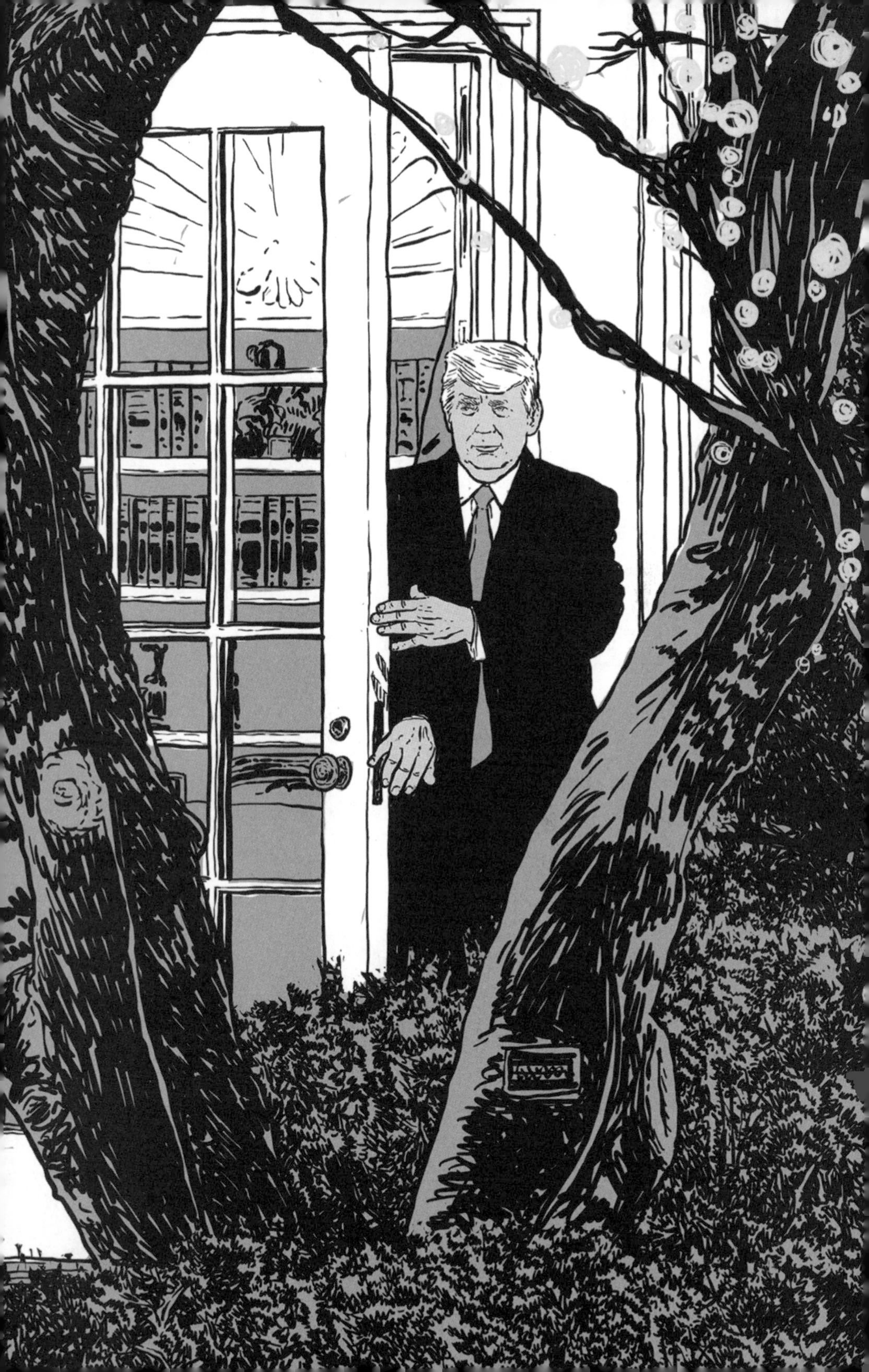

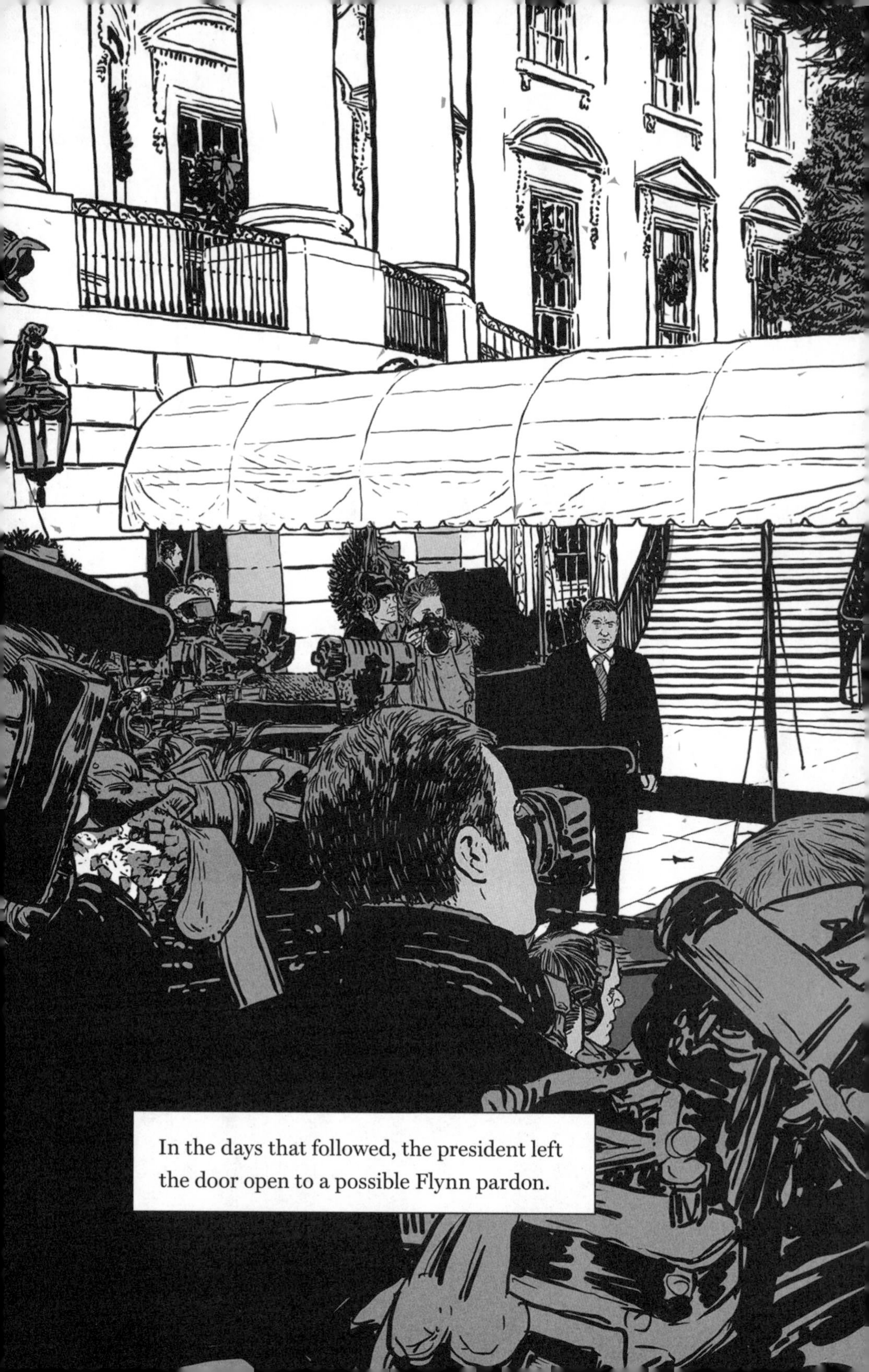
In the days that followed, the president left the door open to a possible Flynn pardon.

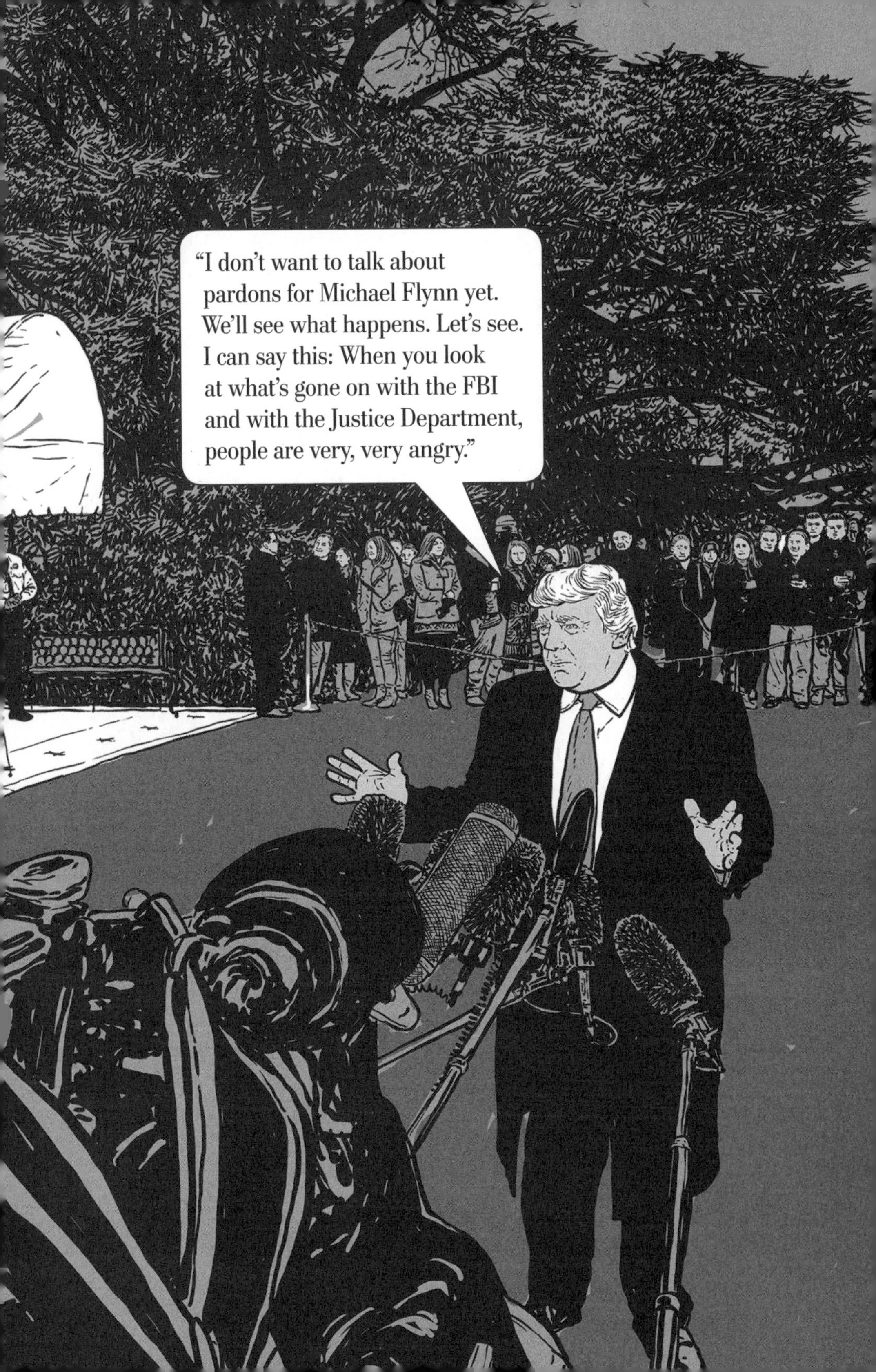
"I don't want to talk about pardons for Michael Flynn yet. We'll see what happens. Let's see. I can say this: When you look at what's gone on with the FBI and with the Justice Department, people are very, very angry."

Meanwhile, the president had two other former aides to worry about. Former Trump campaign chairman Paul Manafort and his deputy, Rick Gates, were charged in October 2017 with conspiracy to defraud the United States and other crimes related to their work as political consultants in Ukraine before joining Trump's campaign.

A few months after they were indicted, Manafort told Gates that he had spoken to the president's personal lawyer. It would be stupid to plead guilty, Manafort said.

"Sit tight."

"We'll be taken care of."

Gates asked Manafort whether anyone had specifically mentioned that the two would be pardoned. Manafort responded that no one had used that wo

On Feb. 22, 2018, additional charges were filed against
Manafort and Gates in Virginia. The next day, Gates
pleaded guilty and agreed to cooperate with prosecutors.
Trump seemed anxious about the development.

He told aide Rob Porter that he never liked Manafort. He
began asking aides whether Manafort might also cooperate
with the investigation and whether the former campaign
chief knew of anything that could hurt him.

In June 2018, prosecutors accused Manafort of trying to tamper with witnesses in his case. They asked a judge to revoke his bail and send him to jail while he awaited trial. On the day of a hearing in the matter, Trump spoke publicly about the case.

Trump was asked if he was considering a pardon for Manafort. He demurred — but did not rule it out.

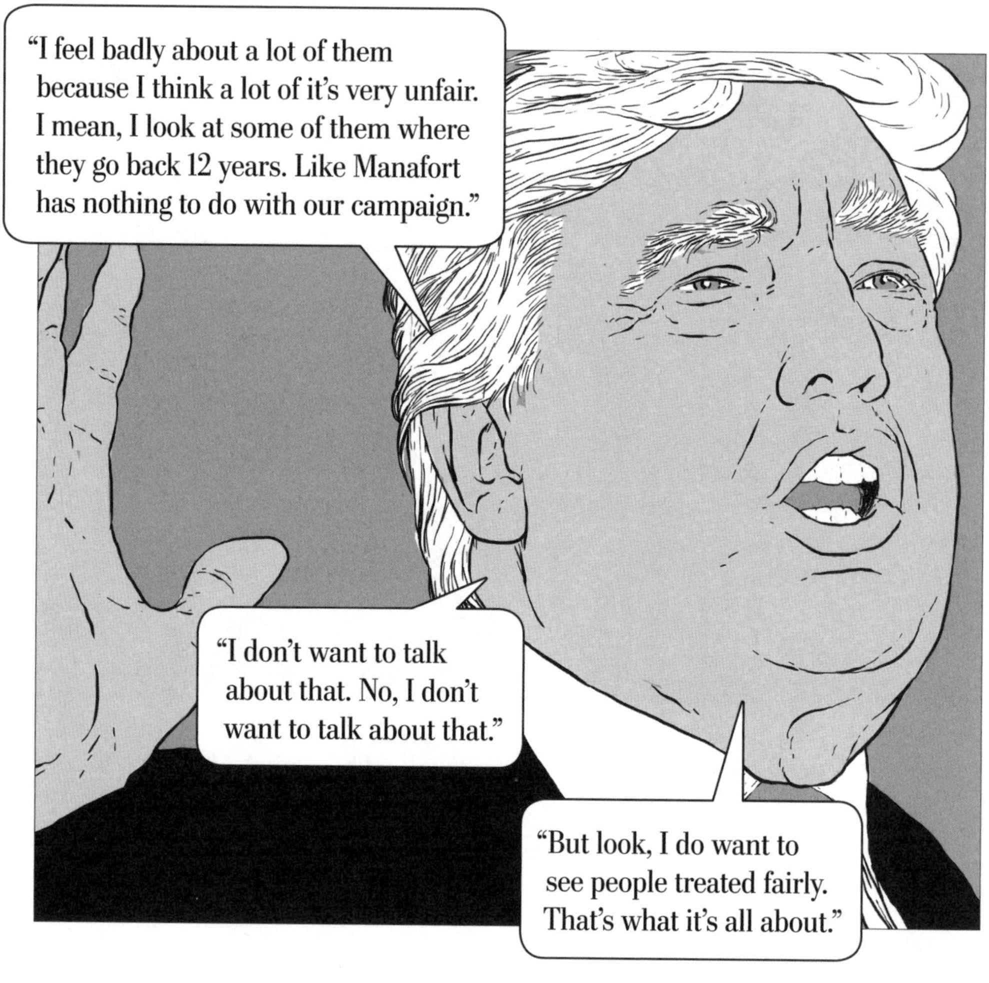
"I feel badly about a lot of them because I think a lot of it's very unfair. I mean, I look at some of them where they go back 12 years. Like Manafort has nothing to do with our campaign."
"I don't want to talk about that. No, I don't want to talk about that."
"But look, I do want to see people treated fairly. That's what it's all about."

U.S. District Judge Amy Berman Jackson of Washington agreed with prosecutors, revoking Manafort's bail and ordering him to jail while he waited for his trial.

In interviews, Trump's personal attorney Rudolph W. Giuliani seemed to reassure Manafort that Trump was on his side. While the president shouldn't issue any pardons during an ongoing investigation, he said, Trump might pardon Manafort at some point in the future.

"When it's over, hey, he's the president of the United States. He retains his pardon power. Nobody is taking that away from him."

As Manafort's criminal trial opened in Alexandria, Va., on July 31, Trump repeatedly tweeted that his former campaign chairman was being treated unfairly.

 Donald J. Trump ✔
@realDonaldTrump

..This is a terrible situation and Attorney General Jeff Sessions should stop this Rigged Witch Hunt right now, before it continues to stain our country any further. Bob Mueller is totally conflicted, and his 17 Angry Democrats that are doing his dirty work are a disgrace to USA!

9:24 AM · Aug 1, 2018

22.5K Retweets   **89.4K** Likes

 Donald J. Trump ✔
@realDonaldTrump

Looking back on history, who was treated worse, Alfonse Capone, legendary mob boss, killer and "Public Enemy Number One," or Paul Manafort, political operative & Reagan/Dole darling, now serving solitary confinement - although convicted of nothing? Where is the Russian Collusion?

11:35 AM · Aug 1, 2018

16.4K Retweets   **66.2K** Likes

Manafort's situation upset the president. But nothing, it
appeared, got him as worked up as the investigation of
Michael Cohen, his longtime personal counsel. Cohen had
been at his side for more than a decade and was intimately
familiar with Trump's personal and financial dealings. In
2016, the lawyer had led failed negotiations to build a Trump
Tower in Moscow — an effort that persisted through much
of the campaign, even as Trump said he had no business
interests in Russia.

In May 2017, Congress asked Cohen to provide documents
and testimony about the Moscow project.

In a May 18, 2017, meeting, Trump told Cohen to cooperate
with Congress. Cohen entered into an agreement to share
information with the president's legal team and began to
speak frequently with them. At the same time, Cohen's legal
bills were being paid by the Trump Organization.

Cohen later recalled that one of Trump's attorneys, Jay Sekulow, told him that he was protected as part of the group, but that he would not be if he "went rogue."

"The president loves you."

Cohen recalled that he was told that if he stayed on message, the president would have his back. Sekulow has denied Cohen's account of their conversations, calling Cohen a liar whose "instinct to blame others is strong."

Cohen spent 10 days in August 2017 drafting his statement for Congress. Phone records show that he and Sekulow spoke nearly every day.

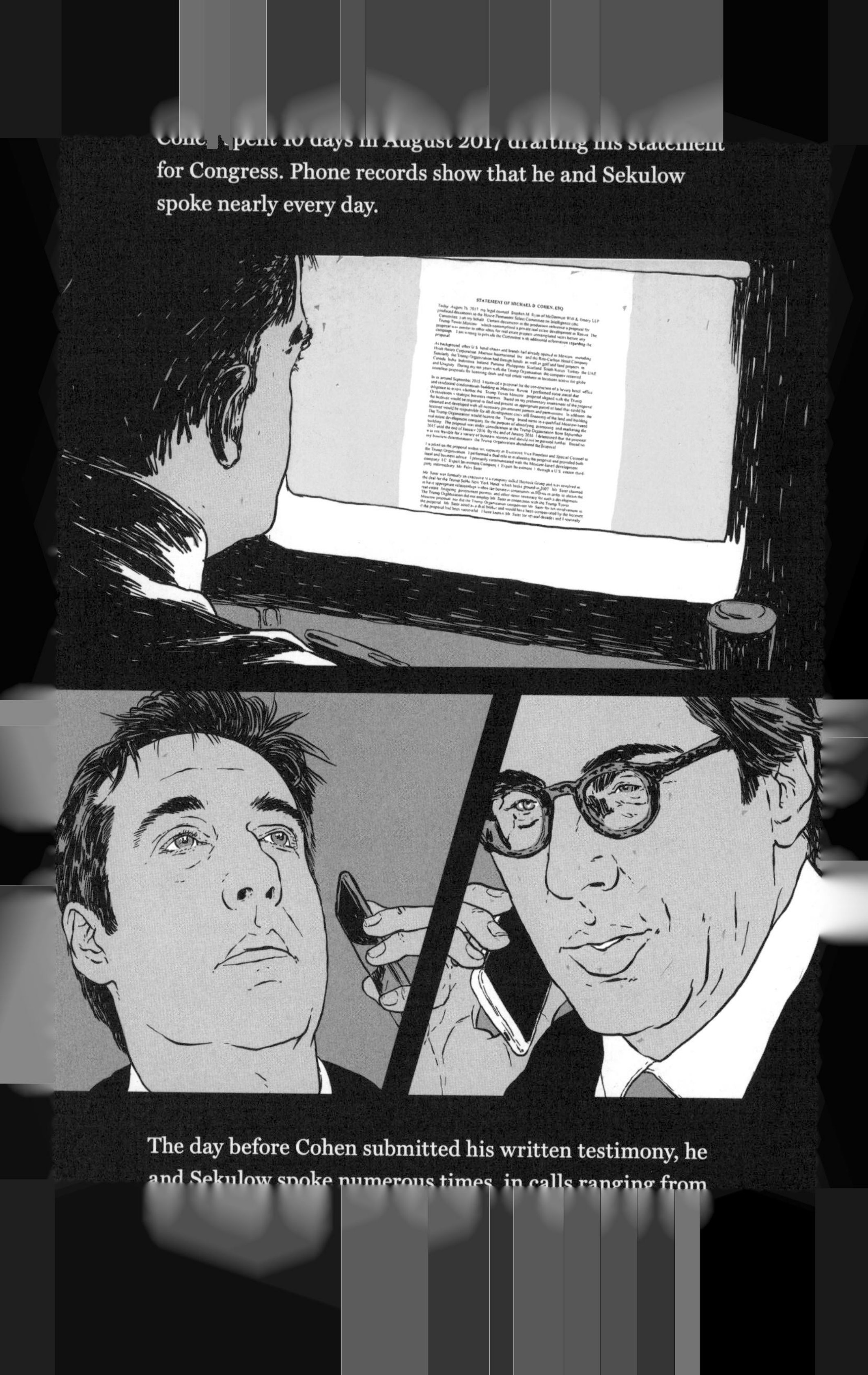
STATEMENT OF MICHAEL D. COHEN, ESQ.

The day before Cohen submitted his written testimony, he and Sekulow spoke numerous times, in calls ranging from

In late October, Cohen testified to lawmakers behind closed doors. Cohen later admitted his testimony included key falsehoods about the negotiations for the Moscow Trump Tower and how long they lasted.

Cohen said later that he was adhering to a "party line" designed to obscure Trump's ties to Russia and that his statement was reviewed by the president's lawyers before its submission.

Cohen was not done lying on behalf of his boss.

In early 2018, the Wall Street Journal revealed that Cohen paid $130,000 to adult-film star Stormy Daniels to keep her quiet before the election about an affair she claimed she had with Trump years earlier.

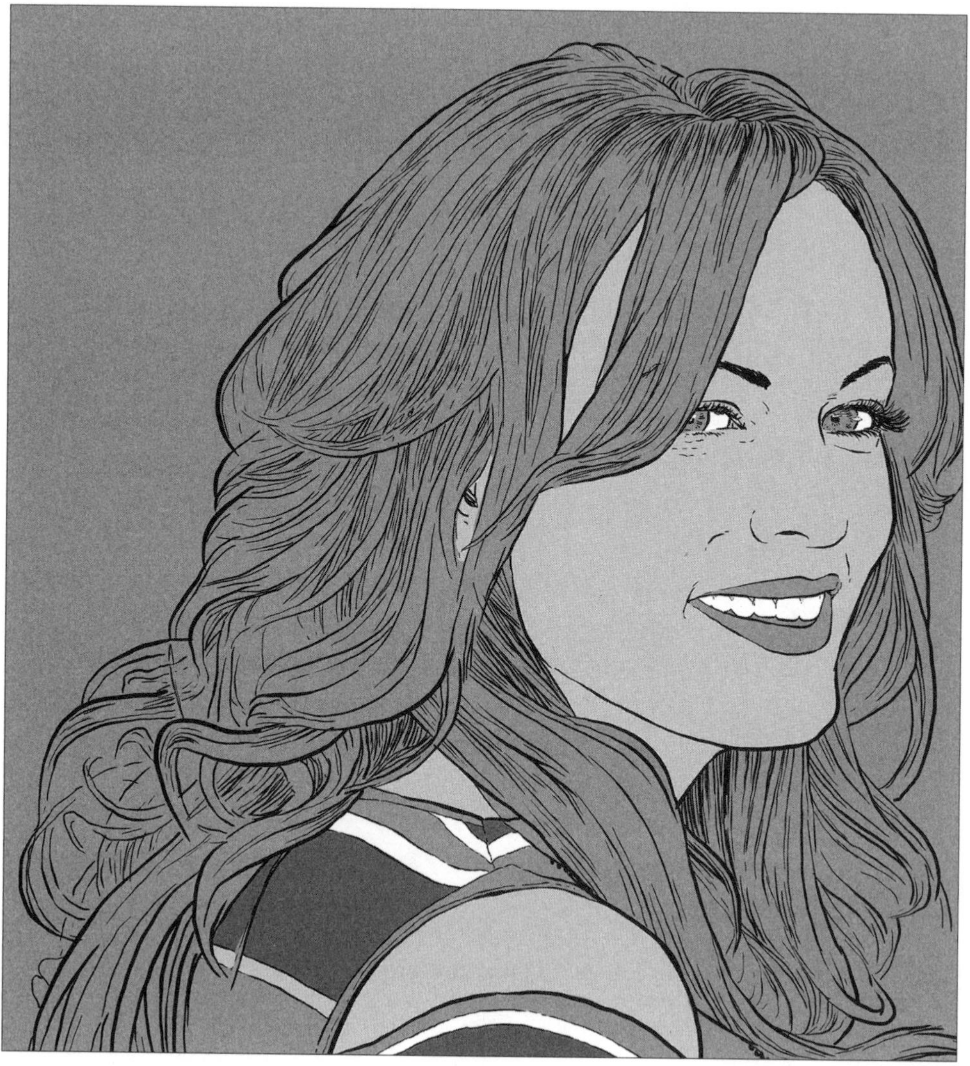

Cohen issued a statement in February saying he used his own money for the payoff.

"Neither the Trump Organization nor the Trump campaign was a party to the transaction ... and neither reimbursed me for the payment, either directly or indirectly."

That was not true. But the president was grateful, according to a text from a Trump lawyer to Cohen.

Client says thanks for what you do.

The pressure on Cohen soon escalated dramatically. On April 9, 2018, FBI agents investigating his finances and the payment to Daniels, among other issues, raided his home,

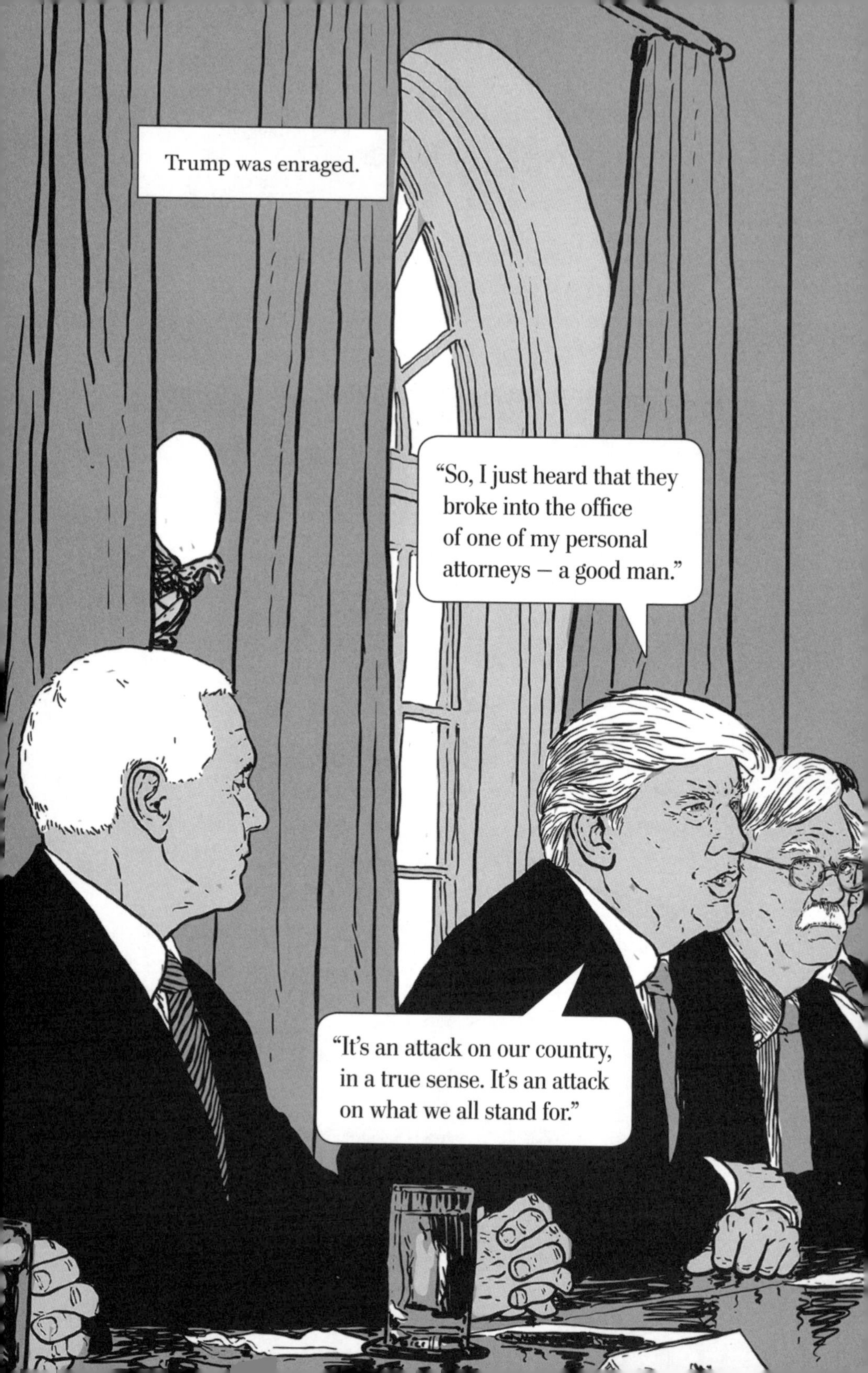
Trump was enraged.
"So, I just heard that they broke into the office of one of my personal attorneys — a good man."
"It's an attack on our country, in a true sense. It's an attack on what we all stand for."

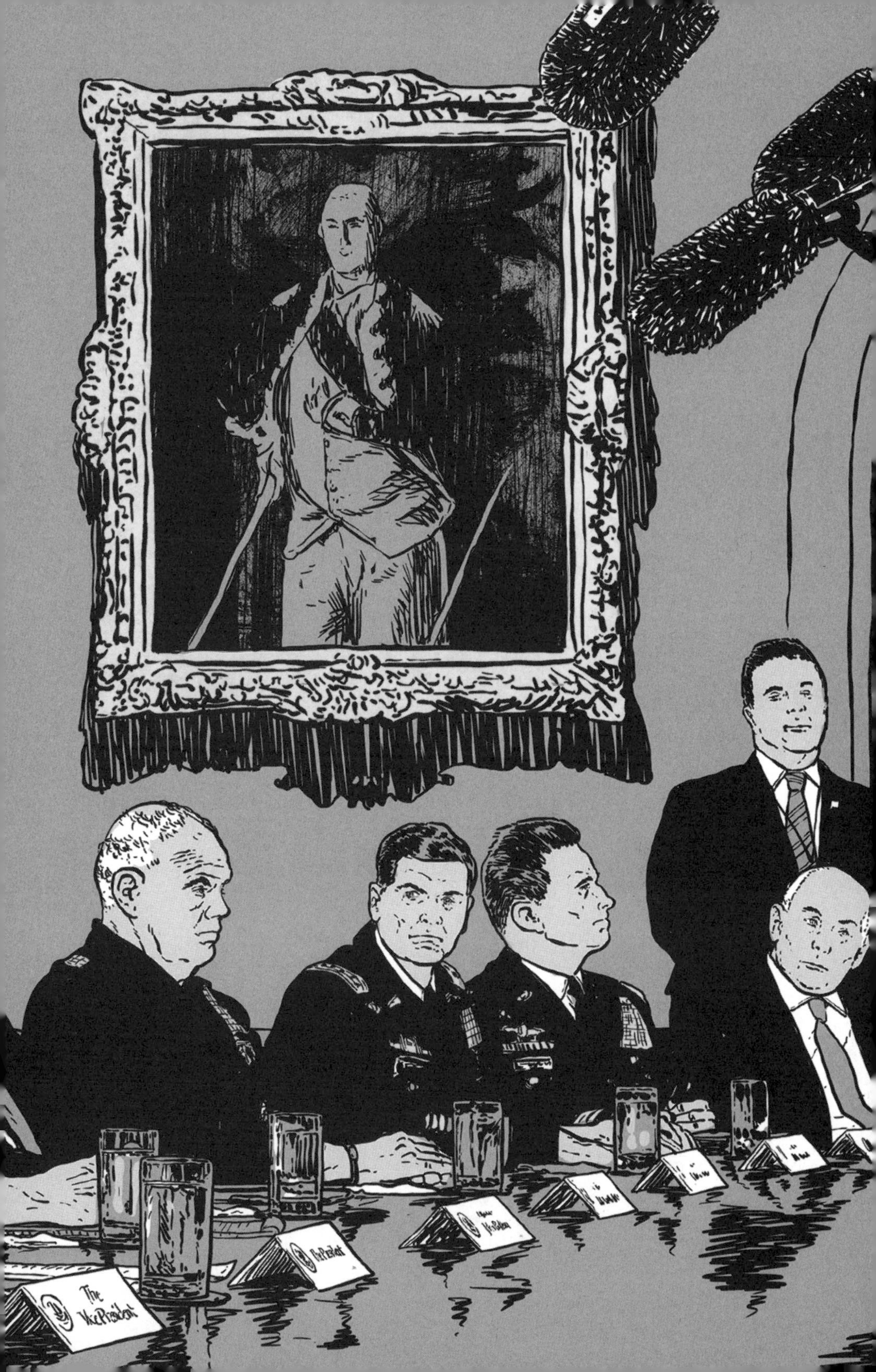
The Vice President

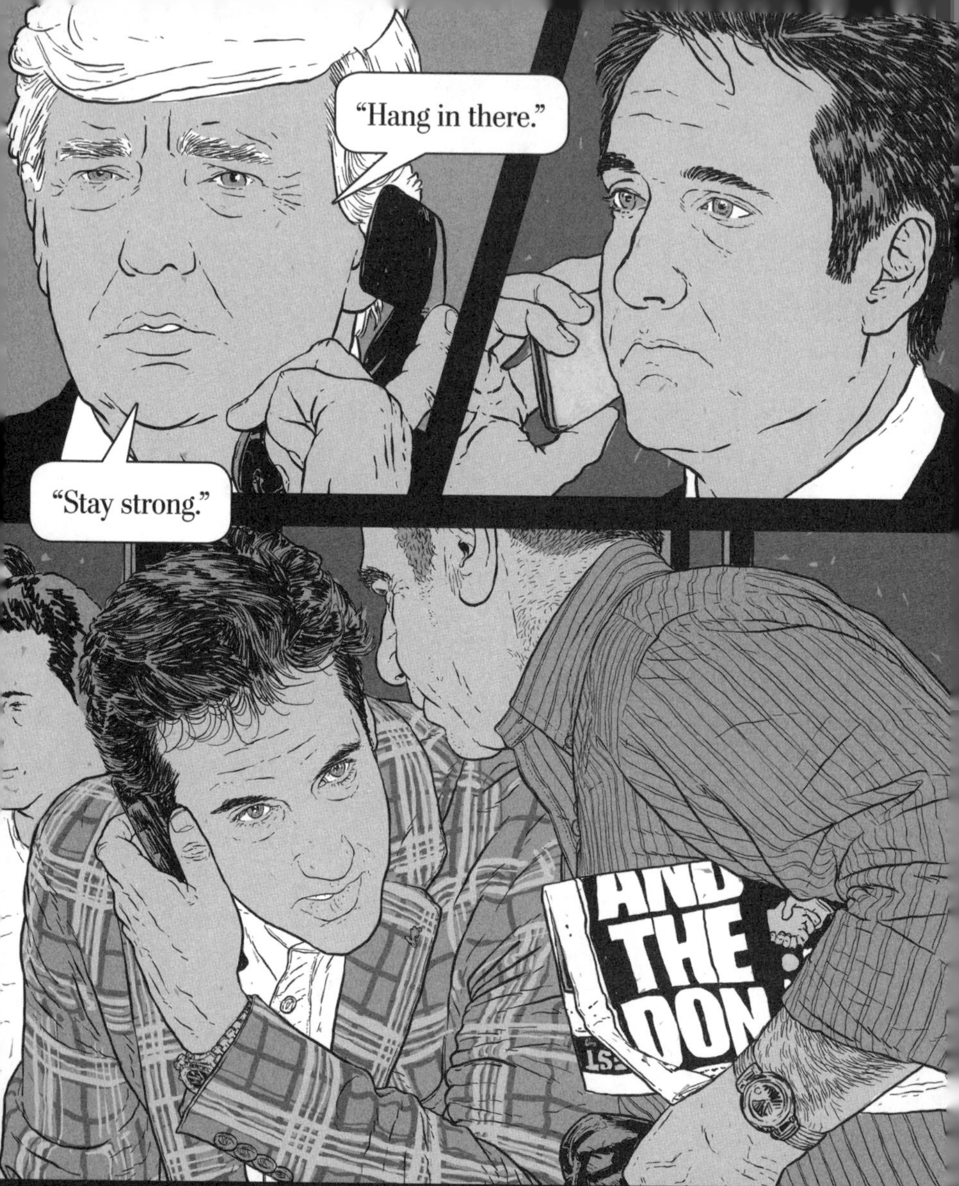
"Hang in there."
"Stay strong."

But after the raid, the New York Times reported that Cohen felt isolated and could turn on the president.

Outraged, Trump insisted that would never happen.

> Donald J. Trump
> @realDonaldTrump
>
> The New York Times and a third rate reporter named Maggie Haberman, known as a Crooked H flunkie who I don't speak to and have nothing to do with, are going out of their way to destroy Michael Cohen and his relationship with me in the hope that he will "flip." They use....
>
> 9:10 AM · Apr 21, 2018
>
> **13.4K** Retweets **55.1K** Likes

> Donald J. Trump
> @realDonaldTrump
>
> ....non-existent "sources" and a drunk/drugged up loser who hates Michael, a fine person with a wonderful family. Michael is a businessman for his own account/lawyer who I have always liked & respected. Most people will flip if the Government lets them out of trouble, even if....
>
> 9:10 AM · Apr 21, 2018
>
> **9.9K** Retweets **45.5K** Likes

> Donald J. Trump
> @realDonaldTrump
>
> ....it means lying or making up stories. Sorry, I don't see Michael doing that despite the horrible Witch Hunt and the dishonest media!
>
> 9:10 AM · Apr 21, 2018
>
> **10.3K** Retweets **49K** Likes

Cohen later told investigators that he received messages from people close to Trump and Giuliani. Cohen said these people stressed to him that the president loved him and had his back. Cohen decided he should stay on message, believing if he did so, Trump would protect him.

Several weeks later, Trump was asked if he might pardon Cohen or Manafort.

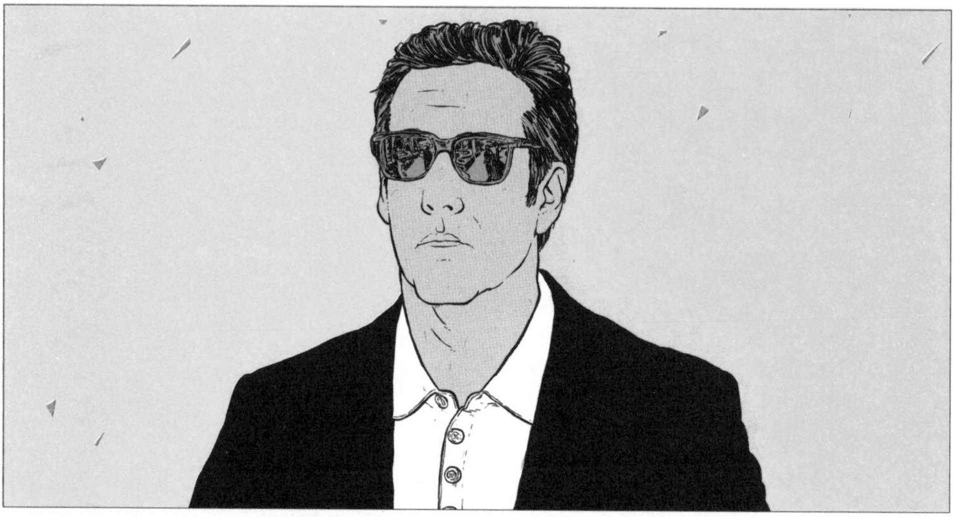

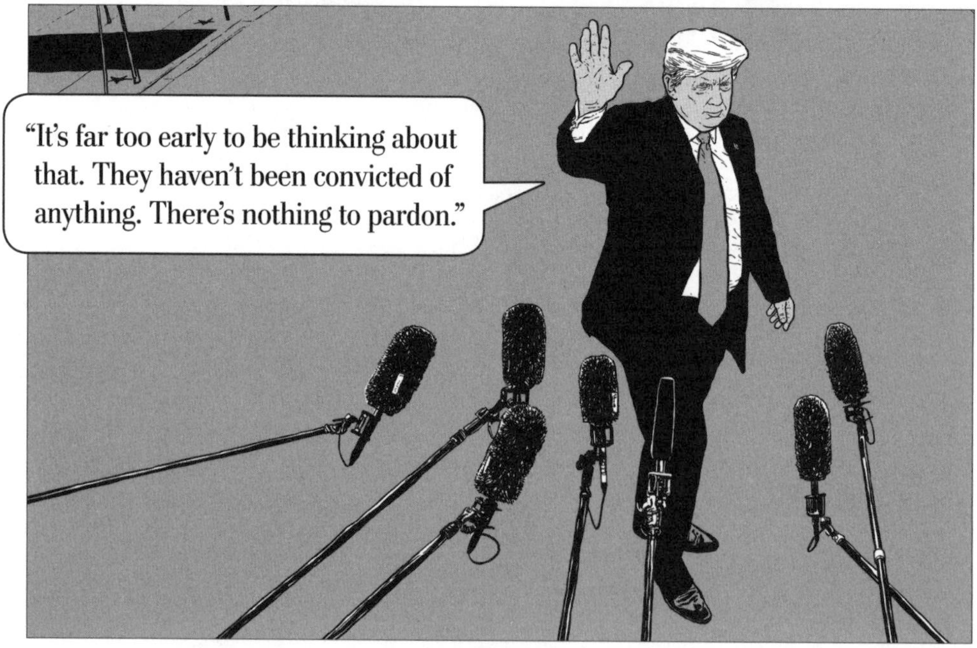
"It's far too early to be thinking about that. They haven't been convicted of anything. There's nothing to pardon."

As Cohen's legal woes intensified, the president's words were not enough.

On July 2, he publicly turned on his longtime boss. Cohen told ABC's George Stephanopoulos that he would cooperate with the government and that he had hired a new lawyer: Lanny Davis, a longtime confidant of former president Bill Clinton and former secretary of state Hillary Clinton.

"I am done being loyal to President Trump, and my first loyalty belongs to my wife, my daughter, my son and this country."

Trump's posture toward his longtime lawyer abruptly changed.

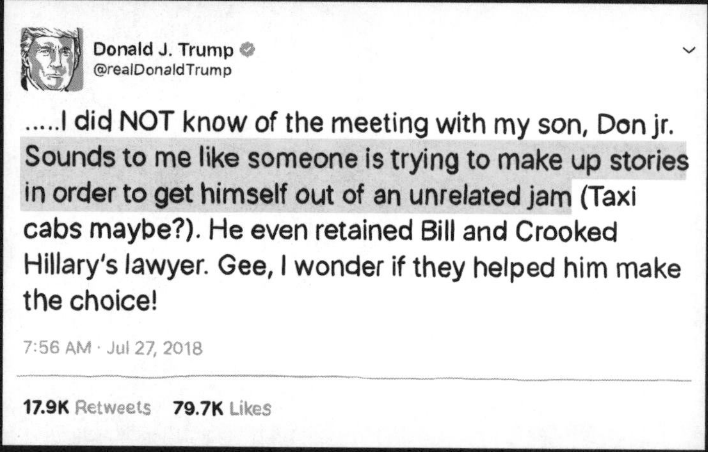

Donald J. Trump ✔
@realDonaldTrump

.....I did NOT know of the meeting with my son, Don jr. Sounds to me like someone is trying to make up stories in order to get himself out of an unrelated jam (Taxi cabs maybe?). He even retained Bill and Crooked Hillary's lawyer. Gee, I wonder if they helped him make the choice!

7:56 AM · Jul 27, 2018

17.9K Retweets   **79.7K** Likes

Critics feared the president was trying to bully Cohen and affect his testimony.

On July 31, 2018, Manafort went on trial in Virginia for bank and tax fraud. Two weeks later, his case in federal court was submitted to the jury. Trump could not resist commenting on the trial, though there were fears that the president's words could influence the jury.

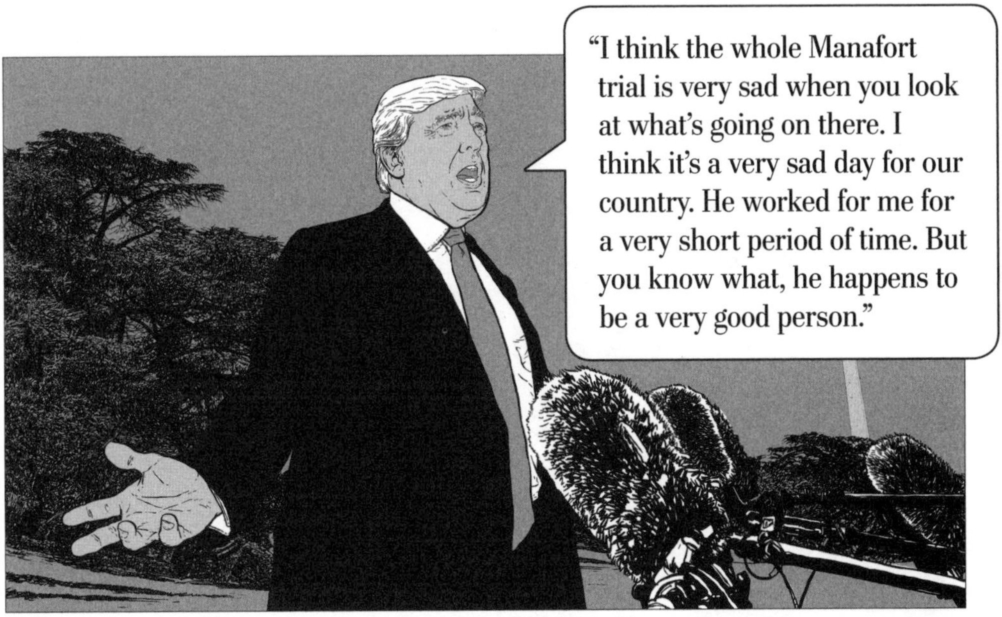
"I think the whole Manafort trial is very sad when you look at what's going on there. I think it's a very sad day for our country. He worked for me for a very short period of time. But you know what, he happens to be a very good person."

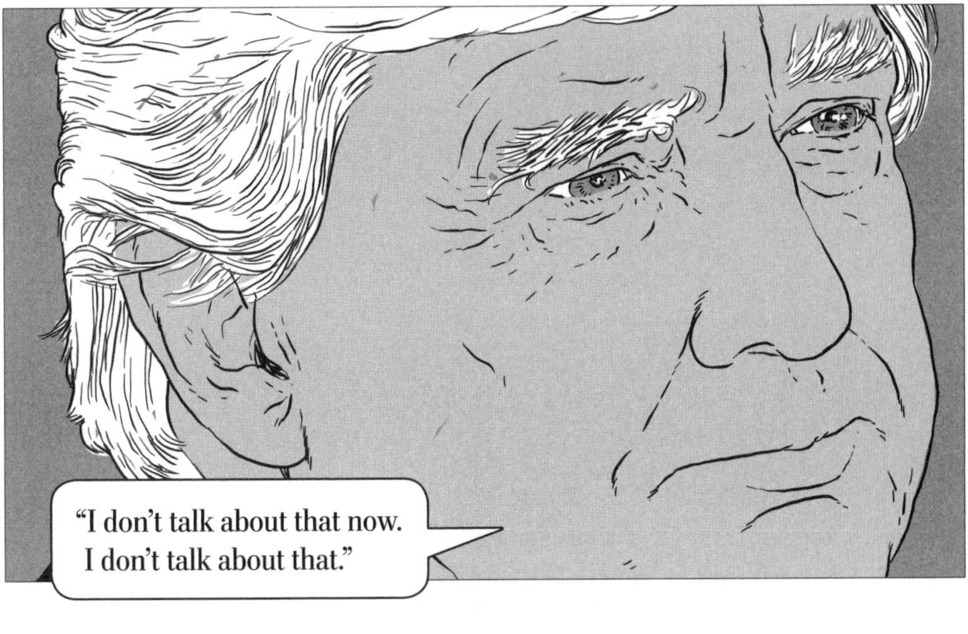
"I don't talk about that now. I don't talk about that."

Trump was asked whether he would pardon Manafort.

Aug. 21, 2018, was a grim day for the president. A jury in Washington found Manafort guilty on eight felony counts — increasing the pressure on him to cooperate with Mueller in the hopes of getting a reduced sentence.

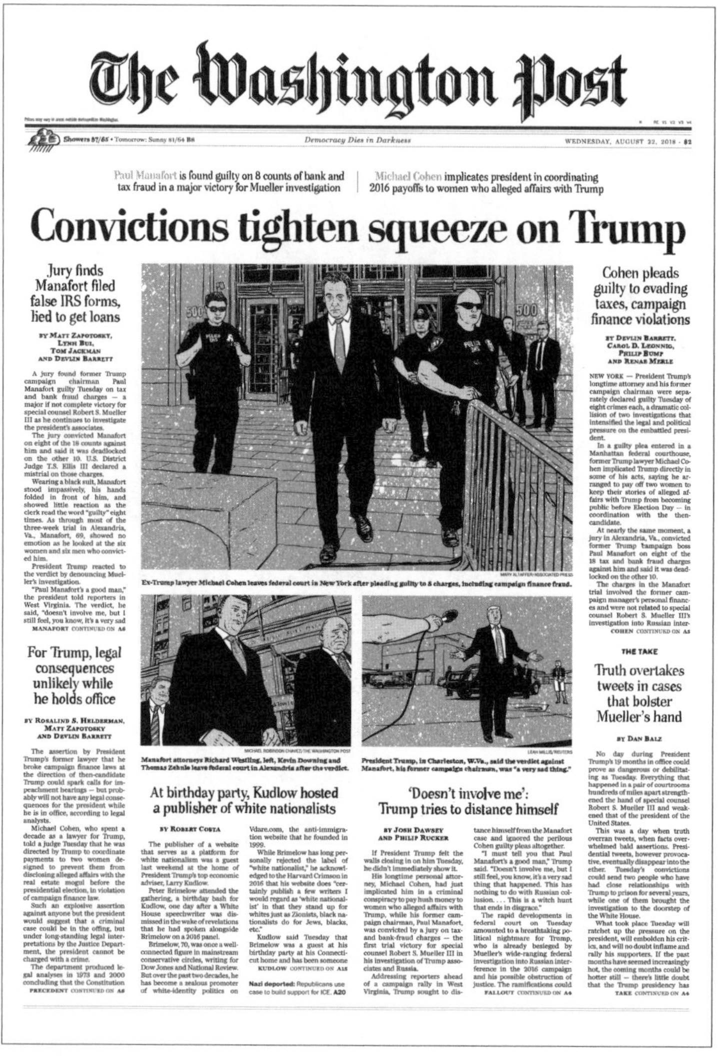

The Washington Post

Showers 87/65 • Tomorrow: Sunny 81/64 B8 — *Democracy Dies in Darkness* — WEDNESDAY, AUGUST 22, 2018 · $2

Paul Manafort is found guilty on 8 counts of bank and tax fraud in a major victory for Mueller investigation | Michael Cohen implicates president in coordinating 2016 payoffs to women who alleged affairs with Trump

Convictions tighten squeeze on Trump

Jury finds Manafort filed false IRS forms, lied to get loans

BY MATT ZAPOTOSKY, LYNH BUI, TOM JACKMAN AND DEVLIN BARRETT

A jury found former Trump campaign chairman Paul Manafort guilty Tuesday on tax and bank fraud charges — a major if not complete victory for special counsel Robert S. Mueller III as he continues to investigate the president's associates.

The jury convicted Manafort on eight of the 18 counts against him and said it was deadlocked on the other 10. U.S. District Judge T.S. Ellis III declared a mistrial on those charges.

Wearing a black suit, Manafort stood impassively, his hands folded in front of him, and showed little reaction as the clerk read the word "guilty" eight times. As through most of the three-week trial in Alexandria, Va., Manafort, 69, showed no emotion as he looked at the six women and six men who convicted him.

President Trump reacted to the verdict by denouncing Mueller's investigation.

"Paul Manafort's a good man," the president told reporters in West Virginia. The verdict, he said, "doesn't involve me, but I still feel, you know, it's a very sad

MANAFORT CONTINUED ON A6

For Trump, legal consequences unlikely while he holds office

BY ROSALIND S. HELDERMAN, MATT ZAPOTOSKY AND DEVLIN BARRETT

The assertion by President Trump's former lawyer that he broke campaign finance laws at the direction of then-candidate Trump could spark calls for impeachment hearings — but probably will not have any legal consequences for the president while he is in office, according to legal analysts.

Michael Cohen, who spent a decade as a lawyer for Trump, told a judge Tuesday that he was directed by Trump to coordinate payments to two women designed to prevent them from disclosing alleged affairs with the real estate mogul before the presidential election, in violation of campaign finance law.

Such an explosive assertion against anyone but the president would suggest that a criminal case could be in the offing, but under long-standing legal interpretations by the Justice Department, the president cannot be charged with a crime.

The department produced legal analyses in 1973 and 2000 concluding that the Constitution

PRECEDENT CONTINUED ON A6

MARY ALTAFFER/ASSOCIATED PRESS

Ex-Trump lawyer Michael Cohen leaves federal court in New York after pleading guilty to 8 charges, including campaign finance fraud.

MICHAEL ROBINSON CHAVEZ/THE WASHINGTON POST

Manafort attorneys Richard Westling, left, Kevin Downing and Thomas Zehnle leave federal court in Alexandria after the verdict.

LEAH MILLIS/REUTERS

President Trump, in Charleston, W.Va., said the verdict against Manafort, his former campaign chairman, was "a very sad thing."

At birthday party, Kudlow hosted a publisher of white nationalists

BY ROBERT COSTA

The publisher of a website that serves as a platform for white nationalism was a guest last weekend at the home of President Trump's top economic adviser, Larry Kudlow.

Peter Brimelow attended the gathering, a birthday bash for Kudlow, one day after a White House speechwriter was dismissed in the wake of revelations that he had spoken alongside Brimelow on a 2016 panel.

Brimelow, 70, was once a well-connected figure in mainstream conservative circles, writing for Dow Jones and National Review. But over the past two decades, he has become a zealous promoter of white-identity politics on Vdare.com, the anti-immigration website that he founded in 1999.

While Brimelow has long personally rejected the label of "white nationalist," he acknowledged to the Harvard Crimson in 2016 that his website does "certainly publish a few writers I would regard as 'white nationalist' in that they stand up for whites just as Zionists, black nationalists do for Jews, blacks, etc."

Kudlow said Tuesday that Brimelow was a guest at his birthday party at his Connecticut home and has been someone

KUDLOW CONTINUED ON A15

Nazi deported: Republicans use case to build support for ICE. **A20**

'Doesn't involve me': Trump tries to distance himself

BY JOSH DAWSEY AND PHILIP RUCKER

If President Trump felt the walls closing in on him Tuesday, he didn't immediately show it.

His longtime personal attorney, Michael Cohen, had just implicated him in a criminal conspiracy to pay hush money to women who alleged affairs with Trump, while his former campaign chairman, Paul Manafort, was convicted by a jury on tax- and bank-fraud charges — the first trial victory for special counsel Robert S. Mueller III in his investigation of Trump associates and Russia.

Addressing reporters ahead of a campaign rally in West Virginia, Trump sought to distance himself from the Manafort case and ignored the perilous Cohen guilty pleas altogether.

"I must tell you that Paul Manafort's a good man," Trump said. "Doesn't involve me, but I still feel, you know, it's a very sad thing that happened. This has nothing to do with Russian collusion. . . . This is a witch hunt that ends in disgrace."

The rapid developments in federal court on Tuesday amounted to a breathtaking political nightmare for Trump, who is already besieged by Mueller's wide-ranging federal investigation into Russian interference in the 2016 campaign and his possible obstruction of justice. The ramifications could

FALLOUT CONTINUED ON A4

Cohen pleads guilty to evading taxes, campaign finance violations

BY DEVLIN BARRETT, CAROL D. LEONNIG, PHILIP BUMP AND RENAE MERLE

NEW YORK — President Trump's longtime attorney and his former campaign chairman were separately declared guilty Tuesday of eight crimes each, a dramatic collision of two investigations that intensified the legal and political pressure on the embattled president.

In a guilty plea entered in a Manhattan federal courthouse, former Trump lawyer Michael Cohen implicated Trump directly in some of his acts, saying he arranged to pay off two women to keep their stories of alleged affairs with Trump from becoming public before Election Day — in coordination with the then-candidate.

At nearly the same moment, a jury in Alexandria, Va., convicted former Trump campaign boss Paul Manafort on eight of the 18 tax and bank fraud charges against him and said it was deadlocked on the other 10.

The charges in the Manafort trial involved the former campaign manager's personal finances and were not related to special counsel Robert S. Mueller III's investigation into Russian inter-

COHEN CONTINUED ON A5

THE TAKE

Truth overtakes tweets in cases that bolster Mueller's hand

BY DAN BALZ

No day during President Trump's 19 months in office could prove as dangerous or debilitating as Tuesday. Everything that happened in a pair of courtrooms hundreds of miles apart strengthened the hand of special counsel Robert S. Mueller III and weakened that of the president of the United States.

This was a day when truth overran tweets, when facts overwhelmed bald assertions. Presidential tweets, however provocative, eventually disappear into the ether. Tuesday's convictions could send two people who have had close relationships with Trump to prison for several years, while one of them brought the investigation to the doorstep of the White House.

What took place Tuesday will ratchet up the pressure on the president, will embolden his critics, and will no doubt inflame and rally his supporters. If the past months have seemed increasingly hot, the coming months could be hotter still — there's little doubt that the Trump presidency has

TAKE CONTINUED ON A4

Minutes later, in Manhattan, Cohen pleaded guilty to bank and tax fraud, as well as campaign finance violations related to hush-money payments to Stormy Daniels and another woman.

Cohen implicated Trump directly, telling the judge he committed the campaign finance violations "in coordination with and at the direction of a candidate for federal office." He agreed to cooperate with prosecutors.

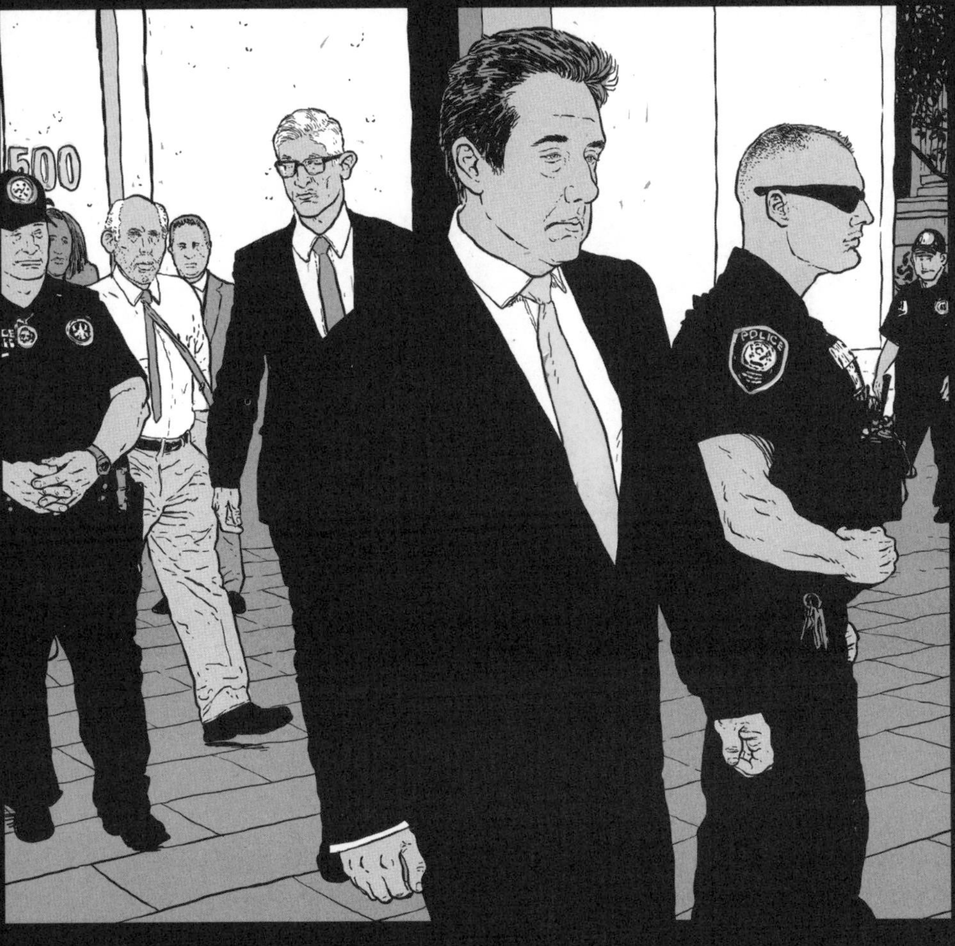
500
POLICE

Donald J. Trump ✔
@realDonaldTrump

I feel very badly for Paul Manafort and his wonderful family. "Justice" took a 12 year old tax case, among other things, applied tremendous pressure on him and, unlike Michael Cohen, he refused to "break" - make up stories in order to get a "deal." Such respect for a brave man!

9:21 AM · Aug 22, 2018

20.6K Retweets   **89.8K** Likes

Trump immediately began contrasting Cohen, who was assisting the government, with Manafort, who was proving more difficult for prosecutors.

Cohen "makes a better deal when he uses me, like everybody else. And one of the reasons that I respect Paul Manafort so much is that he went through that trial — you know they make up stories. People make up stories. This whole thing about flipping, they call it, I know all about flipping." Flipping was "not fair" and "almost ought to be outlawed."

Days later, Giuliani told The Washington Post that Trump had asked his lawyers about pardoning Manafort. Trump was advised against considering a pardon — but not necessarily forever, Giuliani said. The president was told he should put the idea on hold until the investigation had ended.

"They tried to crack him and it didn't work. Over the last two to three weeks, [the president has] expressed anger and frustration about how he's been treated."

On Sept. 14, 2018, Manafort pleaded guilty to a second set of charges in Washington. At that point, he also began to work with prosecutors, sitting for multiple interviews and appearing before the grand jury. News organizations, however, reported that Manafort's attorneys remained in an agreement to share information with Trump's lawyers and regularly briefed them about what Mueller's investigators asked and how Manafort answered.

On Nov. 26, the special counsel's office informed a federal judge that Manafort had breached his plea agreement by lying to investigators.

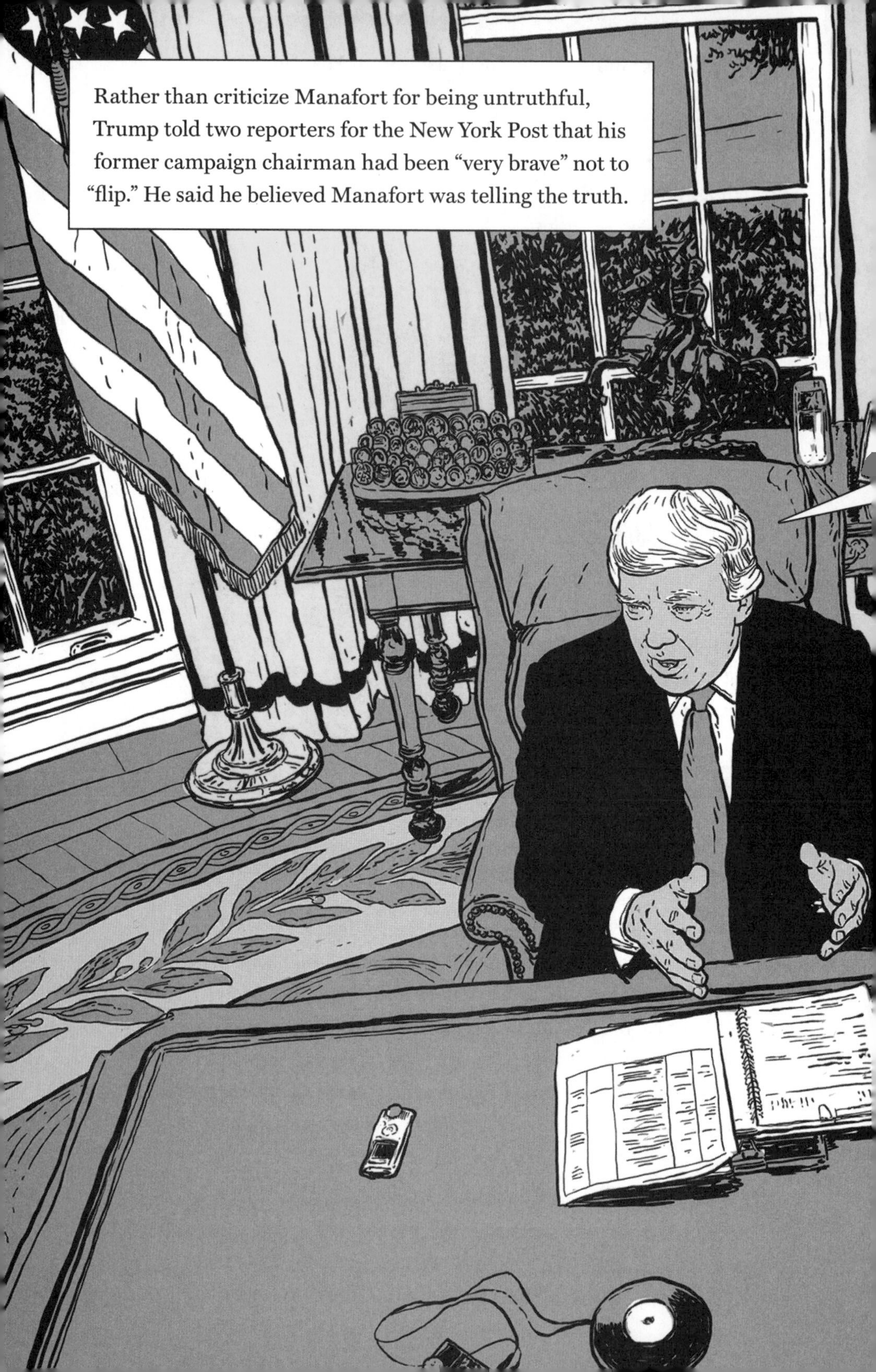
Rather than criticize Manafort for being untruthful, Trump told two reporters for the New York Post that his former campaign chairman had been "very brave" not to "flip." He said he believed Manafort was telling the truth.

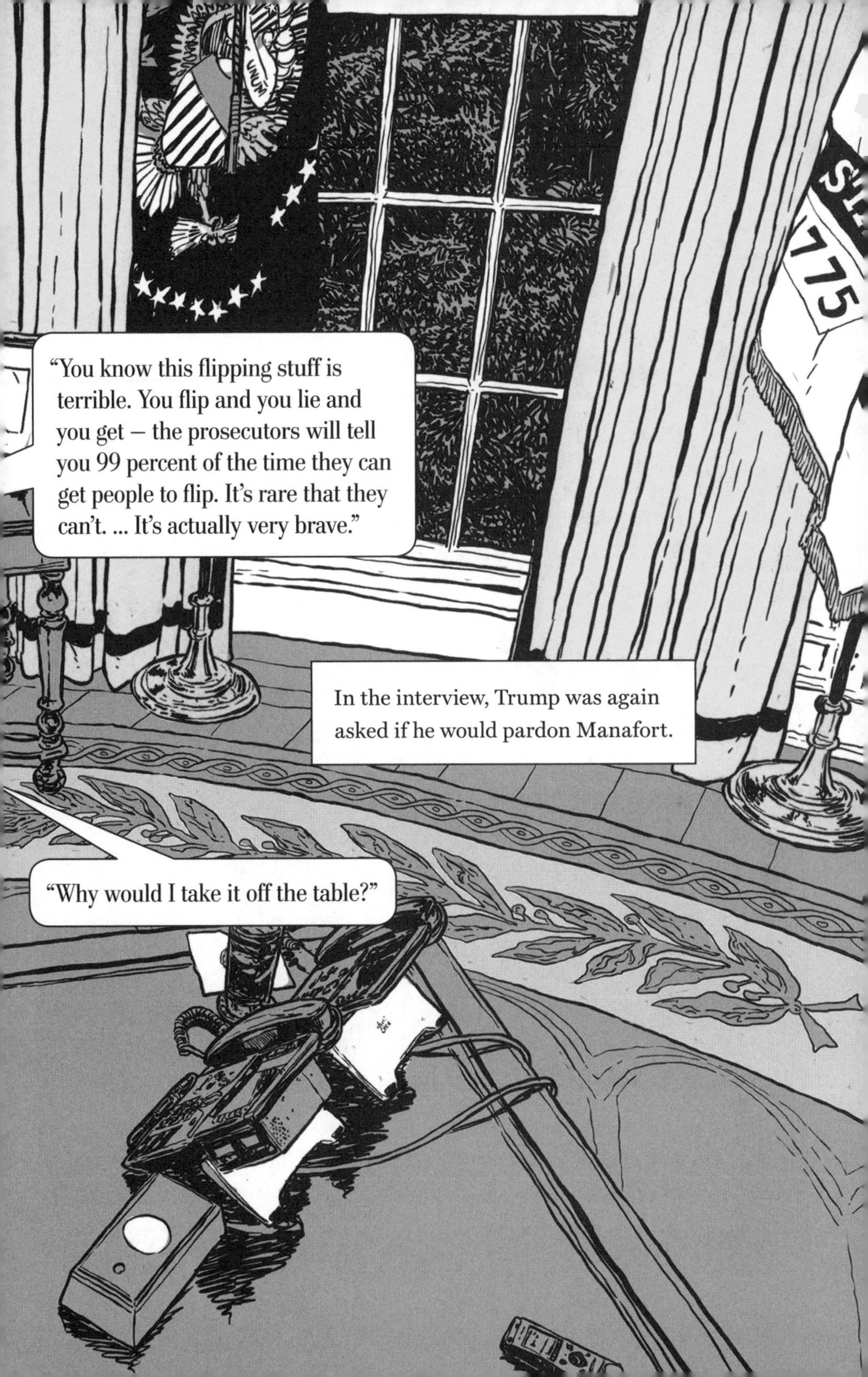
"You know this flipping stuff is terrible. You flip and you lie and you get – the prosecutors will tell you 99 percent of the time they can get people to flip. It's rare that they can't. ... It's actually very brave."
In the interview, Trump was again asked if he would pardon Manafort.
"Why would I take it off the table?"

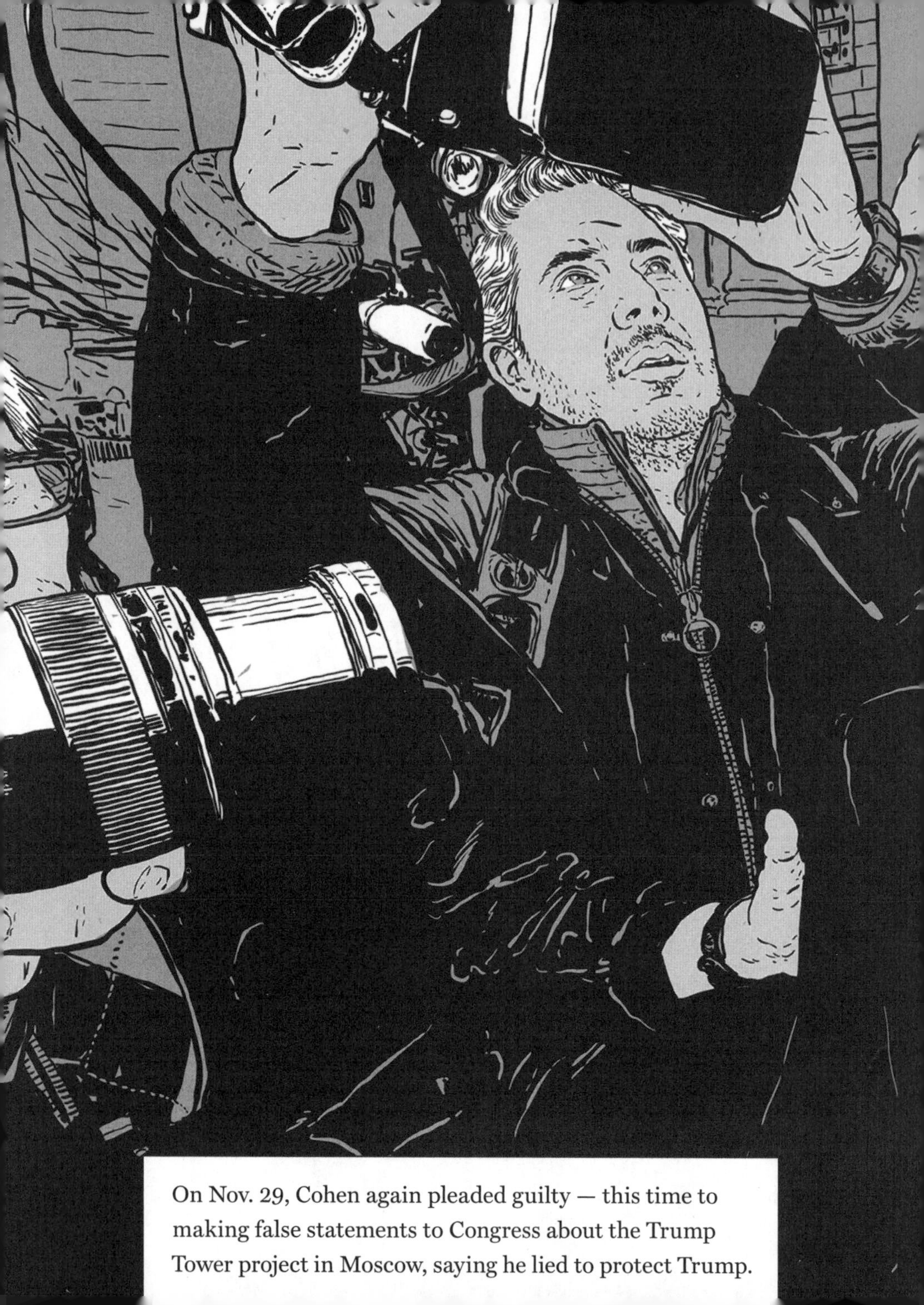
On Nov. 29, Cohen again pleaded guilty — this time to making false statements to Congress about the Trump Tower project in Moscow, saying he lied to protect Trump.

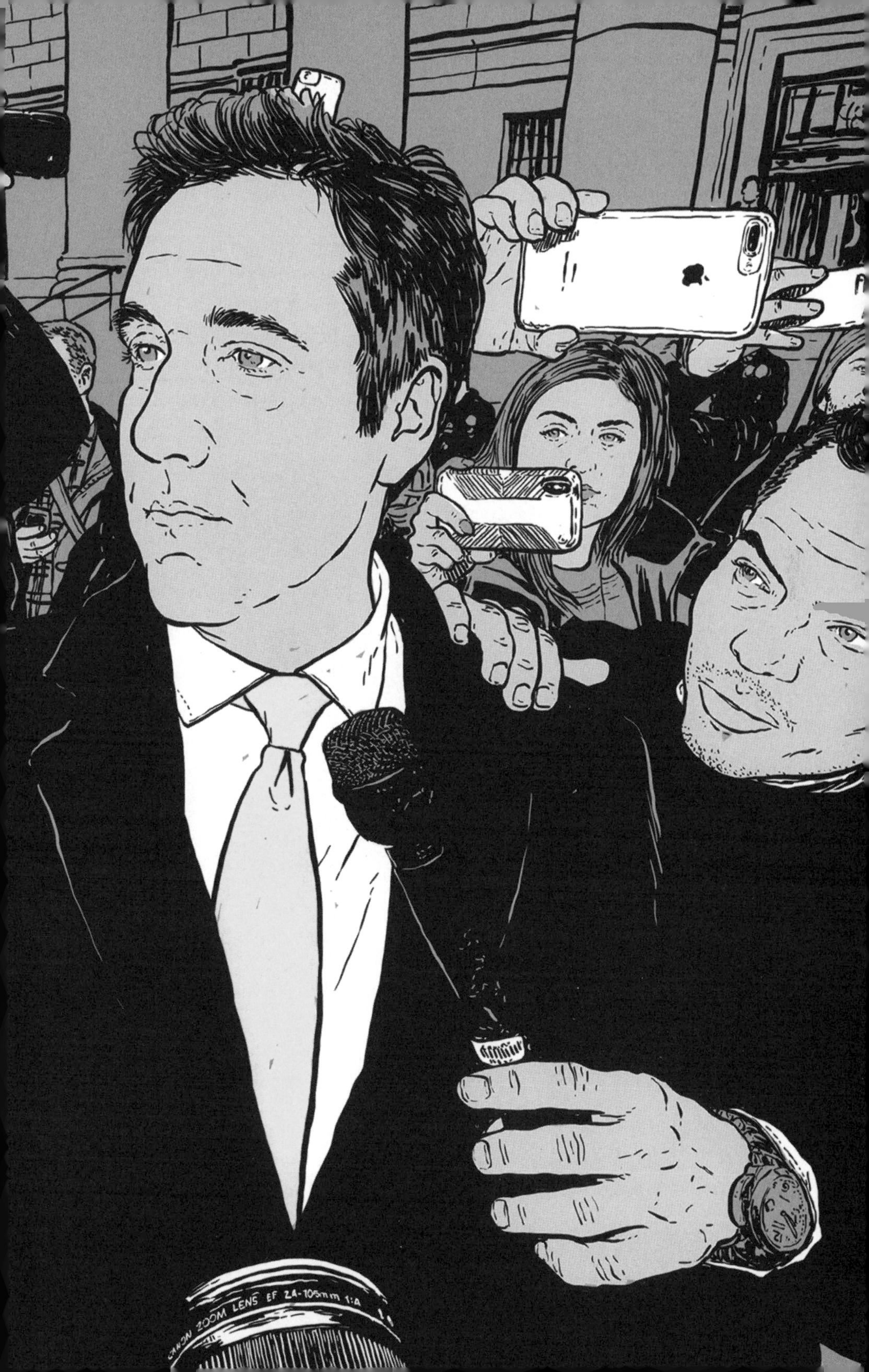
CANON ZOOM LENS EF 24-105mm 1:4

The president went on the attack.

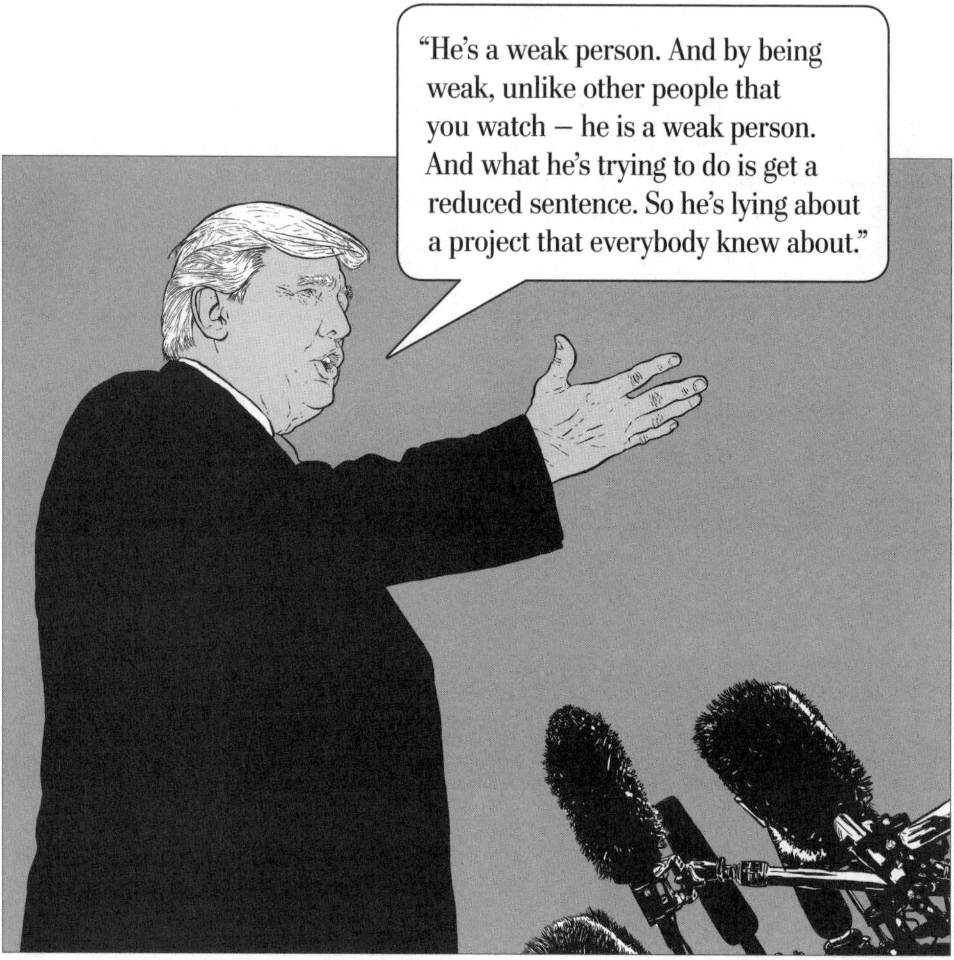
"He's a weak person. And by being weak, unlike other people that you watch – he is a weak person. And what he's trying to do is get a reduced sentence. So he's lying about a project that everybody knew about."

Trump then began to publicly suggest that Cohen's family members were guilty of crimes.

Donald J. Trump ✓
@realDonaldTrump

"Michael Cohen asks judge for no Prison Time." You mean he can do all of the TERRIBLE, unrelated to Trump, things having to do with fraud, big loans, Taxis, etc., and not serve a long prison term? He makes up stories to get a GREAT & ALREADY reduced deal for himself, and get.....

10:24 AM · Dec 3, 2018

16.6K Retweets **70.2K** Likes

Donald J. Trump ✓
@realDonaldTrump

....his wife and father-in-law (who has the money?) off Scott Free. He lied for this outcome and should, in my opinion, serve a full and complete sentence.

10:29 AM · Dec 3, 2018

13.2K Retweets **63.5K** Likes

On Dec. 12, 2018, Cohen was sentenced to three years in prison. Before he reported to serve his time, he spent a day before Congress, offering withering testimony about his former boss.

"Mr. Trump called me a 'rat' for choosing to tell the truth — much like a mobster would do when one of his men decides to cooperate with the government."

On May 6, 2019, Cohen reported to the Federal Correctional Institution in Otisville, N.Y., to begin serving his sentence.

Mueller would ultimately indict or convict six Trump associates for a wide variety of crimes — though none were charged with conspiring with Russia to interfere in the 2016 campaign.

Along with Cohen, there was former Trump foreign policy adviser George Papadopoulos, who served 12 days in prison for lying to the FBI. Manafort was sentenced to 7½ years in prison. Longtime Trump confidant Roger Stone, who was charged with lying, obstruction and witness tampering, was headed to trial in late 2019. Gates, who had assisted the government, was still awaiting his sentencing.

Two years after Flynn pleaded guilty to lying to federal agents, he switched course and changed his legal team. In October 2019, his new attorneys argued that Flynn had not intended to lie and had instead been entrapped by the FBI. They asked the judge to toss out his case.

For Trump, the question remained: Would he pardon his former aides?

As for the president himself, the special counsel stopped short of declaring whether he had broken the law.

"While this report does not conclude that the President committed a crime," Mueller wrote, "it also does not exonerate him."

U.S. Department of Justice

~~Attorney Work Product~~ // ~~May Contain Material Protected Under Fed. R. Crim. P. 6(e)~~

IV. CONCLUSION

Because we determined not to make a traditional prosecutorial judgment, we did not draw ultimate conclusions about the President's conduct. The evidence we obtained about the President's actions and intent presents difficult issues that would need to be resolved if we were making a traditional prosecutorial judgment. At the same time, if we had confidence after a thorough investigation of the facts that the President clearly did not commit obstruction of justice, we would so state. Based on the facts and the applicable legal standards, we are unable to reach that judgment. Accordingly, while this report does not conclude that the President committed a crime, it also does not exonerate him.

Epilogue

The nation waited for nearly two years to learn the results of the investigation by Robert S. Mueller III and his elite team of prosecutors — only to discover that the special counsel punted on the key question of whether President Trump broke the law.

Mueller cited Justice Department legal opinions that concluded a president cannot be indicted while serving in office. The opinions — written in 1973 when President Richard M. Nixon faced the Watergate investigation and in 2000 following an independent counsel inquiry into President Bill Clinton's behavior — found that a criminal indictment would impede the president's ability to carry out his or her constitutional duties. The opinions noted that a president who is accused of breaking the law can be prosecuted, but only after first being impeached by Congress and removed from office.

Mueller accepted the department's position and decided further that, out of fairness, he should avoid coming to any conclusions about whether there was sufficient evidence to indict Trump. The special counsel reasoned it wouldn't be fair to say the president committed a crime but then not proceed with charges and a trial in which Trump would be afforded the opportunity to defend himself.

But unlike a traditional prosecutor, Mueller decided to share the extensive facts he gathered as part of the probe. His investigators had obtained 20,000 pages of internal White House records and interviewed more than 20 White House staffers, including the chief of staff and White House counsel, as well as other Trump advisers.

The special counsel was careful not to conclude whether Trump's actions were criminal. But he analyzed in detail the president's actions in 10 separate episodes, evaluating whether each met the three elements typically required to establish obstruction of justice. That meant looking at whether the president's actions would naturally impede an investigation, whether they appeared connected to a specific probe and whether the president acted with corrupt intent.

The six chapters of this book depict seven of those episodes, ones in which Mueller and his prosecutors identified at least some potential evidence of obstruction. In multiple episodes, the special counsel indicated there was possible evidence of all three legal elements that would be needed to make an obstruction case.

The special counsel found that there was "substantial evidence" that the president's efforts to get White House Counsel Donald McGahn to fire Mueller were connected to the fact that the special counsel was investigating the president.

Likewise, Mueller found there was "substantial evidence" that Trump was trying to prevent further scrutiny of himself and his campaign when he sought to have former campaign manager Corey Lewandowski tell Attorney General Jeff Sessions to limit the scope of the probe. He also found there was "substantial evidence" that Trump was trying to block the investigation of his actions when he tried repeatedly to get McGahn to deny that the president had pressured him to oust the special counsel. And Mueller bluntly stated that he believed the way Trump treated former campaign chairman

Paul Manafort after he was charged was "intended to encourage Manafort to not cooperate with the government."

The special counsel noted that once the president learned he was personally under investigation, Trump stepped up his public attacks on the probe and his private efforts to control it — behavior that could speak to the president's motives, he wrote.

In the end, Mueller said that if he had confidence Trump had not obstructed justice, he would say so. "Accordingly," he wrote, "while this report does not conclude that the President committed a crime, it also does not exonerate him."

For his part, the president ignored the special counsel's assessment and declared on Twitter that the report offered him "complete and total EXONERATION."

Mueller's inconclusive legal analysis has been hotly debated. But his factual narrative provides a singular historical account of Trump's first two years in office. It offers a vivid depiction of a president who sought ways to use the power of his office to halt or curb an investigation he viewed as unfair. He did so even when he was warned he was trampling on traditions of an independent justice system and courting legal jeopardy.

Again and again, Trump was restrained only by the resistance of his aides, who learned that if they ignored or delayed the president's most impetuous orders, his mood and attention would often shift.

Trump emerged from the Mueller investigation battered but politically victorious. He was also more isolated than ever. As he entered the last half of his term, many of the aides who had pushed back against presidential acts they viewed as inappropriate or legally perilous during the investigation were gone. Chief of Staff Reince Priebus, senior strategist Stephen K. Bannon, McGahn and Sessions had all resigned or been fired. The question loomed: With those guardrails gone, how would Trump behave?

A day after Mueller broke his two-year silence and offered concluding testimony about his investigation on Capitol Hill in July 2019, a fateful phone call with the president of Ukraine would provide part of the answer.

In the call, Trump asked Ukrainian President Volodymyr Zelensky to initiate an investigation into his political rival, former vice president Joe Biden. He also asked the Ukrainians to look into an unsubstantiated theory that it had been their country — not Russia — that interfered in the 2016 campaign.

Trump's requests followed a months-long effort by his personal attorney Rudolph W. Giuliani to find information in Ukraine to damage Democrats, discredit the Russia investigation and undermine Mueller's conclusions. Even after the special counsel's probe had concluded, Trump remained consumed by it.

The pressure put on Ukraine would spark a new crisis — and a formal impeachment inquiry in the House of Representatives. Once again, the president was under investigation.

About the illustrator

Jan Feindt is a freelance illustrator who divides his time between Berlin and Tel Aviv. He studied communications design at the Design Factory Hamburg in Germany and illustration at Shenkar College of Engineering, Design and Art in Ramat Gan, Israel.

His clients have included Der Spiegel, Rolling Stone, GQ, Men's Health, The Washington Post, the New York Times and the Wall Street Journal.

In 2005, the art book publisher Taschen featured Feindt as one of 150 contemporary artists to watch in its publication Illustration Now. His work has been displayed in group shows in Tel Aviv, Berlin, Paris, Zurich, New York and London.

Feindt made his graphic nonfiction debut in the 2005 book "Cargo: Comic Reporting From Israel-Germany," in which he illustrated the life of Bedouin women in Israel's Negev desert. His 2015 book, "Weisse Wölfe," produced with journalist David Schraven, depicted neo-Nazi networks in Germany and won the German Reporter Award for innovation, a prize given by a national journalist network.

Acknowledgments

This project would not have been possible without the support of Washington Post Executive Editor Martin Baron, Managing Editors Cameron Barr, Emilio Garcia-Ruiz and Tracy Grant, and National Editor Steven Ginsberg. Many thanks to Senior Politics Editor Peter Wallsten for helping inspire the idea and to Deputy National Editor Lori Montgomery and National Security Editor Peter Finn for their wise counsel. Senior audio producer Matt Collette and designer Lucio Villa provided essential research and web development.

Staff writers Devlin Barrett, Josh Dawsey, Tom Hamburger, Carol D. Leonnig, Ashley Parker, Philip Rucker and Matt Zapotosky contributed audio analysis.

We owe an enormous debt of gratitude to Jan Feindt for his creativity and tireless dedication. Thanks to photo editors MaryAnne Golon and Robert Miller, deputy video director Phoebe Connelly and video editor Sarah Parnass for their help with visual research, along with Cynthia Edorh at Getty Images and Marcia Schiff at the Associated Press. Brian Baracani delivered rapid production assistance. Copy desk chiefs Jesse Lewis, Courtney Rukan and Brian Cleveland lent their unflagging support, and Jay Kennedy, Jim McLaughlin and Kalea Clark gave invaluable legal counsel. Thanks as well to Todd Shuster with Aevitas

Creative Management and Nancy Moore with Gerald & Cullen Rapp for their behind-the-scenes work.

And finally, we're immensely grateful to Nan Graham, Colin Harrison and the entire Scribner team — Jason Arias, Brian Belfiglio, Samantha Cohen, Dan Cuddy, Sarah Goldberg, Erich Hobbing, Jonathan Karp, Irene Kheradi, Roz Lippel, Jaya Miceli, Amanda Mulholland and Jennifer Weidman — for their enthusiasm and collaboration.

A digital version of this project will be available through The Washington Post at *wapo.st/muellerreportillustrated.*

Sources

CHAPTER 1

Mueller, Robert S. III. "B. The President's Conduct Concerning the Investigation of Michael Flynn." In *Report on the Investigation into Russian Interference in the 2016 Presidential Election*, Vol. II: 24-44. Department of Justice, Washington, D.C., 2019.

"To interfere with the US election process." "Joint Statement From the Department of Homeland Security and Office of the Director of National Intelligence on Election Security," October 7, 2016.

"It could be somebody sitting in a bed some place." *Fox News Sunday*. Fox News, December 11, 2016.

"Based on uniform intelligence assessments." Obama, Barack. "Press Conference by the President." The White House, December 16, 2016.

"Tit for tat w Russia not good." Mueller, Robert S. III. Vol. II, p. 24.

"Statement by the President of Russia." Putin, Vladimir V. "Statement by the President of Russia." The Kremlin, December 30, 2016.

"Absolutely no effect." Miller, Greg; Entous, Adam. "Declassified report says Putin 'ordered' to undermine faith in U.S. election and help Trump." *The Washington Post*, January 6, 2017.

"On Jan. 12, 2017, Washington Post columnist David Ignatius reported." Ignatius, David. "Why did Obama dawdle on Russia's hacking?" *The Washington Post*, January 12, 2017.

"What the hell is this all about?" Mueller, Robert S. III. Vol. II, p. 29.

"I want to kill the story." Mueller, Robert S. III. Vol. II, p. 29.

"They did not discuss anything." "Interview with Vice President-elect Mike Pence." *Face the Nation*. CBS, January 15, 2017.

"Even though she said later." Mueller, Robert S. III. Vol. II, p. 29.

"He lied about his conversations with Kislyak." *United States of America v. Michael T. Flynn.* (United States District Court for the District of Columbia. "Statement of the Offense." December 1, 2017.)

"Not again, this guy, this stuff." Mueller, Robert S. III. Vol. II, p. 32.

"I need loyalty, I expect loyalty." Mueller, Robert S. III. Vol. II, p. 34.

"On Feb. 9, 2017, The Washington Post broke the news." Miller, Greg; Entous, Adam; Nakashima, Ellen. "National security adviser Flynn discussed sanctions with Russian ambassador, despite denials, officials say." *The Washington Post*, February 9, 2017.

"Okay. That's fine. I got it."
Mueller, Robert S. III. Vol. II, p. 37.

"We'll give you a good recommendation."
Mueller, Robert S. III. Vol. II, p. 38.

"Now that we fired Flynn, the Russia thing is over."
Mueller, Robert S. III. Vol. II, p. 38-39.

"I want to talk about Mike Flynn."
Mueller, Robert S. III. Vol. II, p. 40.

"On March 31, 2017, the news broke."
Entous, Adam; Nakashima, Ellen. "Flynn offers to cooperate with congressional probe in exchange for immunity." *The Washington Post*, March 31, 2017.

Other sources/supplementary reading:
Comey, James. *A Higher Loyalty*. MacMillian Publishers, 2018.

Christie, Chris. *Let Me Finish*. Hatchette Books, 2019.

McCabe, Andrew. *The Threat*. St. Martin's Press, 2019.

Miller, Greg; Entous, Adam; Nakashima, Ellen. "Flynn's swift downfall: From a phone call in the Dominican Republic to a forced resignation at the White House." *The Washington Post*, February 14, 2017.

Miller, Greg. *The Apprentice*. HarperCollins Publishers, 2018.

Schmidt, Michael S. "In a Private Dinner, Trump Demanded Loyalty. Comey Demurred." *The New York Times*, May 11, 2017.

CHAPTER 2

Mueller, Robert S. III. "D. Events Leading Up To and Surrounding the Termination of FBI Director Comey." In *Report on the Investigation into Russian Interference in the 2016 Presidential Election*, Vol. II: 62-74. Department of Justice, Washington, D.C., 2019.

"The current investigation with respect to Russia."
U.S. Congress. Senate. Committee on the Judiciary. *Oversight of the Federal Bureau of Investigation*. 115th Cong., 1st sess., May 3, 2017.

"This is terrible, Jeff."
Mueller, Robert S. III. Vol. II, p. 63.

"I, and I believe the American public."
Mueller, Robert S. III. Vol. II, p. 64.

"I'm going to read you a letter."
Mueller, Robert S. III. Vol. II, p. 66.

"Not right."
Mueller, Robert S. III. Vol. II, p. 67.

"Put the Russia stuff in the memo."
Mueller, Robert S. III. Vol. II, p. 67.

"Serious mistakes."
Rosenstein, Rod J. "Restoring Public Confidence in the FBI." Department of Justice, May 9, 2017.

"Is this the beginning of the end?"
Mueller, Robert S. III. Vol. II, p. 68.

"Did you fire [Comey] because of what Rod wrote in the memo?"
Mueller, Robert S. III. Vol. II, p. 70.

"It was all him."
Mueller, Robert S. III. Vol. II, p. 70.

Johnson, Jenna. "After Trump fired Comey, White House staff scrambled to explain why." *The Washington Post*, May 10, 2017.

"I just fired the head of the FBI."
Mueller, Robert S. III. Vol. II, p. 71.

"The rank and file of the FBI."
Mueller, Robert S. III. Vol. II, p. 72.

"He made a recommendation."
"Interview with President Donald Trump." NBC, May 11, 2017.

"Broke the news."
Schmidt, Michael S. "In a Private Dinner, Trump Demanded Loyalty. Comey Demurred." *The New York Times*, May 11, 2017.

Other sources/supplementary reading:
Apuzzo, Matt; Haberman, Maggie; Rosenberg, Matthew. "Trump Told Russians That Firing 'Nut Job' Comey Eased Pressure From Investigation." *The New York Times,* May 19, 2019.

Comey, James. *A Higher Loyalty.* MacMillian Publishers, 2018.

Comey, James. "The Memos of James Comey." Department of Justice, April 20, 2018.

Harris, Shane; Dawsey, Josh; Nakashima, Ellen. "Trump told Russians in 2017 he wasn't concerned about Moscow's interference in U.S. election." *The Washington Post,* September 27, 2019.

CHAPTER 3

Mueller, Robert S. III. "E. The President's Efforts to Remove the Special Counsel." In *Report on the Investigation into Russian Interference in the 2016 Presidential Election,* Vol. II: 77-87. Department of Justice, Washington, D.C., 2019.

"Oh my God. This is terrible."
Mueller, Robert S. III. Vol. II, p. 78.

"Pursuant to our conversation of yesterday. "
Mueller, Robert S. III. Vol. II, p. 79.

"Shock collar."
Mueller, Robert S. III. Vol. II, p. 80.

"Ridiculous and petty."
Mueller, Robert S. III. Vol. II, p. 81.

"Ethics officials had cleared him."
Gerstein, Josh. "DOJ releases part of Mueller's conflict of interest waiver." *Politico,* September 14, 2019.

"Knocking out Mueller."
Mueller, Robert S. III. Vol. II, p. 81.

"I don't think it's for me to say."
U.S. Congress. Senate. Select Committee on Intelligence. *Hearing on Russian Election Interference.* 115th Cong., 1st sess., June 8, 2017.

"I think he's considering perhaps terminating the special counsel."
"Trump confidant Christopher Ruddy says Mueller has 'real conflicts' as special counsel." PBS, June 12, 2017.

"Do you know of any reason?"
U.S. Congress. Senate. Appropriations Subcommittee on Commerce, Justice, and Science. *Hearing on Fiscal 2018 Justice Department Budget.* 115th Cong., 1st sess., June 13, 2017.

"The Washington Post broke a bombshell story."
Barrett, Devlin; Entous, Adam; Nakashima, Ellen; Horwitz, Sari. "Special counsel is investigating Trump for possible obstruction of justice, officials say." *The Washington Post,* June 14, 2017.

"You gotta do this. You gotta call Rod."
Mueller, Robert S. III. Vol. II, p. 85-86.

"Do crazy shit."
Mueller, Robert S. III. Vol. II, p. 87.

Other sources/supplementary reading:
Leonnig, Carol D.; Parker, Ashley; Helderman, Rosalind S.; Hamburger, Tom. "Trump team seeks to control, block Mueller's Russia investigation." *The Washington Post,* July 21, 2017.

Leonnig, Carol D. "Watergate had the Nixon tapes. Mueller had Annie Donaldson's notes." *The Washington Post,* May 3, 2019.

Schmidt, Michael S. "As McGahn Emerges as Chief Witness in the Mueller Report, Trump and Allies Ramp Up Attacks." *The New York Times,* April 22, 2019.

CHAPTER 4

Mueller, Robert S. III. "F. The President's Efforts to Curtail the Special Counsel Investigation." In *Report on the Investigation into Russian Interference in the 2016 Presidential Election,* Vol. II: 90-96. Department of Justice, Washington, D.C., 2019.

"I know that I recused myself."
Mueller, Robert S. III. Vol. II, p. 91.

"Most popular guy in the country."
Mueller, Robert S. III. Vol. II, p. 92.

"Lewandowski would later be asked."
"Corey Lewandowski Testimony Before House
Judiciary Committee." C-SPAN, September
17, 2019.

"Sessions should have never recused himself."
Baker, Peter; Schmidt, Michael S.; Haberman,
Maggie. "Citing Recusal, Trump Says He
Wouldn't Have Hired Sessions." *The New York
Times*, July 19, 2017.

"The Washington Post reported that Sessions
had discussed."
Entous, Adam; Nakashima, Ellen; Miller,
Greg. "Sessions discussed Trump campaign-
related matters with Russian ambassador, U.S.
intelligence intercepts show." *The Washington
Post*, July 21, 2017.

"Need a letter of resignation on desk
immediately."
Mueller, Robert S. III. Vol. II, p. 95.

It's "all wrong."
Mueller, Robert S. III. Vol. II, p. 95.

"Did you get it? Are you working on it?"
Mueller, Robert S. III. Vol. II, p. 96.

Other sources/supplementary reading:
Parker, Ashley; Leonnig, Carol D.; Rucker,
Philip; Hamburger, Tom. "Trump dictated
son's misleading statement on meeting with
Russian lawyer." *The Washington Post*, July
31, 2019.

Bade, Rachael; Itkowitz, Colby; Wagner, John.
"Lewandowksi mocks Democrats, talks over
lawmakers, promotes possible Senate bid." *The
Washington Post*, September 17, 2019.

Parker, Ashley; Helderman, Rosalind S.;
Zapotosky, Matt. "Stymied by aides, Trump
sought out loyalist to curtail special counsel
— and drew Mueller's glare." *The Washington
Post*, April 25, 2019.

CHAPTER 5

Mueller, Robert S. III. "I. The President Orders
McGahn to Deny that the President Tried to
Fire the Special Counsel." In *Report on the
Investigation into Russian Interference in the
2016 Presidential Election*, Vol. II: 113-118.
Department of Justice, Washington, D.C.,
2019.

"The New York Times broke the news that,
during the previous summer. "
Schmidt, Michael S.; Haberman, Maggie.
"Trump Ordered Mueller Fired, but Backed
Off When White House Counsel Threatened
to Quit." *The New York Times*, January 25,
2019.

"The Washington Post quickly followed with its
own report."
Helderman, Rosalind S.; Dawsey, Josh.
"Trump moved to fire Mueller in June,
bringing White House counsel to the brink
of leaving." *The Washington Post,* January 26,
2019.

"Fake news, folks. Fake news."
Mueller, Robert S. III. Vol. II, p. 114.

It's "bullshit."
Mueller, Robert S. III. Vol. II, p. 115-116.

"I never said to fire Mueller."
Mueller, Robert S. III. Vol. II, p. 116.

"What you said is, 'Call Rod.' "
Mueller, Robert S. III. Vol. II, p. 117.

They "did have that conversation."
Mueller, Robert S. III. Vol. II, p. 117.

"Fine" with McGahn.
Mueller, Robert S. III. Vol. II, p. 118.

Other sources/supplementary reading:
Dawsey, Josh; Helderman, Rosalind S.;
Zapotosky, Matt. "White House counsel walks
a fine line in serving Trump's demands." *The
Washington Post*, February 18, 2018.

Rucker, Philip; Dawsey, Josh; Costa, Robert.
"Trump blames McGahn after Mueller paints
damning portrait with notes from White
House aides." *The Washington Post*, April 19,
2019.

CHAPTER 6

Mueller, Robert S. III. "J. The President's Conduct Towards Flynn, Manafort" and "K. The President's Conduct Involving Michael Cohen." In *Report on the Investigation into Russian Interference in the 2016 Presidential Election*, Vol. II: 120-152. Department of Justice, Washington, D.C., 2019.

"Flynn is a fine person."
Trump, Donald. "Remarks by President Trump in Press Conference." The White House, February 16, 2017

"Maybe, I — I'm sympathetic."
United States of America v. Michael T. Flynn. (United States District Court for the District of Columbia. "Document 86." June 6, 2019.)

"Tenor and the contents."
"Mueller appears to have edited voicemail transcript between John Dowd and Flynn lawyer." *Hannity.* Fox News, June 3, 2019.

"We'll see what happens."
"President Trump Remarks on Tax Reform and Michael Flynn's Guilty Plea." C-SPAN, December 2, 2017.

"I don't want to talk about pardons for Michael Flynn yet."
"President Trump White House Departure." C-SPAN, December 15, 2017.

"Sit tight."
Mueller, Robert S. III. Vol. II, p. 123.

"I feel badly about a lot of them."
Trump, Donald. "Remarks by President Trump in Press Gaggle." The White House, June 15, 2018.

"When it's over, hey, he's the president of the United States."
"State of the Union with Jake Tapper." CNN, June 17, 2018.

One "of Trump's attorneys, Jay Sekulow."
U.S. Congress. House of Representatives. Permanent Select Committee on Intelligence. *Deposition of Michael Cohen.* 116th Cong., 1st sess., March 6, 2019.

"The president loves you."
Mueller, Robert S. III. Vol. II, p. 140.

"Party line."
Mueller, Robert S. III. Vol. II, p. 138.

"In early 2018, the Wall Street Journal revealed. "
Rothfeld, Michael; Palazzolo, Joe. "Trump Lawyer Arranged $130,000 Payment for Adult-Film Star's Silence." *The Wall Street Journal*, January 12, 2018.

"Neither the Trump Organization nor the Trump campaign was a party."
Berman, Mark. "Longtime Trump attorney says he made $130,000 payment to Stormy Daniels with his money."
The Washington Post, February 14, 2018.

"Client says thanks for what you do."
Mueller, Robert S. III. Vol. II, p. 145.

"So, I just heard that they broke into."
Trump, Donald. "Remarks by President Trump Before Meeting with Senior Military Leadership." The White House, April 9, 2018.

"Hang in there."
Mueller, Robert S. III. Vol. II, p. 146.

"But after the raid, the New York Times reported."
Haberman, Maggie; LaFraniere, Sharon; Hakim, Danny. "Michael Cohen Has Said He Would Take a Bullet for Trump. Maybe Not Anymore." *The New York Times*, April 20, 2018.

"It's far too early to be thinking about that."
Mueller, Robert S. III. Vol. II, p. 148.

"I am done being loyal."
"Michael Cohen says family and country, not President Trump, is his 'first loyalty.' " ABC, July 2, 2018.

"I think the whole Manafort trial is very sad."
"President Trump Remarks on John Brennan and Mueller Probe." C-SPAN, August 17, 2018.

Cohen "makes a better deal when he uses me, like everybody else."
"Fox & Friends Exclusive Interview with President Trump." Fox News, August 23, 2018.

"Giuliani told The Washington Post."
Leonnig, Carol D.; Dawsey, Josh. "Trump recently sought his lawyers' advice on possibility of pardoning Manafort, Giuliani says." *The Washington Post*, August 23, 2018.

"You know this flipping stuff."
Schultz, Marisa; Schwab, Nikki; "Trump says pardon for Paul Manafort still a possibility." *The New York Post*, November 28, 2018.

"He's a weak person."
"President Trump Departure Remarks." C-SPAN, November 29, 2018.

"Mr. Trump called me a 'rat.'"
U.S. Congress. House of Representatives. Committee on Oversight and Reform. *With Michael Cohen, Former Attorney to President Donald Trump*. 116th Cong., 2nd sess., February 27, 2019.

Other sources/supplementary reading:
Hsu, Spencer S. "Michael Flynn fires his attorneys and retains new counsel as he awaits sentencing." *The Washington Post*, June 6, 2019.

Schmidt, Michael S.; Becker, Jo; Mazzetti, Mark; Haberman, Maggie; Goldman, Adam. "Trump's Lawyer Raised Prospect of Pardons for Manafort and Flynn." *The New York Times*, March 28, 2018.

Helderman, Rosalind S.; Weiner, Rachel; Fisher, Marc. "The Manafort scramble: Raising millions for himself even as he ran Trump's campaign." *The Washington Post*, August 10, 2018.

Helderman, Rosalind S.; Hamburger, Tom. "How Manafort's 2016 meeting with a Russian employee at a New York cigar club goes to 'the heart' of Mueller's probe." *The Washington Post*, February 12, 2019.

Confessore, Nicholas; Meier, Barry. "How the Russia Investigation Entangled Rick Gates, a Manafort Protege." *The New York Times*, June 16, 2017.

Schwartzman, Paul. "Michael Cohen's secret agenda."
The Washington Post, February 9, 2019.

PHOTO REFERENCES

Many of the photographs used as reference in this book were created on assignment for The Washington Post.

Alexey Agarishev/Sputnik/Associated Press
Drew Angerer/Getty Images
J. Scott Applewhite/Associated Press
David Becker/The Washington Post
Jabin Botsford/The Washington Post
Bruce Boyajian/The Washington Post
Ricky Carioti/The Washington Post
Jahi Chikwendiu/The Washington Post
Timothy A. Clary/Agence France-Presse/
    Getty Images
Oliver Contreras/The Washington Post
Shealagh Craighead/The White House
D. Myles Cullen/Department of Defense
Al Drago/CQ Roll Call/Getty Images
Richard Drew/Associated Press
Patrick Dove/Getty Images
Tia Dufour/The White House
Jonathan Ernst/Reuters
Katherine Frey/The Washington Post
Salwan Georges/The Washington Post
Zach Gibson/Agence France-Presse/Getty
    Images
Yuri Gripas/Reuters
Aude Guerrucci/Getty Images
Sait Serkan Gurbuz/Associated Press
Andrew Harnik/Associated Press
Andrew Harrer/Getty Images
Evelyn Hockstein/The Washington Post
Andrew Innerarity/The Washington Post
iStock Photos
Nicholas Kamm/Agence France-Presse/
    Getty Images

Carolyn Kaster/Associated Press
Andrew Kelly/Reuters
Dan Kitwood/Getty Images
Justin Lane/EPA/Shutterstock
Jin Lee/Bloomberg News/Getty Images
Saul Loeb/Getty Images
Melina Mara/The Washington Post
Cheriss May/NurPhoto/Getty Images
Matt McClain/The Washington Post
Brendan McDermid/Reuters
Leah Millis/Reuters
Thomas Mukoya/Reuters
NBC News
Mandel Ngan/Agence France-Presse/
    Getty Images
Bill O'Leary/The Washington Post
Yana Paskova/Getty Images
Kate Patterson/The Washington Post
PBS NewsHour
William B. Plowman/NBC/Getty Images
Michael Reynolds/EPA/Shutterstock
Russian Foreign Ministry Photo/Associated
    Press
Markus Schreiber/Associated Press
Mike Segar/Reuters
Ting Shen/Xinhua/Zuma
Marlena Sloss/The Washington Post
Brendan Smialowski/Agence France-Presse/
    Getty Images
Chip Somodevilla/Getty Images
Justin Sullivan/Getty Images
Carolyn Van Houten/The Washington Post
Sarah L. Voisin/The Washington Post
Evan Vucci/Associated Press
Tom Williams/CQ Roll Call/Getty Images
Michael Williamson/The Washington Post
Alex Wong/Getty Images
123RFstockimages.com